W9-AXJ-471

The Plantation Overseer

As Shown in His Letters

THE
Southern Plantation Overseer

As Revealed in His Letters

By JOHN SPENCER BASSETT, *Ph.D., LL.D.*
Professor of AMERICAN HISTORY *on the* SYDENHAM
CLARK PARSONS FOUNDATION *in* SMITH COLLEGE

NEGRO UNIVERSITIES PRESS
NEW YORK

PREFACE

ALL *the letters in this book deal with the affairs of an ante-bellum Southern cotton plantation. Most of them were written by plantation overseers, and all of them were written about the things with which the overseers were closely concerned. All of them are taken from the Correspondence of James Knox Polk, president of the United States from* 1849 *to* 1853. *So far as the editor knows none have been published hitherto, and all are preserved in manuscript form in the Library of Congress, Washington, D. C. Taken together they constitute a remarkably full and interesting record of some phases of the life on a cotton plantation in the old régime.*

The letters of the overseers have been copied with great care. It is believed that they are as correctly reproduced as is possible under the circumstances; for where handwriting is so grotesquely distorted it is often impossible to be certain that it is correctly deciphered. In cases like those before us, where composition as well as spelling mean so much in revealing to the reader the mental qualities of the writer, it is highly important that exact reproductions be offered to him. The editor dares not claim that no errors of copying have crept in, but he has tried hard to reduce them to the lowest number possible.

Collecting and editing these letters has excited his warmest interest. The good qualities they reveal in their writers have won his admiration, which only the exercise of historical detachment has enabled him to keep subordinate. In many of the respectable things of life the overseer was less than a full man. In the things that concerned his craft he

iii

was, in typical cases, all that the situation required, which is saying much for any man.

The editor acknowledges his pleasure in having an opportunity to return for a time to the field in which his earliest efforts in history were made. After residing nearly two decades in New England, always a hospitable home for a student, he has found a special joy in getting back into the history of Southern conditions. Of the South the overseer was a veritable son. He was true to its social genius, expressing in his letters the views and desires of that portion of Southern society from which he was sprung. It is very interesting to be able to introduce this man to the public in a more faithful attire than he has hitherto been made to wear when held up for observation. He was a part of that rich Old South which will always command the interest of the world and the love of its descendants.

The work of preparing these letters for publication has been lightened for the editor by the assistance of many friends; but special interest has been taken in the project by President Wm. Allan Neilson, of Smith College, to whom I wish at this place to express my thanks for his personal sympathy and encouragement. I must also acknowledge my indebtedness to Messrs. E. D. Beanland, of Oxford, Miss., and John A. Bergland, of New Orleans, for information about Ephraim Beanland, and to Messrs. C. V. Beadles and H. B. Johnson, of Coffeeville, Miss., for information about the Polk plantation.

Northampton, Mass.,

September 10, 1925.

JOHN SPENCER BASSETT.

CONTENTS

ILLUSTRATIONS

CHAPTER I

The Overseer and His Work

T HE overseer on the old Southern plantation has departed this life with the institution that made him a necessity. Unnoticed in society, with no friends to record his services, he lived and disappeared without leaving a record of his existence. The planter had his books, newspapers, and journals; and from them we may learn what he did and tried to do. Now and again he left diaries and letters that throw light on his manner of living. He has found writers of imagination to picture the life in his mansions. Taken altogether we have had and are likely to continue to have a mass of pleasant literature, more or less accurate, that perpetuates what he did for his time and what he was in it. The sable race at the bottom of the system has had its champions also. Their lives have been told in prose and poetry. Their trials, virtues, and joys have been portrayed with great effect by persons who wrote with more or less truthfulness. These things are well in their ways. Master and slave have a right to all that can be said fairly about them. But the overseer, who was in fact the essential centre of the industrial operations of the plantation system, has been almost wholly neglected. Little is known of him, and that little is distorted. This book is written to present to the reader some of the memorials of his life: letters written by his own untutored hands, eloquent in their evidence of society's miserly gifts to him, and a veracious record of many of the things he did to make possible the pleasant living of the planter class.

The overseer's position was central in the Southern system. The planter might plan and incite, and the slave might dig, plow, and gather into barns: it was the overseer who brought the mind of the one and the muscle of the other into coöperation. As he did his part well or poorly the plantation prospered or failed. If there was money in the bank, or festivities in the "great house" or gay silks for my lady's wardrobe, he had his part in putting them there. I do not mean he was supreme in the process, but he was so high in the sharing of responsibility that he stood close to the master as a creator of wealth and happiness.

It was not even his fortune to be esteemed for what he did. He was patronized by the benign planters and contemned by the heedless. He might belong to the same church with the planter, but he usually preferred some plain form of worship, as in the churches of Methodists or Baptists. If the two found themselves worshipping in the same place they sat apart quite distinctly. Their children did not visit one another nor intermarry. Each was a class in society and between them in social matters was a frozen ocean.

When there was illness in the overseer's family there was much kindness for him in the mansion. The mistress on a Southern plantation knew no caste in time of distress. Her broth, jelly, cordial, and plasters were as freely given to him and his as to her neighbors on other plantations. But she knew, and the overseer knew, that her visits of mercy were not visits of social equality. And he suffered nothing in his mind because of his lower place on the ladder. He was born to it. His wife was born to it. His children would never have aught else so far as the existing environment was concerned. Being a sensible man he was not discontented. He took the best he could get of what life offered to overseers, finding his wife and marrying off his children in the ranks of such people as himself. If he did not like this prospect, and sometimes he was in revolt against it, he might turn to the frontier which always had a welcome for a man with courage and industry.

The planters, that is the owners of large farms, were but a small part of the white people of the old South. The great mass were small farmers, owners of small groups of slaves or of none at all, men who had land and lived independently without leisure, education, or more than simple comforts. These people were the descendants of the original settlers, all poor at first, who had not prospered in the new environment. Many of them were descended from the indented servants who had originally bound themselves to serve for a number of years in order to pay their passage out of old England to the land of opportunity. It was from this class of small farmers that the overseer came. He was often a man whose father had a few slaves, or some ambitious farmer youth who had set his eyes upon becoming a planter and began to "manage," as the term was, as a stepping stone to proprietorship in the end.

Slight as was the respect the overseer had from the planter it was greater than the respect he had from the slaves. To them he was the master's left hand, the burden layer and the symbol of the hardest features of bondage. From his decisions an appeal was to the owner who as a dispenser of mercy and forgiveness had some degree of affection from the slaves. As a giver of food and clothing and of largesses at Christmas time and as a protector in extreme calamity the master stood high in the respect of the slave.

The Plantation Overseer

If he was a man of distinction his slaves were apt to be pleased that he and not a less prominent man was the master. But the slave was not proud of his overseer nor boasted of his overseer's virtues. It was the fate of this man, standing in the place of the owner, to absorb the shock of bitterness felt by the slaves for their enslavers and in so doing keep it away from those who were in reality the responsible parties.

It was natural that the slaves thought of the overseer as the symbol of slavery. Who rang the plantation bell before dawn, calling the hands to prepare for the day's labor? Who kept his eye fixed on the workers and passed judgment on the quality of the work? Who gave the signal for leaving the field when the sun had passed below the rim of pine trees on the western horizon? Who punished the slothful and discovered the wiles of the deceitful? It was he, the vigilant overseer, who did these things, standing ever in the way of any slave who had liberal ideas of the comforts of bondage.

The overseer was not loved: as a rule he was not lovable. The life in the South was hearty rather than gentle. It dealt with the direct virtues and vices of plain country people. For the class out of which the overseer sprang it was crude. The days a boy of this class spent in school were few and plain. The small learning he got he used for very simple purposes. He rarely read a book and his newspapers were insignificant. With a mind having this imprint he looked out on a narrow horizon. The itinerant clergyman might hammer the simpler rules of righteousness into his mind, a good mother might reinforce them with the blessing of a virtuous example, but there was not much more that could inspire him with the purpose of making his stewardship gentle or liberal for the slaves. His words were apt to be severe, his epithets might be strong, his standards of justice might be crude. Negro slavery did not invite liberal ideas. The relation was primeval and the subject race was childlike. When, therefore, this uneducated white man and this child race of black men came together under the aegis of slavery there was much groping in the dark.

In Professor Ulrich B. Phillips's excellent book, "American Negro Slavery" (1918), we may find much information about the life of the overseer, what kind of a man he was and what he did as a part of the plantation system. The ideal held for him by the planter was high, demanding a man of many qualities and much enlightenment. James H. Hammond, an eminent South Carolina planter, is quoted by Phillips to the following effect: "The overseer will never be expected to work in the fields, but he must always be with the hands when not otherwise engaged in the employer's business." To work side by side with the slaves was thought to weaken one's authority over them. "The overseer," continues Hammond, "must never be absent a single night, nor an entire day, without permission previously obtained. Whenever absent at church or elsewhere he must be on the plantation by sundown without fail. He must attend every night and morning at the stables and see that the mules are watered, cleaned and fed, and the barn locked. He must keep the stable keys at night, and all the keys in a safe place, and never allow anyone to unlock the barn, smoke-house, or other depository of plantation stores but himself. He must endeavor, also, to be with the plough-hands always at noon." Exacting as these rules were on the overseer's time, they were reasonable. Barns and storehouses had to be kept locked, and if the slaves were left to lock them the contents would not be secure. Mules had to be curried and fed, and if the task were left to the slaves without supervision it would often be neglected. It took a lot of effort to get the ordinary amount of work out of a slave.

For his many services the overseer received a salary varying from $250 to $600 a year, but on some very large plantations it was more. Polk thought he paid high wages in the early thirties when he was paying Ephraim Beanland $350 a year. In the older seacoast region of the cotton belt the pay was as high as $600 on the large plantations and even ran up to $1000 in exceptional times. Added to the pay was the use of a house and the services of a cook and even of a man servant, with board and the use of a horse. In the early history of the plantation the overseer was given a share of the crop but experience showed that it was a bad system. The tendency under it was for the overseer to work the slaves so hard that he injured their health, and for this reason the practice was given up.

Some of the overseers took up the calling with the idea of acquiring experience and a start in the world, after which they might embark on the career of planter on their own accounts. Out of their savings they bought slaves whom they hired to their employers or to others. When the time seemed fitting they moved off to the frontier where land was cheap. Arrived there they set up as planters on a small scale. If industrious and practical they increased in wealth and in social position. For such men two generations were enough to bleach out of the family all traces of the overseer taint. Its representative members now became men of solid worth, their children assumed the status of pillars of society, and their grandchildren might be noted for personal charm and distinguished manners. In the third generation very little memory was held of the origin of the family, a trait in which the grandchildren of an overseer were by no means unique.

Comparatively few of the overseers were of this ambitious and advancing class. The majority were men of little imagination and saw no further into the future than the contentment that came from doing well the task of the year. Among them were many good and many indifferent managers. The good were the comfort and the bad were the despair of their employers. A planter was fortunate who had an overseer whom he trusted thoroughly and who understood the land and managed the slaves in a satisfactory manner. He could visit the springs in the summer or the city in the winter without anxiety. He had leisure for hunting, reading, or politics, as his taste led him.

The overseers had the vices common to the class in society from which they sprang, the small farmers and the landless whites. They had little education, as their fathers before them had. They often drank spirituous liquors to excess, or were idle and ineffective. They inherited the slovenness that their fathers had inherited from the indented servants whom the colonists had brought over from the sodden mass of English laborers of the seventeenth century. There was nothing in their lives to induce them to throw off these limitations. They had the powers of a proconsul in a narrow province, and their subjects were the African slaves, the plantation mules, and the cattle. Sometimes they ruled, despite the vices inherent in this position, in such a way that the province smiled with plenty and contentment.

George Washington, who was a man of excellent business method, had much to say to the discredit of his overseers.

He spoke of their bad habit of "running about," meaning, no doubt, leaving the estate for country frolics, thus giving the slave opportunity to go where he chose. One he described as intelligent and honest but vain and talkative and slow in getting the work done. Another neglected his duties in order to visit his friends, so that the slaves did things during his absence for which they had to be whipped when he came back. Of another it was said that he had "no more authority over the slaves. . . . .than an old woman would have." Another was described as sickly and stupid and another as a failure because he put himself on a level with the slaves and lost their respect. These qualities were probably typical of the run of the overseers. They give us an idea of what the members of the class were like who were neither exceptionally good nor exceptionally bad; and it was out of this intermediate class that most planters had to be served.

We may see Washington's idea of overseers in general in his advice to a new steward who was placed in charge of his several plantations. In telling him how to deal with these men Washington said: "To treat them kindly is no more than what all men are entitled to; but my advice to you is, keep them at a proper distance, for they grow upon familiarity and you will sink in authority, if you do not. Pass by no fault or neglects, particularly at first, for overlooking one only serves to generate another."

The overseer took the place assigned to him without complaint. He was a solitary figure on the plantation, whether the master lived there or not. To the slaves he was "Buckra," a word expressing scorn for a man of no standing. He could not touch the life above nor the life below him. If his employer did not reside on the place the overseer gained little in standing; for he was apt to be more disliked by the slaves and no better received by the owners of the surrounding plantations. It was even more necessary for him to stay on the place, since he was the only white man there. He gained, however, in opportunity to violate his instructions; and it is not to be wondered at if he was tempted to slip off at night to a country dance through sheer revolt at his state of isolation.

The letters published in this book are the clearest possible evidence of the mind, character, and culture of those who wrote them. They show what kind of men stood at the actual centre of the plantation system and made it go. We see men who rarely had the learning acquired by their descendants in the second grade of the modern Southern schools. To them were entrusted the care of property worth from $50,000 to $100,000. I can think of no other form of industry in which so much property was under the management of such illiterate men. The things needed in the overseer were courage, industry, and common sense, and if these qualities existed he would succeed though illiterate.

The reader will make a mistake if he dismisses the overseer as insignificant because he was illiterate. Literacy is not the same thing as being intelligent; and it is probable that nature gives her gifts about as freely in a community where there are few good schools as in communities where there are many. At any rate, the overseer, despite his illiteracy, generally met the emergency thrust upon him. In proportion to what he did he was underpaid. What other agent in our industrial history ever took under his direction so much property for the salary of the average overseer?

From many sources the present generation has received statements purporting to describe the life on the plantation. In fiction and in the reminiscences of persons who look back at the life they loved they have built up a picture of a joyous and sparkling life.[1] In the letters of the overseers one finds another view. It is in gray shades, reflecting a life that was not what the novelists have presented. True, it was not a picture of the whole life on the plantation. But it referred to the doing of work, the health of the slaves, and the general problem of making crops. So far as they can go these letters give us in a way we may not question the definite assurance that the plantation had its dreary side.

[1] For an excellent discussion of what he aptly terms the "Plantation Tradition" see Professor Francis Pendleton Gaines's *Southern Plantation* (Columbia Press, New York, 1925). It traces the "Tradition" through American fiction, essays, drama, poetry, popular music and travel from the early decades of the nineteenth century and presents a good comparison of the "Tradition" with the actual state of living on the plantation.

CHAPTER II

The Duties of the Overseer

HE Old South had its quota of gentlemen farmers who employed their leisure in writing for the newspapers and other periodicals. One of their topics was farm management, and out of their observations upon it Professor Phillips[1] has collected an interesting mass of information. I have drawn from it liberally in the preparation of this chapter and begin by making acknowledgments to my benefactor. A word of caution, however, seems to be necessary. The planters who wrote for the press were not always the most successful of their class, nor did they put into operation all of the precepts they thought out in their own chambers. Their observations are, therefore, to be understood as something more or less than the actual state of affairs. In what follows here an attempt has been made to make a fair deduction for this margin of error.

The first duty of the overseer, or manager, as he was frequently called, was to take care of the slaves and the stock. Next he was to see that enough food was produced for use on the place. By food was meant corn, bacon, potatoes, and vegetables for the slaves and corn, fodder, hay, and oats for the stock. These two duties done, he was to raise as much cotton, or rice in the rice region, as possible without overworking the slaves. Placing the production of supplies be-

[1] Phillips, Ulrich B., "American Negro Slavery" (N. Y., 1918).

[11]

fore the raising of a money crop was sound judgment. Now and again came a devastating drought and frequently some calamity tended to reduce the yield of food. It did not pay to run too close to the margin of safety in such a respect. A wise planter sought to insure against such inconvenience by having more supplies than he needed rather than not enough.

The routine of the overseer was as follows: An hour before dawn he rang the bell or blew the horn that called the hands from their beds. On some places they prepared their breakfasts in their cabins, on others they had breakfast brought to them in the fields after they had begun to work. It was always desired that they be assembled in the yards by the time it was broad daylight, and when the sun appeared above the horizon it was expected that they should be at their tasks. They worked in groups, each with a leader, or driver, who was one of the slaves. Throughout the day the overseer went from one to the other group to see that the labor was performed properly. At noon dinner was brought to the fields, if the gangs were working at a distance from the cabins, or eaten in their cabins if the cabins were close at hand.

The overseer was to inspect the food and see that it was wholesome. He gave the signal for leaving the fields when the sun had set. He looked after the feeding of the stock, the closing of the barns and stables, which must be locked and the keys taken by him and kept safely. One of the bad habits of the slaves was to take out horses or mules during the night and ride to remote places, and the overseer was expected to see that no such thing happened. At half past nine he rang a curfew bell and then went the rounds of the cabins to see that the occupants were abed. He was also expected to visit the houses unexpectedly during the night lest some of the people had slipped away after his inspection. If he did all these things continually he was a very busy man. No slave on the place served as long hours as the overseer was expected to serve. From an hour before dawn to ten at night was seventeen or eighteen hours. And if he got up to make inspections during the night he had little sleep. It is not likely that the details as here outlined were carried out with exactness.

The overseer was instructed to take the best possible moral care of his charges and to afford them fair opportunity, as far as he could, for getting religious instruction. "I want all my people," wrote one planter to his manager, "encouraged to cultivate religious feeling and morality and punished for inhumanity to their children or stock, for profanity, lying and stealing. . . . When ever the services of a suitable person can be secured have them instructed in religion. In view of the fanaticism of the age, it behooves the master or overseer to be present on all such occasions. They should be instructed on Sundays in day time if practicable; if not, then on Sunday night."

Judging by the overseer letters that have come into my hands the writers of them were not men of sufficient enlightenment to qualify as censors of preaching, to determine whether it was incendiary or not. They were probably safe enough to say that an open incitement to insurrection was objectionable. But such an incitement was not likely to be made by any man permitted to preach to the slaves. On utterances less open and direct the overseers were not safe judges. To make them censors of the sermons delivered to the slaves was ridiculous.

In all the preaching to slaves there was, in fact, something incongruous. In the first place the slave was not to be taught to read — this after the initiation of the active anti-slavery propaganda in 1831 by William Lloyd Garrison. If a slave could not read the Bible, the guide of his Christian life, how could he be expected to absorb the spirit of Christianity? He could not "search the scriptures" in which was eternal life. More than half of the Christian religion was diverted from him by condemning him to illiteracy.

Another incongruity was in the narrow range of the preaching that could be made to the slaves within the limits imposed by slavery. There must be no argument based on such texts as "The truth will make you free," and "The laborer is worthy of his hire." Doctrines that would make a man wish to raise himself to something better and higher were impossible; for they were sure to create dissatisfaction with slavery. The religious instructors of these people so unhappily placed had to recognize these facts and to preach a doctrine of contentment and humility. In an instinctive reaction against the hard lot of this world they dwelt at large upon the joys and beauties of a world to come.

Lunsford Lane, who was born in North Carolina, purchased his freedom and became an abolitionist lecturer in the North just before the civil war, gives the negro's views on this subject in the following words: "I often heard select portions of the Scriptures read in our social meetings and comments made upon them. On Sunday we always had one sermon prepared expressly for the colored people, which it was generally my privilege to hear. So great was the similarity of the texts that they were always fresh in my memory: 'Servants, be obedient to your masters' — 'not with eye-service, as men-pleasers.' 'He that knoweth his master's will and doeth it not, shall be beaten with many stripes;' and some others of this class. Similar passages, with but few exceptions, formed the basis of most of these public instructions. . . . I will not do them the injustice to say that connected with these instructions there was not mingled much that was excellent. There was one very kind-hearted clergyman whom I used often to hear; he was very popular with the colored people. But after he had preached a sermon to us in which he argued from the Bible that it was the will of Heaven from all eternity that we should be slaves, and our masters be our owners, many of us left him, considering, like the doubting disciple of old, 'This is a hard saying, who can hear it?'"[1]

As the representative of the owner the overseer had the duty of sitting as judge over the wrongdoing of the slaves. He had wide authority, for evidence of guilt, procedure, and extenuating circumstances were within his discretion. In view of his slight degree of culture this fact placed the slave's case at the mercy of an unenlightened judge. On the other hand the thing needed was not a knowledge of law, but common sense; and it will be allowed that when a man had proved himself a successful manager of a plantation he had a fair store of that quality. Also, we must not forget that the negro did not make the same distinctions as men of higher degrees of progress in civilization. He recognized the propriety of discipline and quick and firm punishment when orders were violated. If now and then a man was punished too much, or when innocent, it nevertheless remained that most of those who were punished were not given more than was considered just, and most of those who were punished were believed to be guilty. By and large the slave did not feel very deeply any lapses the overseer

[1] Hawkins, W. G., "Lunsford Lane," p. 65.

may have made in awarding punishment unless it was done cruelly.

The decision once made the overseer saw that the execution of punishment was done in such a way as to make the victim respect the power that inflicted it. Some masters insisted that their slaves should be sent to a public official for the whipping. In most cases the overseer did the whipping himself. Sometimes he stood by while a driver, that is, a slave, applied the lash. In stubborn cases the victim was "salted." This process was very painful and it was dreaded by the slaves. It consisted in whipping the victim on the bare back until the thongs cut the flesh and then washing the back down with strong brine. In some cases this was repeated several times. In general, public opinion was against "salting" and other forms of extreme punishment. Humane masters did not resort to such means of breaking the resistance of a slave unless they thought the case an unusual one. If a slave had to be dealt with as severely as this they believed it was better to sell him to a trader.

Some planters believed that a plantation could be run without whipping. Few overseers agreed with the idea. For whipping the benevolent ones would substitute tact, patience, and a careful study of the peculiarities of the individual slaves. Not many masters and even fewer overseers had the address to carry out such ideas. It was the ordinary view that whipping was "the only thing that would do a negro any good." Probably most of the slaves would have accepted the view in an abstract way. The power to whip within his discretion was held to be a necessary thing for the overseer's success with the slaves under him. At the same time it placed an alarming power in the hands of men who were not always likely to use it with discretion.

In the absence of the master the overseer administered the regulations governing the marriage of slaves. It was a common rule that slaves should not marry slaves living off the plantation, since such marriages involved visiting and brought up the problem of discipling such visitors when on the plantation of the wife's master. One master whose ideas we have in writing directed his overseer to permit separation when sufficient cause was shown on either side, the overseer, evidently, to be the judge of what was sufficient cause; but it was added, the offending party must be severely punished. If both were guilty both must be punished, and if after that they insisted on separation they must have a hundred lashes each. After such separation neither was to marry again for three years. For the first marriage a bounty of $5.00 was allowed to be invested in household articles. But if either had been married before the bounty was to be $2.50. A third marriage was not to be allowed.[1]

It has been said that failure to breed was considered grounds for separation: the charge was denied by the masters as a class. Probably it was unusual for a separation to occur for this cause; but it was one of the peculiarities of slavery that great latitude was allowed to the owner, so that he might do as he chose about most things. Consequently things done by one master might not be done by another. Some were not ruled by feelings of humanity nor even by public opinion. If a man of this class decided that a young slave woman was not bearing children by the husband she had he probably made it as easy for her to separate and form another marriage as she desired. The law did not look on the union of slaves as legal marriage; and

[1] Phillips, "American Negro Slavery," 269.

one of the first things to be done after emancipation was to take steps for remedying that defect.

It ought to be remembered that the negroes themselves did not esteem marriage as the white people esteemed it. In Africa a wife was considered property, and polygamy was practiced by many tribes. Divorce was easy and it was resorted to freely. The negro therefore arrived in America with ideas favorable to a loose marriage bond. Contact with the whites taught them to hold it in stricter esteem, but the old standards did not disappear suddenly. It is doubtful if the separations that occurred produced great distress in the minds of either party involved.

Dealing with runaways was one of the overseer's most difficult problems. Nearly every plantation had slaves who were accustomed to flee to the woods when they thought the discipline too severe. To get these persons back to their work was a thing that demanded address. Punishment for the liberty they had taken was a matter of course. It was expected by the runaway himself, and sometimes a form of negotiation seems to have been employed through the medium of some slaves who had not run off, by which it was agreed that the runaway would return provided his punishment did not go beyond a stipulated amount. The approach of cold weather could be counted on to bring many back. These conditions did not maintain in the parts of the South that permitted escape into the free states. In such sections the runaway was apt to turn his steps northward.

In the letters that follow are many allusions to runaways. None of them show such a group tendency to deal with the overseer in retaliation as the following incident related by a Georgia overseer and quoted by Professor Phillips: "I write you a few lines to let you know that six of

The Duties of the Overseer

your hands has left the plantation — every man but Jack. They displeased me with their worke and I give some of them a few lashes, Tom with the rest. On Wednesday morning they were missing. I think they are lying out until they can see you or your uncle Jack, as he is expected daily. They may be gone off, or they may be lying around in this neighborhood, but I don't know. I blame Tom for the whole. I don't think the rest of them would of left the plantation if Tom had not of persuaded them of for some design. I give Tom but a few licks, but if I ever get him in my power I will have satisfaction. There was a part of them had no cause for leaving, only they thought that if they would all go it would injure me moore. They are as independent set for running as I have ever seen, and I think the cause is they have been treated too well. They want more whiping and no protector; but if our country is so that negroes can quit their homes and run off when they please without being taken they will have the advantage of us."[1]

The tone of this letter indicates that the writer of it was not a man who should have been permitted to correct slaves. It shows that he lacked firmness and good judgment. Washington seems to have had a similar overseer, and he gives us a view of the man's character by writing: "Let Abram get his deserts when taken, but do not trust Crow to give it to him, for I have reason to believe he is swayed more by passion than by judgment in all his corrections."[2]

Testimony shows that the overseer had more trouble with the slave women than with the men. Travelers in Africa have noticed that the women there have a marked ascendency over the men, that they keep them in awe of

[1] Phillips, "American Negro Slavery," p. 303.
[2] *Ibid.*, p. 285.

[19]

their sharp tongues and that they are in general of violent passions as compared with the men. These qualities appeared in the slaves in the South. As a result many plantations had women who kept the rest of the slaves in a state of unrest and thereby made it hard for the overseer to keep order.

Phillips mentions several slave women who stood out for one bad quality or another. The case of one, a certain Suckey, is so suggestive that I give it here in the words of the Virginia overseer who reported it to his employer. "I sent for hir to come in the morning," he wrote, "to hep Secoure the foder, but She sent me word that She would not come to worke that Day, and that you had ordered her to wash hir Cloaiths and goo to Any meeting She pleased any time in the weke without my leafe, and on Monday when I come to Reckon with her about it she said it was your orders and she would do it in Defiance of me. . . . .I hope if Suckey is aloud that privilege more than the Rest, that she will be moved to some other place, and one Come in her Room."[1]

In nothing was the master more concerned than in the increase of his slaves through the birth of children. He resented the charge that he was breeding slaves as other men bred horses. Nevertheless, he watched carefully the statistics of births and within the bounds of humanity he took pains to promote conditions that made for large families. He encouraged marriage because he thought they made for orderly living and a large number of children. In some states it was a common saying that a slave child was worth a hundred dollars as soon as it breathed.

In realization of this desire it devolved on the overseer

[1] Phillips, "American Negro Slavery," 280.

to see that the women were taken care of that childbirth might be attended with no serious mishap. The ignorance of the women made it necessary to take many precautions. A large number of children died soon after being born. In many cases it was reported that the mothers lay on them in the night. How much this was due to sheer ignorance, how much to the alleged indifference of the slave women for their offspring, and how much to a desire to bring no children into the world to live under slavery it is impossible to say. Perhaps each cause contributed to the result.

The instructions of the employers required the overseer to see that mothers did not nurse their children in hot weather for fifteen minutes after they had come from the fields, that they were not put to difficult labor when they were not physically able to perform it, that they had the proper food for nursing women, that they had time from their work to go to the houses to nurse their children, that a midwife was on the plantation, or nearby, and many other things pertaining to safe childbearing. I find no evidence that doctors were summoned in childbirth, and it seems to have been the custom to leave the case entirely to the midwife, who was invariably a slave. On the other hand it should be remembered that most of the early white settlers in this country followed the same practice.

Crude as this method may seem it was greatly better than anything the negro had been used to in Africa. In marriage, religion, the use of language, treatment for disease, ideals of industry and private property, low as he was in slavery, he was nevertheless higher than in his ancestral home. In Africa most of the negroes who came to America had never seen a plough, a metal implement of agriculture, nor any animal domesticated to help man do his work. After a hundred years of slavery he had learned the fundamentals in all these lines. After another hundred years he was still higher up in the scale of progress. Hard as it was slavery had its service for him. He would never have come into the contact with the white man's civilization if it had not been for slavery. Had he been brought into touch with it by any other means he would not have absorbed it. It was the force in slavery that taught him to labor with some degree of regularity, it was the authority of the master that taught him to improve his ideas of morality, it was the superior authority of the white race that induced him to change fetishism for a rude and simple kind of Christianity. In many ways slavery instilled in him the fundamentals of civilization. This truth is just beginning to be understood: some day it will be better realized. Slavery was a hard school but in it the Africans learned some good lessons.

These people disliked much the overseers who themselves knew so little of the things of culture. But they knew enough to teach the benighted black people. They taught them by making them do. They stormed at them for not doing, lashed them for doing badly, and made them acquire habits they would not have acquired but for this rough tutelage. Nor were they always rough teachers, though their methods were frequently primitive. That they were usually men of sense and good intention is seen in the fact that the institution of slavery did not go to pieces under their supervision but actually became more firmly rooted in the minds of masters and slaves. As a rule they were men of ability and administered their many duties toward the slaves with a fair amount of efficiency.

CHAPTER III

Terms of the Overseer's Contract

T HE contract incorporated in this chapter was prepared by Plowden C. J. Weston, a South Carolina rice planter, for use on his several plantations. It was printed originally as a small pamphlet with blank spaces to be filled out as occasion demanded with the names of the overseers and the plantations on which they were employed. The actual contract was simple enough, but attached to it were a number of rules which when signed became a part of the instrument. The form in which the contract was printed suggests that the employer expected the overseer to keep it at hand, familiarize himself with the contents, and use it as a guide in his operations.[1]

It is probable that overseers did not follow the terms of this instrument exactly. Nor did all the employers attempt to have so complete a body of rules put into operation. The paper is interesting chiefly because it indicates a high standard for the conduct of a good overseer. As a statement to be lived up to it gives us an ideal for measuring the purposes of the slaveowners. Many of its rules were un-

[1] Weston's rules were published in *De Bow's Review,* XXII, 38-44. In the same periodical (XXI, 617-620, Dec., 1856 and XXII, 376-381, April, 1857) are rules of a similar general nature prepared by Joseph A. S. Acklen of Louisiana. In Professor Phillips's "American Negro Slavery," 261-290, is much on the same subject. See also his "Plantation and Frontier," I, 109-129. *De Bow's Review* of this period contains many other pieces on plantation management, which was a favorite subject for planters when writing for the press.

doubtedly fairly put into operation. Like most everything
else about slavery it depended to a great extent on the kind
of men who had to execute it. The contract was in the following form:

RULES FOR THE GOVERNMENT AND MANAGEMENT OF................
PLANTATION TO BE OBSERVED BY THE OVERSEER.[1]

"Memorandum of an Agreement between...
.....................................on the one part, and Plowden Charles Jennett Weston
on the other part:

"IT IS AGREED That...shall live at..........
....Plantation as Overseer for the year 18.........;
and that he shall follow all and every the printed rules hereunto
annexed.

"IT IS AGREED That Plowden Charles Jennett Weston shall pay him,
for his services as Overseer, at the rate of...
Dollars a year; and shall find him in a house, a woman, and a boy,
and in feed for one horse during the year 18.........

"IN WITNESS of which Agreement, we have hereunto set our hands
and seals, this ....day of ...., in the
year of our Lord Eighteen hundred and...................................., and of the
Independence of the United States the..

(L. S.)
(L. S.)

RULES, &c.

"The Proprietor, in the first place, wishes the Overseer *MOST
DISTINCTLY* to understand that his first object is to be, under all
circumstances, the care and well being of the negroes. The proprietor
is always ready to excuse such errors as may proceed from want of
judgment; but he never can or will excuse any cruelty, severity, or
want of care towards the negroes. For the well being, however, of
the negroes, it is absolutely necessary to maintain obedience, order,
and discipline, to see that the tasks are punctually and carefully performed, and to conduct the business steadily and firmly, without weak-

[1] It was printed in pamphlet form by A. J. Burke, 40 Broad Street, Charleston.

ness on the one hand, or harshness on the other. For such ends the following regulations have been instituted:

"LISTS, TICKETS. — The names of all the men are to be called over every Sunday morning and evening, from which none are to be absent but those who are sick, or have tickets. When there is evening Church, those who attend are to be excused from answering. At evening list, every negro must be clean and well washed. No one is to be absent from the place without a ticket, which is always to be given to such as ask it, and have behaved well. All persons coming from the Proprietor's other places should shew their tickets to the Overseer, who should sign his name on the back; those going off the plantation should bring back their tickets signed. The Overseer is every now and then to go round at night and call at the houses, so as to ascertain whether their inmates are at home.

"ALLOWANCE, FOOD. — Great care should be taken that the negroes should never have less than their regular allowance: in all cases of doubt, it should be given in favor of the largest quantity. The measures should not be *struck,* but rather heaped up over. None but provisions of the best quality should be used. If any is discovered to be damaged, the Proprietor, if at hand, is to be immediately informed: if absent, the damaged article is to be destroyed. The corn should be carefully winnowed before grinding. The small rice is apt to become sour: as soon as this is perceived it should be given every meal until finished, or until it becomes too sour to use, when it should be destroyed.

"Allowances are to be given out according to the following schedule. None of the allowances given out in the big pot are to be taken from the cook until after they are cooked, nor to be taken home by the people.

SCHEDULE OF ALLOWANCES
Daily, (Sundays Excepted)

"*During Potato-time.*
To each person doing any work.. 4 qts.
To each child at the negro-houses... 2 qts.

"*During Grits-time.*
To the cook for public-pot, for every person doing any work........ 1 qt.

To the child's cook, for each child at the negro-houses.................. 1 pt.

Salt to cook for the public-pot .... pt.

Salt to child's cook .... pt.

"On every Tuesday and Friday throughout the year.

To cook for public-pot, for whole gang of workers, trades, drivers, &c., Meat .... lbs.

To child's-cook for all the children, Meat .... lbs.

"On every Tuesday and Friday from April 1st to October 1st.

To the plantation cook for each person doing any work, instead of the pint of grits, Small Rice .... 1 pt.

To the child's-cook for each child instead of the ½ pt. of grits, Small Rice .... ½ pt.

To plantation cook for the whole gang of workers, tradesmen, drivers, &c., Peas .... qts.

"Every Thursday throughout the year.

To the child's-cook, for all the children, Molasses..................... qts.

"Weekly Allowance throughout the year — To be given out "Every Saturday Afternoon.

To each person doing any work, Flour .... 3 qts.

To each child at negro-houses .... 3 pts.

To each person who has behaved well, and has not been sick during the week, 2 Fish or 1 pt. Molasses.

To each nurse....................................4 Fish or 1½ pt. Molasses.

To head-carpenter; to head-miller;
To head-cooper; to head-ploughman;
To watchman; to trunk minder;
To drivers; to mule-minder;
To hog-minder; to cattle-minder; and
To every superannuated person,

} 3 Fish or 1½ pt. Molasses each.

"Monthly Allowance — On the 1st of every Month.

To each person doing any work, and each superannuated per-son .... Salt, 1 qt.

Do... Tobacco 1 hand.

Terms of the Overseer's Contract

"Christmas Allowance.

To each person doing any work,
      and each superannuated person

	Fresh Meat,	3 lbs.
	Salt do. ...	3 lbs.
	Molasses	1 qt.
	Small Rice	4 qts.
	Salt	½ bushel.

To each child at negro-houses

	Fresh Meat	1½ lbs.
	Salt Meat	1½ lbs.
	Molasses	1 pt.
	Small Rice,	2 qts.

Additional Allowance.

Every day when rice is sown or harvested, to the cook, Meat,   lbs.
      for the whole gang of workers in the field   Peas   qts.
No allowances or presents, besides the above, are on any con-
      sideration to be made — except for sick people, as specified
      further on.

"WORK, HOLIDAYS, &c. — No work of any sort or kind is to be permitted to be done by negroes on Good Friday or Christmas day, or on
any Sunday, except going for a Doctor, or nursing sick persons; any
work of this kind done on any of these days is to be reported to the
Proprietor, who will pay for it. The two days following Christmas
day; the first Saturdays after finishing threshing, planting, hoeing,
and harvest, are also to be holidays, on which the people may work
for themselves. Only half task is to be done on every Saturday, except during planting and harvest, and by those who have misbehaved
or been lying up during the week. A task is as much work as the
meanest full hand can do in nine hours, working industriously. The
Driver is each morning to point out to each hand their task, and this
task is *never* to be increased, and no work is to be done over task
except under the *most urgent necessity;* which over-work is to be reported to the Proprietor, who will pay for it. No negro is to be put
into a task which they cannot finish with tolerable ease. It is a bad
plan to punish for not finishing task; it is subversive of discipline to
leave tasks unfinished, and contrary to justice to punish for what

cannot be done. *In nothing does a good manager so much excel a bad, as in being able to discern what a hand is capable of doing, and in never attempting to make him do more.*

"No negro is to leave his task until the Driver has examined and approved it, he is then to be permitted immediately to go home; and the hands are to be encouraged to finish their tasks as early as possible, so as to have time for working for themselves. Every negro, except the sickly ones and those with suckling children, (who are to be allowed half an hour,) are to be on board the flat by sunrise. One Driver is to go down to the flat early, the other to remain behind and bring on all the people with him. He will be responsible for all coming down. The barn-yard bell will be rung by the watchman two hours, and half an hour before sunrise.

"PUNISHMENTS. — It is desirable to allow 24 hours to elapse between the discovery of the offence and the punishment. No punishment is to exceed 15 lashes: in cases where the Overseer supposes a severer punishment necessary, he must apply to the Proprietor, or to ——————————————————, Esq., in case of the Proprietor's absence from the neighborhood. Confinement (*not* in the stocks) is to be preferred to whipping; but the stoppage of Saturday's allowance, and doing whole task on Saturday, will suffice to prevent ordinary offences. Special care must be taken to prevent any *indecency* in punishing women. No Driver, or other negro, is to be allowed to punish any person in any way, except by order of the Overseer, and in his presence.

"FLATS, BOATS, &c. — All the flats, except those in immediate use, should be kept under cover, and sheltered from the sun. Every boat must be locked up every evening, and the keys taken to the Overseer. No negro will be allowed to keep a boat.

"SICKNESS. — All sick persons are to stay in the hospital night and day, from the time they first complain to the time they are able to go to work again. The nurses are to be responsible for the sick not leaving the house, and for the cleanliness of bedding, utensils, &c. The nurses are never to be allowed to give any medicine, without the orders of the Overseer or Doctor. A woman, beside the plantation nurse, must be put to nurse all persons seriously ill. In all cases *at all* serious the Doctor is to be sent for, and his orders are to be strictly attended to: no alteration is to be made in the treatment he directs. Lying-in women are to be attended by the midwife as long as is necessary, and by a woman put to nurse them for a fortnight. They will remain at the negro houses for 4 weeks, and will then work 2 weeks on the highland. In some cases, however, it is necessary to allow them to lie up longer. The health of many women has been entirely ruined by want of care in this particular. Women are sometimes in such a state as to render it unfit for them to work in water; the Overseer should take care of them at these times. The pregnant women are always to do *some* work up to the time of their confinement, if it is only walking into the field and staying there. If they are sick, they are to go to the hospital, and stay there until it is pretty certain their time is near.

"Nourishing food is to be provided for those who are getting better. The Overseer will keep an account of the articles he purchases for this purpose, during the Proprietor's absence, which he will settle for as soon as he returns.

"BLEEDING IS UNDER ALL CIRCUMSTANCES STRICTLY PROHIBITED, EXCEPT BY ORDER OF THE DOCTOR. — The Overseer is particularly warned not to give strong medicines, such as calomel, or tartar emetic: simple remedies such as flax-seed tea, mint water, *No.* 6, magnesia, &c., are sufficient for most cases, and do less harm. Strong medicines should be left to the Doctor; and since the Proprietor never grudges a Doctor's bill, however large, he has a right to expect that the Overseer shall always send for the Doctor when a serious case occurs. Dr. _____is the Physician of the place. When he is absent, Dr._____. Great care must be taken to prevent persons from lying up when there is nothing or little the matter with them. Such persons must be turned out immediately; and those somewhat sick can do lighter work, which encourages industry. Nothing is so subversive of discipline, or so unjust, as to allow people to sham, for this causes the well-disposed to do the work of the lazy.

"LIVE STOCK. — One man is to be put to take care of all the oxen; he will do only half-task ploughing, and will be responsible for them. The Overseer must see them well provided with straw, tailing, and coarse flour. The ploughing and carting tasks will be regulated by the appearance of the oxen. It is better to be a fortnight later in work, and have cattle in good order, than to kill any of them.

"Mules should also be under the care of one person *all the year round,* who shall be responsible for them. Their ordinary food shall be flour and tailing cut up, and during hard work, corn; crab grass cut, with straw and flour, is also a good food. In summer they must be turned out on the marsh, when not in use. No mule must ever be worked with a gall; on the first appearance of one, the man in charge must inform the Overseer. It must be recollected, *that it is easy to keep an animal once fat in good condition, but extremely difficult to get one into condition who is worked down.*

"The harness, chains, yokes, ploughs, &c., should always be kept under cover, as well as the carts and wagons. The stables and ox-houses should be cleaned out every week, and the oxen and mules cleaned down every evening. No animal can do well whose skin is covered with dirt.

"THRESHING, &c., MACHINERY. — The mill is to be closed in time to allow the whole yard to be cleaned up by sunset. The Proprietor considers an Overseer who leaves *any* straw or tailing during the night within 300 yards of the mill, as unfit to be trusted with the care of valuable property. He should keep a constant and vigilant inspection on the machinery, to see that no part of it heats; he should also stay in the yard whilst threshing, and not leave the keys to the drivers. As soon as the people come in, in the morning, the barn-yard doors should be locked, and not be opened again until work is over, except to admit the meals, and the suckling children. As soon as anything goes wrong in the mill, or other machinery, Mr.⎯⎯⎯⎯⎯⎯⎯⎯⎯⎯⎯⎯ should be informed of it.

DUTIES OF OFFICIALS

"Drivers are, under the Overseer, to maintain discipline and order on the place. They are to be responsible for the quiet of the negro-houses, for the proper performance of tasks, for bringing out the people early in the morning, and generally for the immediate inspection of such things as the Overseer only generally superintends. *For other duties of Drivers, see article* WORK.

"WATCHMEN are to be responsible for the safety of the buildings, boats, flats, and fences, and that no cattle or hogs come inside the place. If he perceives any buildings or fences out of repair, or if he hears of any robberies or trespasses, he must immediately give the Overseer notice. He must help to kill hogs and beeves.

"TRUNK-MINDERS undertake the whole care of the trunks, under the Proprietor's and Overseer's directions. Each has a boat to himself, which he must on no account let any body else use.

"NURSES are to take care of the sick, and to be responsible for the fulfilment of the orders of the Overseer, or Doctor, (if he be in attendance.) The food of the sick will be under their charge. They are expected to keep the hospital floors, bedding, blankets, utensils, &c., in perfect cleanliness. Wood should be allowed them. Their assistants should be entirely under their control. When the Proprietor and Overseer are absent, and a serious case occurs, the nurse is to send for the Doctor.

"YARD WATCHMAN is responsible for the crop in the yard, and for the barns.

"COOKS take every day the provisions for all the people, the sick only excepted, *(see article Allowance.)* The Overseer is particularly requested to see that they cook cleanly and well. One cook cooks on the Island, the other on the Main, for the carpenters, millers, highland hands, &c.

"The child's cook cooks for the children at the negro-houses; she ought to be particularly looked after, so that children should not eat anything unwholesome.

MISCELLANEOUS OBSERVATIONS

"The Proprietor wishes particularly to impress on the Overseer the criterions by which he will judge of his usefulness and capacity. *First* — by the general well being of the negroes; their cleanly appearance, respectful manners, active and vigorous obedience; their completion of their tasks well and early; the small amount of punishment; the excess of births over deaths; the small number of persons in hospitals, and the health of the children. *Secondly* — the condition and fatness of the cattle and mules; the good repair of all the fences and buildings, harness, boats, flats, and ploughs; more particularly the good order of the banks and trunks, and the freedom of the fields from grass and volunteer. *Thirdly* — the amount and quality of the rice and provision crops. The Overseer will fill up the printed forms sent to him every week, from which the Proprietor will obtain most of the facts he desires, to form the estimate mentioned above.

"The Overseer is expressly prohibited from three things, viz.: bleeding, giving spirits to any negro without a Doctor's order, and letting any negro on the place have or keep any gun, powder, or shot.

"When carpenters' work is wanted, the Overseer must apply in writing to Mr._____Miller.

"When the Overseer wishes to leave the plantation for more than a few hours, he must inform the Proprietor, (if he is in the Parish.)

"Whenever a negro is taken seriously ill, or any epidemic makes its appearance, or any death or serious accident occurs, the Proprietor (if in the Parish) must be immediately informed, as well as of any serious insubordination or breach of discipline.

"No gardens, fowl-houses, or hog-pens, are allowed near the house; a space will be fenced out for these purposes, and they will be under the charge of the watchman.

"No trees are to be cut down within 200 yards on each side of the houses.

"Women with six children alive at any *one* time, are allowed all Saturday to themselves.

"Fighting, particularly amongst women, and obscene or abusive language, is to be always rigorously punished.

"During the summer, fresh spring water must be carried every day on the Island. Anybody found drinking ditch or river water must be punished.

"*Finally.* — The Proprietor hopes the Overseer will remember that a system of *strict justice* is necessary to good management. No person should ever be allowed to break a law without being punished, or any person punished who has not broken a well known law. Every person should be made perfectly to understand what they are punished for, and should be made to perceive that they are not punished in anger, or through caprice. All abusive language or violence of demeanor should be avoided: they reduce the man who uses them to a level with the negro, and are hardly ever forgotten by those to whom they are addressed.

Hagley

PLOWDEN C. J. WESTON."

Terms of the Overseer's Contract

By the side of this paper I am able to place the following contract in what was no doubt the more usual form of such documents. It was made by George Jones, of Savannah, Georgia, and applied to one of his two plantations near Tallahassee, Florida.[1] It reads as follows:

This agreement made and entered into this twenty fourth day of December in the year of our Lord eighteen hundred and Forty nine Between George Jones of the first part and Jesse W. Whatley of the second part Witnesses that the said Jesse W. Whatley for and in consideration of the sum of one dollar to him in hand paid by the said George Jones the receipt whereof is hereby acknowledged and also in consideration of the Covenants and agreement hereinafter contained agrees to oversee and manage the plantation of the said George Jones situated in Leon County State of Florida and known by the name of Cheemoonie for and during the term of one year from date, that is to say, until the twenty fourth day of December eighteen hundred and fifty unless sooner discharged. To take care of the Negroes on the said plantation in sickness and in health and to treat them with humanity, to obey the lawful instructions of the said George Jones his agent or agents and generally to do and perform all acts usually required of a faithful overseer. And in consideration of the premises aforesaid George Jones agrees to pay Jesse W. Whatley at the end of the year aforesaid, That is to say on the twenty fourth day of December eighteen hundred and Fifty the sum of Four hundred dollars or at that rate for a less time, viz. at the rate of thirty three dollars and thirty three cents a month if the said George Jones should wish to terminate this agreement before the end of the year aforesaid. George Jones also agrees to furnish the said Jesse W. Whatley with a woman to cook and wash, Corn and fodder for one horse and bread and meat sufficient for his own use and such as the plantation affords.

In witness whereof the parties to these presents have hereunto set their hands and seals the day and year first above written.

JESSE WHATLEY
GEORGE JONES

[1] The original is in the possession of Mr. J. C. Yonge, Tallahassee, Florida.

The Plantation Overseer

It is understood between the parties to the above agreement that if John Evans should prefer to remain on the Chemoonie Plantation then the said Jesse W. Whatley will take charge of George Jones' El Destino plantation in Jefferson County, Florida, upon the same terms as he has agreed to oversee the Chemoonie Plantation and George Jones agrees to pay him the same wages and grants to him the same privileges.[1]

Jesse Whatley
Geo. Jones

In the same collection which contains this contract is another, made for one of the George N. Jones plantations for the year 1879. It is interesting as showing the terms on which overseers were employed after the civil war. It provided that the overseer, James S. Curry, should receive for his services $400 in money, the feed of one horse, and 500 pounds of bacon or "its equivalent for the whole year and likewise bread for his family," which was not much unlike the remuneration of *ante-bellum* days. Curry on his part agreed to discharge faithfully the duties of an overseer, to refrain from trading with the laborers, to refrain from leaving the place "except under urgent circumstances," and not to raise poultry for sale. He agreed to give his whole time to the duties of his office and not to "make a practice of receiving visitors." It thus seems that the fall of slavery made little difference in the wages, treatment, and ordinary duties of an overseer on a Georgia plantation. It created, however, a tendency to subdivide the large holdings of land and thus to establish the cropping system; and both of these developments tended to make the overseer unnecessary.

---

[1] Indorsements on the contract show that Jones paid $400, the amount in full of the wages specified, on December 24, 1850, and that the contract was renewed on the same day for the following year on the same terms. Another entry shows that on May 30, 1851, Jones paid Whatley $25 "for the use of the plantation."

CHAPTER IV

The Plantation Experience of James K. Polk

M OST of the letters in this volume were written by overseers on two plantations owned by James K. Polk, eleventh president of the United States. Simple as they were they were filed by Polk in his well preserved correspondence and are now in the Polk Papers in the Library of Congress. It would be agreeable to suppose that Polk had some realization of the service he rendered to future students of our social history in saving letters of a class of men who wrote very badly and whose letters were so slightly esteemed that few specimens have been preserved. But there is no reason to suppose that Polk knew how important these letters might become. Saving them seems to have been but the result of habit. Polk had an honest, efficient, routine mind to which small things were as important as large things. His overseer letters had their place in his files as truly as his correspondence with important political leaders.

Polks ancestry, Scotch-Irishmen, settled in Mecklenburg County, North Carolina, before the beginning of the war for independence. One of the family, Colonel Thomas Polk, was a leader in the revolution and was associated with the men of Mecklenburg who voted for the celebrated resolutions of May 31, 1775, which went far in disputing the authority of the king. Colonel Polk's brother, Ezekiel, was an early associate in the same movement, but when Cornwallis appeared in 1780 Ezekiel swore loyalty to the king and thus saved his considerable estate from confiscation. Many of his neighbors did likewise. About 1800 he became dissatisfied with Mecklenburg and turned his eyes westward. Looking around for fields of speculation he became interested in Tennessee lands. He bought claims in the fertile region south of Duck River, then allotted to the Cherokees; but when the Indians ceded it to the federal government in 1806 his claims became realities and he moved to his newly acquired possession in the same year. The state set up a new county, calling it Maury, with the court house at Columbus, forty miles south of Nashville. Here Ezekiel Polk lived in high esteem until he died in 1824.

Accompanying him when he moved to Tennessee was his son Samuel, with his wife and small children. Samuel was a surveyor and like most other surveyors had an eye for good land. He arrived in Maury the year it was set up as a county. He acquired many a fine acre for a song and as the country grew in population his lands grew in value. When he died in 1827 he left a fair estate to be divided among nine children, or their heirs; for some of them had preceded him to the grave. His eldest son, James Knox Polk, he made one of the executors and the guardian of some of the minor children and grandchildren. This eldest son was then a lawyer in Columbia, a hardworking, reliable, and industrious man by whom no task was ever assumed without careful and conscientious execution.

For the guidance of the reader of the letters that follow it will be well to say that one of Polk's sisters was married to James Walker, who long had a stage route with contracts to carry the mails, another to Dr. Silas M. Caldwell, who seems to have been more of a planter than a physician, and another to A. O. Harris. They all lived in Columbia. It will be seen that Polk transacted business with most of these relatives, and it is not always possible to tell whether a particular action was taken by him for himself or as acting for a ward. For example, some of the slaves mentioned in the correspondence as his were in reality the property of one of his wards, and they were only in his hands as guardian.

The management of this property in trust has a peculiar interest. It was, naturally, mostly in the form of land and slaves. To place the slaves on the land and carry on farming operations demanded much time from the guardian, and Polk, who was ever in politics, had little leisure for it. The method followed was to get a court of chancery, after allotting the slaves to the heirs on a basis of equitable division, to consent that they might be hired out for the benefit of the particular heirs to whom they had been allotted. Some of them Polk hired himself, with the approval of the court. It was characteristic of the South in the era of slavery that almost the only opportunity for the investment of money was in land and slaves. Few corporations existed and of those that did exist not many were so sound that their shares and bonds were good investments. Inherited property, if not in the form of slaves and land when inherited, could hardly be invested in anything else.

When Samuel Polk was acquiring his large property in land the Chickasaw Indians held the part of Tennessee that lay west of the Tennessee River. In 1818 by treaty they ceded this territory to the whites. Much of it had already been disposed of by the Indians in what was known as "floats," grants made by them very cheaply, the grantees taking chances to get their bargains confirmed by the federal government after a treaty had been made. "Floats" were not worth anything against the government; but on a frontier filled with men who held them it was not the custom to dispute their validity, and it rarely happened that he who held one had a competitor when he made his bargain with the government land office. Samuel Polk got much of the land in this cession, which became known locally as the Western District, shortened to "The District." When he died in 1827 he still held a considerable portion of such land, waiting for the price to rise with the increase of population, and these scattered holdings were distributed among the heirs, thus coming to some extent under the direction of James Knox Polk, trustee.

On one of these tracts this story opened in 1833. It lay in Fayette County not far from the town of Somerville. Fayette is in the southern tier of counties in southwest Tennessee and on the west joins Tipton, in which is the city of Memphis, the market for the produce of a wide region. In 1833 Polk and his brother-in-law, Dr. Silas M. Caldwell, were conducting farming operations on two of these tracts, raising cotton, hauling it to Memphis for sale. The operations of the overseers on the two places were directed by means of infrequent visits made by Dr. Caldwell.

By the prevailing standards Polk's plantation was not a large plantation. In 1833 it "made" 25 bales of cotton averaging 489 pounds each. The corn raised was so little that it was necessary to kill the hogs in December before they were fat, and the yield in bacon was only 4,000 pounds. When the place was sold a year later the supplies and cattle included 13 plows, 29 sheep and goats, and 9 cows, besides 22 calves and "young cattle." I have no way of knowing the acreage, and I can only guess at the number of slaves on it, making it not more than twenty-five, male and female, young and old. While Polk conducted this plantation in 1833, Dr. Caldwell carried on operations on a place he owned in the adjoining county of Haywood. There is some reason to believe that Polk began his operations on the Fayette County place with the year 1833, though on that point the evidence is not conclusive.

When we get our first glimpse of the plantation it was under the care of Ephraim Beanland, overseer, who was a young man and unmarried. A tradition in his family says that he was born in England, but his style of expressing himself and his illiteracy were so much like those prevailing among the poorer whites of the South that I cannot be satisfied with the statement. My doubt is strengthened by the fact that he had a younger brother named Jefferson, which does not sound like English birth or early association. He received wages of $350 a year and conducted the place with fair efficiency. He did not have the confidence of Dr. Caldwell, who was a temperamental man and hard to please. Of all the overseers who fall into these pages he was the most picturesque and the man who makes the strongest appeal to my sympathy. He seems to have entered Polk's service late in 1833, taking the place of another overseer, the cause of whose departure from the plantation is not revealed.

The Fayette County plantation was not very successful. In 1834 it gave its owner 39 bales of cotton from 85 acres, which was small return for the time and labor involved. It happened at that time that the Tennesseeans were being swept away in a tide of enthusiasm for establishing plantations in Mississippi where much of the land was very fertile. Persons traveling through the settlements painted alluring pictures of the country to the southward, and Polk yielded to the temptation. He entered into partnership with Dr. Caldwell for the purchase of a plantation in Mississippi. For that purpose he authorized James Brown, who seems to have been a land agent, to go to Mississippi and buy a tract of land for the partners. "I am determined to make more money or lose more," said Polk. In 1832-1833 cotton sold in Nashville for about 9 cents a pound. In the season of 1833-1834 it began at 10 cents and went up to 15. With this staple rising so rapidly the popular mind was filled with hopes of great wealth in the rich country where it was said to be possible to produce a bale, or more, on an acre. The dream had a disastrous ending in the panic of 1837.

The Fayette plantation brought $6,000, probably sold on the usual terms of three or four annual payments. The new place was to be bought on the same terms. It was characteristic of the times to buy and sell for part cash and part in deferred payments. It was also characteristic of the adventurers to buy land with the hope of making the land yield, above expenses, enough profit to meet the deferred payments as they fell due and thus to pay off the purchase obligation in the time allowed out of the proceeds of the investment. Probably the hope was as often defeated as fulfilled, but it shows to what rates of progress the men settling this large region were accustomed in building up their fortunes.

Polk and Caldwell decided to take Beanland to Mississippi as their overseer, and it was agreed that each should furnish his fair portion of the hands needed to work the place. Caldwell was to give the enterprise as much personal supervision as possible by visiting it at periods, and one of their Tennessee friends in Mississippi was appointed the local representative of the proprietors. He promised to aid the overseer with advice in emergency and to keep a general watch over the progress of the enterprise.

Buying the place in the new country did not prove as easy as was anticipated. James Brown, the agent, disappeared in the South leaving high expectations behind him. After a long wait there came from him a letter dated "Chickasaw Nation, November 4, 1834," which cooled to some extent the hopes of the partners; but it is extremely interesting to us because it shows the actual process of taking up land and trading in it, and settling upon it, on the frontier in the flush days of the early Southwest. The text of the letter is as follows:

DEAR SIR:

I wrote you a short time since that I expected to buy a tract of land on Tellatoby for you. I have since then examined the land and find it not to come up to the description given of it. I can enter land at government price that I would as leave have. I find it all most impossible to find a tract of land that would suite you, that can be bought, in fact such places are very scears, and when I find the body of land, I cant find the owner, and most generally the good lands are owned in small parcels and by speculators, that are non-resident and have no agents in the country. I shall be at the land sales first Monday in December, where it is likely that I shall see the most of them and will I think be able to get a tract to my notion.

I have bought a section and a half of land of a Chickasaw lying on the Yocknepetauphy, but the title to it is as yet uncertain. But if I can get the title complete in time and can do no better for you, I will let you have it so that you

will be certain of a place. It is a most beautifull lying tract,
has good water, a handsome situation to build, a fine running small creek on one line, 500 acres of the 640 tilable
that lies well, but it is not quite as rich as I should like to
get for you tho it is good second rate. The growth is a vari-
ety of oak, hickory, dogwood, etc. It is very handsome land
and very easy cleared. Hands to be on the place by 1st
December could clear as much land by planting time as
they could cultivate. It has two or three small cabins, and
20 acres of cleared land. When I have a place certain I will
wright Beanland at Somerville where it is, how to get to
it, etc. Corn will cost about 75 cents per bushel. There
is plenty in the country for sale hoping that I shall get a
place to suite my own views before I wright you agane I
remain

Yours truly

N. B.   Sales of Chickasaw land are not yet to be relyed
on, as they have not yet got the certificates authorizing
them to trade nor have they yet got the entrys made. I think
about the 1st of December will bring about some certainty
as to the lands. Speculation runns high. I have not been
able to stand the prices offered for some of these lands. If I
trade with them I must make a profit on the land. The 640
I bought cost $2000 the section. The $\frac{1}{2}$ section not being
located cost me $500. I think the trade I have made will be
confirmed.

James Brown proved a broken reed. He was buying land
for himself, expecting to sell it at an advance; and he did
not find more bargains than he was willing to take for himself. Dr. Caldwell, who was inclined to run to suspicion,
believed that the agent would delay until the partners would

have to take some of Brown's own lands, paying him a handsome profit on them. The doctor, who did not number idleness among his faults, was no sooner convinced of this state of affairs than he set out for Mississippi himself. The results of his search are told in the following letter to Polk, written from the Fayette County plantation, January 2, 1835:

DEAR SIR:

I returned from Mississippi a few days since after a long laborious trip of four weeks   I met with James Brown at *Chocchuma*[1] he had not Bot a plantation nor did he know of any. I went below there fifty miles down the Yazoo River, a fine country of Land but very high and very sickly returned followed Brown about a week, quit him and in a day or two found a tract of Land in Yella Busha County near the river Yella Busha. then had to go to Manchester to find the owner the distance 220 miles from Chocchuma I gave Ten Dollars pr. acre I Bot 880 acres, payments one-third down the Balance in two equal annual payments there is no improvement on it.

The distance from the state line is about 100 miles south there is a fine spring on it it is a splendid tract of Land said to be among the best tracts in the county   Brown had been on the land and it could have been bot at that time for $5000 cash   Land is rising in that county very fast   Small Steam Boats run the Yella Busha River in the Winter within 10 Miles of where I will settle   By hauling 40 Miles we get to the Yazoo River which is large enough for large Steam Boats at the Junction of the Yella Busha and Tallahatcha Rivers.   I think where I will settle we can make

1 The government land office was at Chocchuma.

from 12 to 15-Hundred pounds of cotton to the acre[1] the prospect of health is good   I selected a place where I thot the cotton crop would be a certain one and a prospect of health.

Beanland has got your crop out he made 39 Bales of cotton 33 of them at Memphis 3 at home 3 at Colo. Alexanders within 12 Miles of Memphis all of which I have directed to [be] sent there as soon as practicable the roads are very bad at this time   Your Corn Fodder Cattle Hogs and other articles we let Bookers overseer have amounted to $809.25 the hire of Bookers hands amounted to $86 which left a Balance of $723.25.[2]

We leave this in morning for Mississippi with the following negroes Reuben, Caesar, Phil, Addison, Abram, Giles, Elizabeth, old Sarah, and the girl you Bot. of Gregory, Wally, Gilbert, Harvey, Alfred, Jane, Patsey, Marino, John, and a little boy Henry, in all Eighteen. Your Boy Hardy is not able to go he has had a breast complaint about five months, has a very violent cough. I will leave him at my place with Jones   I think his recovery very doubtful indeed it will take the Balance to cultivate my farm one of my women *Judy* I will loose in a day or two I think the smith tools have not come to Memphis yet we will not be able to take them with us which will be a very serious disappointment   I will write to Lawrence and Davis of Memphis, to send them to some point, on the Yella Busha River when he receives them. My corn cost me 66⅔ cents pr. Bushel, the 150 Barrels, $500

We have a desperate time to move, mud and high waters, now raining, the first payment for the Land and corn cost

[1] This was doubtless unginned cotton. The rule in the South is to expect seed cotton to yield one-third its weight in ginned cotton.

[2] Polk's Fayette plantation had been sold to Booker.

near $3500 Cash, which has taken all my money. Write to me who you Bot the Smith tools of in Nashville perhaps they have not shipped them to Memphis yet. Beanland only collected the sixty two dollar note from Silliman could not get the other discounted. I shall make 39 or 40 Bales of Cotton and about 400 Barrels of corn. Bookers overseer took all the Ploughs, Harrows, Hogs, etc., in payment for the hire of the hands. I have recd no letter from you yet. I expect to return to the District about the first of February after you receive this write to me at Columbia. I will write to you after I get to Mississippi. I procured some cotton seed when I was down. I shall put in what corn I think will do us and plant as much cotton as I can   Cotton does tolerable well the first year. 12 O'clock and I am sleepy. Very respectfully, etc. *Beanland is married*

Records preserved in the office of the Register of deeds of Yalabusha County, Mississippi, show that the land bought by Polk and Caldwell comprised two grants by the state to Edward C. Wilkinson, October 31, 1833, and one grant by the state to S. M. Caldwell, December 19, 1834. To these was added another grant by the state to James K. Polk, December 5, 1842. The history of this plantation as shown in these records is that Caldwell sold his share of the estate to James K. and William H. Polk September 4, 1836. Since he had held one-half, it resulted that one-half of his half went by his transfer to each of these grantees, so that James K. Polk now held three-fourths of the plantation and William H. Polk held one-fourth. Edward C. Wilkinson gave a warranty deed to J. K. and W. H. Polk October 15, 1838, which seems to show that it was only at that time that the Polks had completed payment. W. H. Polk sold his fourth to J. K. Polk by a warranty deed of November 3,

1838. The property went after J. K. Polk's death to his widow, Mrs. Sarah Childress Polk, who sold it to James M. Avent January 25, 1860. After that it passed through several hands and at present (1925) is the property of Mr. C. V. Beadles of Coffeeville, Mississippi.[1]

As a by-product of his exertions Dr. Caldwell became interested in "floats" while in Mississippi and thought to do something in that line, if he could get inside information from his friend Polk, who at that time was speaker of the house of representatives and in a position to do a stroke of business for a friend, and for himself, if so inclined. Accordingly, after his return to Tennessee Dr. Caldwell made the following inquiry of Polk in a letter dated February 13, 1835:

DEAR SIR:

Nothing has transpired since I wrote to you. in that Letter I intended to have Requested you [to] ascertain if you could how the Lands belonging to the Chickasaw Indians *To wit* (the Reserves and Floats, as they are called) will be disposed of There was some provisions made in the Treaty for Indians who were not competent to transact their own business. There are a great many persons among the Indians buying their Reserves and Floats One Indian will sell his Reserve perhaps to 8 or 10 persons Now which of the purchasers will get the Land perhaps the Second purchaser will agree to pay Double what the first agreed to pay. It might be of advantage to you and myself to have the necessary information on that subject I dont care about the information until you return

[1] For the information in this paragraph the editor is indebted to Mr. H. B. Johnson, Deputy Chancery Clerk of Yalobusha County, Coffeeville, Mississippi.

Plantation Experience of James K. Polk

I understand since I Returned that the B. Smith Tools have been shipped from Nashville to Memphis on the Boat *Pacific* I have not heard from Memphis whether they have been received or not.

Yours Truly

Having bought the land he liked, Dr. Caldwell lost no time in taking thither Beanland and the slaves who were expected to reduce it from a state of virgin nature to a thriving cotton plantation. In the Polk Papers is the following list, probably intended for the slaves furnished by Polk and Caldwell for their new venture.[1] It refers to none but the young and healthy slaves, one of them a blacksmith, and it is interesting to notice that Jack, whom Beanland called an "old scoundrel," was not in the group. Beanland had acquiesed in the plan to sell him. Ben and Jim also were not included, but Hardy and Wally, who had been most troublesome runaways, were among them, although Hardy, as we have seen, had developed tuberculosis and was not taken to Mississippi. The list was as follows:

Polk's

Abe, blacksmith	$1200	Mariah's child, Henry	200
Reuben	600	Mariah's second child	75
Cæsar	600	Dicey	450
Hardy	600	Elizabeth	450
Addison	600	Eve	450
Henry	600	Eve's child	75
Phil	650	Barabar	300
Giles	600	Young Charles	320
Mariah	450		

[1] This list does not coincide with the list of eighteen given by Dr. Caldwell in his letter of January 2, 1835; but some of the slaves he does not mention on the above list were later on the plantation and Polk in buying supplies had three dozen hats and pairs of shoes sent to the plantation. It is probable that a second group of slaves followed the first to Mississippi.

Caldwell's

Harvey	$600	Claiborne	400
Alfred	600	Patsy	450
Gilbert	600	Jane	450
Wally	600	Mauria [Marina?]	400
Park	600	Judah	450
Hinson	600	Judah's 2 children	200
John	500	Sarah	450
Manuel Monroe	450	Sarah's 2 children	75
Monroe	450	Henry	350

The totals of the valuations in each column was $8,025. It was agreed that if any of the negroes died in the enterprise the plantation should repay the owner at the prices affixed. Nothing was said about fixing the values of children who might be born in either group, but it is likely that such increases belonged to the partner owning the mother. From the list we see that a young man was valued at $600, a young child-bearing woman at $450 and an infant at $75.

The transfer to Mississippi was made under very difficult conditions. The roads were for the most part new trails laid out through the forests and travel was slow and painful. The weather was bad and the season was so far advanced that it was not possible to halt to escape its inclemency. Dr. Caldwell may have been crotchety, but he had an indomitable spirit and he urged the slaves on each day as far as he could get them to go. The journey of about one hundred miles was made in eight days, the negroes traveling on foot and the wagon[1] toiling forward with pork, meal, tools, bedding, household furniture for the cabins and for Beanland, who was evidently accompanied by his new wife. It was rapid journeying taking all things into consideration. Doctor Caldwell pushed forward the work of build-

---

[1] Caldwell speaks of repairing the wagon, indicating that Polk had only one.

ing houses to cover the eighteen slaves he took with him, saw everything stowed in them, gave directions for the continuation of operations, and then set out for Columbia, Tennessee, where he arrived on February 9, one month and a week after he had taken the road at the Fayette County plantation. He described all that had been done in the interval in the following letter to Polk, dated at Columbia, February 10, 1835:

DEAR SIR:

I reached Columbia last night after a three months Laborious tour I got to Mississippi with our negroes on the 10 day of January I remained there Eighteen Days put up a house for Beanland four Houses for the negroes a Smokehouse and a kitchen and made a lot for out Stock I met with no bad luck going down Mr. Beanland is very much pleased with his situation, the negroes only tolerably well satisfied.

I gave you a partial description of the Land I will now describe it more fully the Land lies in Yella Busha County six miles from Yella Busha River on a Creek called Perry's Creek the tract one Mile and a half Long and a Mile wide two good springs on it I have not settled at either a great portion of the land is fit for cultivation and lies well and I think very rich said to be equal if not superior to any tract in the County I procured some Cotton Seed some I Bot and some I got without Buying directed Beanland to plant about 75 acres in corn and all he could in cotton, it does very well in that country the first year.

I have heard not[hing] of the Smith Tools.

I got Abram in a shop to do some work we needed I sent by a waggon to Memphis for the tools and if they are there

they will be at the plantation shortly. I wrote to Lawrence
and Davis to send them if they had got there you requested
in a letter you wrote me to give the amount of the valuation
of our property I had left it at home and therefore could
not do it sooner my property was valued at $1477.42 yours
at $1331.42 there [are] some other articles sold to Booker
that are not included in the valuation of your property.

I have sent by Capt. Lake of Jackson Tennessee to Cin-
cinatti for 2500 pounds of bacon which he is to deliver within
six Miles of our farm in March at cost. and two Dollars pr.
Hundred for carriage therefore you need not buy any for
us. we drove down with us 2500 pounds of Pork.

If James Brown had felt as much interest in procuring
you Land as I expect you did in procuring the Mail Contract for him and Walker he might have saved us two or
three thousand Dollars I wrote to you I had no confidence
in him and I still have none. I lost while I was down a
negro woman named Juda and the day I got back to my
farm in Haywood your Boy Hardy died with a disease of
the Breast which he has had five or six months. which leaves
not enough of hands to cultivate the farm in Haywood. It
will be necessary for you to Buy another hand as soon as
you can Negroes are very high here I have no money
to Buy with I drew on Simpson Walker for $150 of your
money and will need some more before you return I expect
the first payment for the land was near $3000, the corn $500
and Expenses of moving, etc., I paid for you at Somerville
$170 to A. L. Smith and Cooper and for repairing your wag-
gon near $30. I think with good management we can make
money in Mississippi I think we are settled in a good Cotton Country where in a first rate season we can make a

Bale pr. Acre this may be rather extravagant at al events we can make money.

This letter seems rather restrained. In fact the writer's mind was effervescing with dreams of a brilliant future. Mrs. Caldwell, his wife, poked fun at him in a letter, February 16, 1835, to Mrs. Polk. "The Dr. is rather amusing than otherwise," she said. "Town life is strange to him and I amuse myself at him walking in the middle of the street up and down the town 20 times a day Says the Yellow Busha suits him best by odds tho he has come off it already and thinks by the time brother James gets home he will be [*illegible*] polished It is to be hoped he is in high spirits as respects his purchase he thinks he made six thousand Dollars by the purchase three for you and three for himself, if the expenses does not give him the *slipper* at the start." We shall see later that he became discouraged when the crops failed to meet his expectations, with the result that he withdrew from the partnership.

CHAPTER V

Ephraim Beanland's Struggle for Plantation Supremacy

ROM allusions in his letters it seems that Ephraim Beanland assumed control of the Fayette County plantation late in 1833, taking the place of another overseer who had not filled out the term of his contract. By his own assertion he found the slaves in a state of disorganization. He alleged that their unruliness was due to the influence of some disorderly white people who lived near the place. No evidence exists to prove or disprove the assertion; but it is certain that he had trouble to keep them from running away, that he used stern measures to correct their habits, that members of Polk's family in Tennessee, listening to the stories of the slaves, thought him too severe, and that he had to make a stiff fight before he got Polk to allow him full sway in his attempts to enforce obedience.

Dr. Caldwell, who considered himself Polk's authorized agent, A. O. Harris, who did not visit the place but remained in Columbia whither the runaways were apt to go, and James Walker, who, with Harris, had a contract for carrying the mails in his stagecoaches, obtained through the efforts of Polk, were the three brothers-in-law who interfered in the matter. They acted from benevolent motives, no doubt, but they did not wait to hear the overseer's side, and Polk, who was of a judicious mind, after hearing both sides, sustained his overseer.

Ephraim Beanland's Struggle

That Beanland exercised a strict authority over the slaves is hardly to be disputed. He worked them hard and was a man of ready fist and unwavering courage. He does not seem to have tried to rule by stimulating the pride or good will of his subjects. He talked plainly to them — the slaves said he swore roundly at them, which was not proper in a good overseer. But we must admit that he had a hard task and was a man who tackled is by the methods he best understood. He gave his orders and enforced them in the manner most familiar to him.

His trouble at the plantation began late in 1833. Three of the slaves fled the place, two going to Columbia. The other fled to Memphis, drawn thither it seems, by love of town life. Beanland's story of the situation is contained in a letter to Polk, written from the plantation near Somerville, December 22, 1833. Incidentally it contains much interesting information about the ordinary state of affairs on the plantation. It is reproduced here verbatim, in order that the reader may have an idea of the mind and culture of the man who wrote it.

DEAR SIR:

We are all well and lisabeth and mriah [sic] has both fine living children, and garisan and the mule has come long since, and I am sorry to tell you that Jack and Ben hath left the plantation on the 28 of November and I have not heard from them since on the night before I was a bailing until a 11 oclock and Jack went alf and broke into a grocery which he was caught and when I was thorely convinced that it was him I corected and I corected him for telling em 5 or 6 positif lyes and whilste I went to diner they boath left the fields and I have not heard of them since and sir I dont say that I am able to advise you but I do not want any arangements maid for either of them. I want them boath brought back if they aint the rest will leave me also I have sent to Maury after them by George More if they are theire he will fetch them back and I also I sent Sillva and her family to Maury and on crist mas day I am going to see George More he is going to be back.

Dear sir on this day I finished my crop boath corn and [c]oten ageathering and on to morow I look for hardy back from Memphis which he carried the last load of your coten I have sum repairing to do which it will take me until new-ers day and then I shall begin to clear land and on this day I sent him Jim to Maury and I want Jack and Ben verry much indeade My corn is verry short indeade I have not got wan of my cribs full in the shuck and you said sir that you wanted to now how much coten you had in the seede I cant tell for sum was so wet and sum days all hands did not get 200 hundred pounds but they is wan thing it is all gind and it is all in Memphis and I have the receits for it and by the last lode which hardy will be back on tomorow and sir your negroes has traded with white people and bin let run at so loce rained that I must be verry cloce with them they is a set of white people that lives cloce hear that would spoile any set of negroes

Dear sir I cant give you the amount of your seede coten but I can give you the weiggt of the pict coten and the num-bers of every baile an the weights of every baile:

No. 1	477	
No. 2	502	
No. 3	438	
No. 4	581	
No. 5	550	
No. 6	514	
No. 7	484	
No. 8	481	
No. 9	552	
No. 10	498	

No. 11	440		No. 19	458
No. 12	440		No. 20	480
No. 13	470		No. 21	520
No. 14	480		No. 22	526
No. 15	420		No. 23	532
No. 16	450		No. 24	540
No. 17	438		No. 25	520
No. 18	444			

On last munday I cilled my hogs. my corn was so scearse that I could not feede them any longer which they was 4000 weight of it undly it was not verry fat the reason of it I had not corn to ceap it and sir Dr Edwards caime the other day and wanted me to settle his bill against the plantation which it was $34 and sum sence and I tolde him that I cold not but I told him that I would let you [know] about the mater he is A going to moove away and he wants it settled before he goes Nothing more but remaining your respected friend.

The other side of the matter is to be gathered from a letter to Polk written by A. O. Harris from Columbia, December 30, 1833. It rests upon statements made by the runaway slaves themselves and must be received with some caution. Even if they did not consciously exaggerate the severity of Beanland's punishment, we must admit that they were in a state of high excitement in reference to the occurrence and for that reason not able to tell a judicious story about it. The letter is as follows:

MY DEAR SIR:

You have no doubt been advised by Mr. Beanland that Jack and Ben had runaway from your plantation in the District, the cause, etc. I can give you no information on the subject further than I have collected from the negroes Ben and Jim, who a few days ago arrived here. They say that Jack was very badly whip'd indeed, that Beanland salted him four or five times during the whipping, that Ben was also whip'd but not so badly. How much of this is true I cannot undertake to say, but as highly as I approved of your choice in the selection of an overseer, I am very much afraid that he will not treat your negroes as you would wish. As to his other qualifications, there will probably be no objection.

Ben and Jim are both here and both wish to stay here. Ben will not go back. He says he relys on your promise of keeping him here, of selling him or hireing him in this county. He is afraid if he goes back of being whip'd for running away and says that he cannot live with Mr. Beanland. Jim says that Beanland is very severe, that he gives them no encouragement, that if they exert themselves to please him they get nothing but curses for it, and on the whole they give a gloomy account of things.

I do not know what to do with them. Mr. Walker could not make the exchange you wished. I cannot exchange Ben for a hand to go to the District in his place. Skipwith will hire Jim and will probably give me a hand in his place. What I shall do with them finally I do not exactly know, but will do the best I can and will let you know in a few days.

All well. Very truly yours.

January 3, 1834, Harris wrote again telling Polk what he had done with these runaways. He said:

My dear sir:

I have made such a disposition of your boys Ben and Jim as will I hope be satisfactory. At all events it was the best I could do under the circumstances. Ben had resolved that he would not go back to Mr. Beanland again, and no inducement that we could offer him appeared to have any effect in changing his determination, and sooner than send him back confined (where he would not have staid perhaps if we had got him there) I have hired him at the Iron Works at $100 per year and have written to Mr. Beanland to hire a hand in his place, even if he has to give $100, and have but little doubt he will be able to get a good hand at 80 or 90$. I have agreed that he shall come up when you return and you are at liberty to take him at that time or let him continue at the works the year out. Jim has consented to return to the plantation until your return and has gone back. Beanland has very probably been too severe, but Mr. Walker, when he visits the District, will, I presume, go to your place and set all things right. Bills[1] in a letter to Mr. Walker of the 30th ulto. says that "Chunky Jack" has not yet been heard from. I hope all things may get right after a little and that you may receive no more such crocking epistles as the last two or three that I have written to you.

. . . .

Dr. Caldwell added to the story in the following letter, written from Polk's Fayette County Plantation, January 4, 1834, as follows:

DEAR SIR:

I am now sitting at the fire at your plantation. I reached this place on yesterday evening and regret very much I am not able to give as much information about your business here as should wish. You, I suppose, have heard before this that Jack and Ben had run away from

---

[1] Major John H. Bills of Bolivar, Tenn.

your farm. Two or three days since a man by the name of Hughs who was in pursuit of some men who had stolen a negro on the Mississippi River stopped at a Hut on the bank of the river to make some enquiry. Whilst there two white men and Jack came up to the house to make some enquiry about the same men that Hughs was. That circumstance gave rise to suspicion and they having Jack chained Hughs judged they had stolen Jack and that the other men were partners of theirs, took the white men and Jack and put them all in jail in St. Helena, in Arkansas Territory, about 80 miles below Memphis. Jack confessed they had stolen him at Memphis and that he belonged to William Polk and was hired at your farm. They all were going down the river in a scift. He caught them 150 miles below Memphis. They were going to the province of Texas. Hughs got on a steamboat, came to Memphis, from there here, and up to George Moore's. I got George to come down and him and Beanland started the eveng. I got here after Jack. Hughs says it requires two to prove property in Arkansas. In consequence of that I had no time to chat with Beanland.

Mr. Hughes charge for apprehending Jack and expenses is about $140. I refused to pay that amount but authorized George if he got Jack to pay him $100 which I tho't a fair compensation. I also directed George to sell Jack there if he could get a fair price for him. If he bro't him back to take him up to his house and let you have a hand in his place, which he will do. I expect he will not stay here. Ben is in Maury and refuses to come back. If Jim is not exchanged he will return. I wrote today to Harris to iron Ben and send him back (Ben is a bad boy). Your negroes here are very much dissatisfied. I believe I have got them quieted. Some others spoke of running away. Harris wrote to Beanland to hire a hand down here in the place of Ben. I judge from that he is not to be sent back. I told Mr. Parker today to hire one if he could. Harris authorized Beanland to give $100. I directed Parker to give that if not for less. . . . . .

Beanland has got your crop gathered: made 25 bales of cotton, has about one of the cribs full of corn in the shuck, about 4 stacks of fodder, killed 4000 pounds of pork. He will need at least 50 barrels corn. It is worth $2.50 pr. barrel. I know of none for sale in the neighborhood nor has he money to buy with. I expect I shall have some to spare. I will know by April. Beanland has just commenced his new ground. I can't tell how he will do but I am fearfull not quite as well as you expected. I think he lacks stability. I think he has got along badly with the negroes. The negroes say he likes his liquor, but let that rest as negro news. If it is the fact it will appear. Elizabeth's child died last night. She smothered it somehow. No person knew it was dead until this morning. It was a very fine child born the day you and me left this. I had it buried today. Maria has a fine boy about one month old. I bo't you a very fine mule and bro't down with me. I gave $100 for it out of a drove. Your stock looks very well here. Your negroes have plenty of milk. I think if Beanland would be more mild with the negroes he would get along with them better, tho' I don't know this from observation. I shall leave this in the morning for my farm. Any information I can [get] from your farm at any time I [shall] give it to you. Write me as soon as you receive this. Very respectfully your friend, etc.

Beanland's statement of the expenses incurred in recovering Jack and taking him home to Fayette County from the jail in Helena, Arkansas, is an interesting document.

It reveals the simple directness of the man's mind and shows us, incidentally, how closely the agents of the law fastened on the opportunity to make a slaveowner pay well for the recovery of a slave. The statement is dated January 3, 1834, and is as follows:

EXPENSES INCURRED IN THE RECOVERY OF SLAVES[1]

Expensis going to the arcensis and back   *January 3, 1834*

At hals in Sumerville	$ 1.62½
pasage by stage to Memphis, 3 fares	8.75
Hus[2] bill of faire at the first stand	1.12½
Hus bill of faire in rally	1.12½
Hus passage by steam bote from memphis to healeney	15.00
Jaile fease and balcksmiths acount	11.86
The first nite at Clarksvill	.75
And on monday bill of feriage	1.75
And on tusday bill of feriage	1.75
And on wensday bill of feriage	1.25
And Jacks tavern bill	.75
And the hyring of an yawl	1.00
Hus bill of fair at hermete	0.75
Hus bill at the woad yarde and the race ground	2.50
Pasage on steam bote from healeney aup to memphis	18.00
Hus bill of faire at moshis [?]	00.75
The hire of horsis at memphis	4.00
The hire of 2 mules	2.00
Hus bill of faire at arnets	1.37
And Hues expenssis	50.00

Jack's bold break for freedom indicated so strong a spirit of revolt that Polk's Columbia advisers were inclined to question the wisdom of having him continue a member of

---

[1] In Beanland's handwriting. It seems to refer to the expenses of George More and himself to Helena, Arkansas, to recover Chunky Jack.

[2] Hughes'.

the slave group on the plantation. They feared that he would persist in his defiance and corrupt the minds of the other slaves. The man himself, it will be remembered, belonged to Polk's minor brother, William H. Polk, and was held and hired by the elder Polk as guardian for his brother. Beanland heard that the relatives advised that Jack should be sold and protested against such a course. He wished to keep Jack and bring him into a state of obedience as an example to the other slaves, a view in which he was supported eventually by James Walker. This view prevailed with Polk, Jack came back to his fate and continued to struggle against the stout will that was placed above him. He did not subside readily and in one encounter, as we shall see, struck the overseer with a stick which he had concealed about his person. He struck so hard that the stick broke over Beanland's head but that individual gave blow for blow and with the aid of a knife reduced the slave to submission. In the end Beanland agreed that Jack should be sold.

With Jack back from Arkansas Beanland turned with equal earnestness to the establishment of his authority over Ben and Jim, who, as we have seen, had reached Columbia. His demands that they be sent back to him were stated with force in the following letter to Polk, dated February 1, 1834:

DEAR SIR:

Wear all well and I am sorry to informe you that Elisabeths childe is dead[1] and I have got Jack at home I got him out of helany jaile in the arcansis which he cost verry near $200, and as for ben he went back to Maury and Mr.

---

[1] Elizabeth's child died on January 3, which shows that Beanland was slow in reporting the occurrence to his employer.

Haris has sent him to the iron works and I think that haris done rong for I ought to af had him hear at the plantation. This night I will finish fensing my new ground and leaving the work of them to fellews [?] I have not clearde a fot of land as yet and they has so much timber fallin in the plantation that I must go to cleaning up my old land for loosing ben it is felt verry sensible. And when it is so wet that I cant werk in the old land I will celar. I now that it will take me 1 month to get the timber of uve the old land and in that time I must begin to plant which I do not think that I can clear much

I have fensed about 65 acres tho you can tell it is 650 wan way and 525 the other[1] . . . and garisan is a verry waekly boy and I will take good cear of him. The winter is verry harde and colde and my negro shoes is worn out but I am a mending them to make them last as long as posseable and my dear sir my corn is but little I am oblige to fed it on consequence of the winter beinge so harde and as for byinge corn there is none hear in the neighborhood to sell under $3 per bariel tho it is cheaper on big hachy but by sowing oats and be saving with my corn I want to do without bying as little as posiable my stock looks verry bad I shood like for you to rite to me and let me now what to do in the respect of corn for it is rising daily

Mr. haris rote to me and dyrected me to hire a fellow in bens place and I did not do it because at the hyringe they was fellows hyred at $130 and another thing ben ought to be brought back to the plantation for he is a grand scoundrel and I do not think that he ought to be befriended in any such an maner now if I corect any of the others they ar

---

[1] Beanland evidently means yards. On that assumption the amount of land fenced was 70½ acres.

shore to leave me thinking that if they can get back to [*sic*] that will do for they must be youmered to as well as ben and sir I do not think any such foolishness as this is write for I caime her to make a crop and I am determined on doing of it and sir on yesterday I seen Dr. Edwards and he told me that he was not A going away this year but wold still remain in the neighborhood this year if you please rite to me and let me now about these fiew things nothing more but remaining your respectful

The arguments in this letter were supported by the writer in another, written to James Walker, on February 6, 1834. Walker had objected to the treatment of Ben and Jim, but Beanland did not know it. He had favored the return of Jack, which probably led the overseer to expect similar support with respect of the return of the other runaways. The letter to Walker follows:

DEAR SIR:

On last weak I got a letter from Co J. K. Polk and he stated in his letter that he had ritin to you and had tolde you that he wanted ben sent back to the plantation and my dear sir if he is a going to be sent back I would like to see him or otherwise hear wheather he is a cominge or not my reasons are this and I think they are good for if he is not sent back I do not think that Jim or Wally or Hardy any man of them will stay hear on yesterday hardy left his team a standing in the field and has not been seean since which I never corected him tho I talked to him and it insulted him and he went off and as for Jack he has not gone yet but I am confident that he wonte stay and another thing thinge is that I do not like in the first plase I must please Calwell and Mr. Haris as it apeares and then if I donte please everry negro on the place they rin away rite strate and then if I do not make a crop my imploier of corse will not like it and I would like to now how I can please them all and make a crop two and another thinge is it is considered that I am a getting high wages and I consider that they are shore and I want to escape if poseable. But I will be candid I do intend to stay if they everry man run of my time out   Nothing more   you most respectfully

Jim was persuaded to return but his spirit was not tamed, and, as we have seen, it was influencing the other slaves. It reached Hardy, who had been so much trusted that he was the slave who had been given the task of hauling the cotton to Memphis, going alone and coming back faithfully, which shows that he was considered a man of parts among the slaves. His reversal of form is described by Beanland in the following letter to Polk, written February 13, 1834:

DEAR SIR:

Wear all well and I am sorry to informe you that I do get alonge so slowly. I have started my plowse ondly 4 of them yet and on this day a week ago hardy left his teame standing in the field and on last night I got him home and on this morninge Jim and Wally when I calde them they both answered me and I tolde them to starte there plowse and they boath started to the stabile and I have not hearde of them since which I had not struck them a lick nor threeened to do it nor in fact I did [not] now that they was insulted any way and Dear Sir I will be candid with you if ben is not brought back mister haris had beter take the rest of them until I get ben I now that they will run away untill I get ben and you will do me a never to be forgotten if you will have ben sent to me and in the saime time oblige

February the 13th 1834

Mr J R Sather dear Sir we are all well and I am sorry to git for me you that I do git alonge so slowly I have shouted my plouese only 4 of them yat and on this day a weeke ago hardis left his teame standing in the field and on last night I got him home and on this morninge Tim and mally where I calde therm they both insinered me and I tolde them to starte there plouse and they heath Started to the stable and I have not heardo of them since which I had not struck them a lick nor thre can to do it nor in fact I did not now that they was iring inlted ny may and down sir I will be canded with you if hen is not braught back mister hanis had beter take the rest of them untill I get hen I now that they will run a way untill I get hen and you will do me a never to be forgoten if you will have hen sent to me and in the same time iblige your self if he is not sent heare and

maids stay, all the rest of the
fellows, had better be sent to
... for I will be damnde if
I can do any thinge with them
and they all ... in the mean
and if you do any thinge in this
matter I want you to do it
as ... passable and you
will oblige your friend

yourself if he is not sent heare and maide stay all the rest of the fellows had beter be sent to Maury for I will be damde if I can do anythinge with them and they all ways in the mads and if you do anythinge in this matter I want you to do it as soon as poseable and you will oblige your friend,

These arguments were hard to deny and Polk, who had to make the decision, was too practical to ignore them. He gave his decision for the overseer. Slavery was a hard school for the human emotions. It rested on the bitter basis of a denial of equality. Its first law was that slavery should be made safe. To relax this law in order to satisfy impulses of kindness meant the weakening of the institution itself. Polk knew that he would have to back up the authority of his overseer or make it impossible to hold the slaves in a state of submission. He chose the first of these courses and ordered that Ben be taken back to the plantation whence he had fled. Walker, acting for him, wrote a letter which was read to the slaves giving them to understand that they could hope for nothing by running away from Beanland. The overseer's letter to his employer of March 7, 1834, gives us an idea of the effect of the master's action on the plantation slaves. It reads as follows:

DEAR SIR:

I did not rite to you on the firste of the month my reasones was that Squire Walker detained me on Wally acounte which in his last letter said that he had solde Wally and that he must go to the iron works which he shall starte amediately Dear sir wear all well and have bin since the last letter and I have got all of the negroes at home but Jim. I have got Jack and I have got hardy and I wente to the iron works and got ben and on last monday I got Wally which they have bin runaway and I have got them all backe on the plantation and since I have brought ben back the all apear satisfied ande Squire Walker rote me a letter which I redit to all of them which he sayes that they shall stay heare or he will sell them to negro trader and by otheres in there plases which they do not like to solde to a negro trader I thinke that they ar all very well aweare that if they go to runninge away that it will not do for I am determined to brake it aup this set of white people that they had so much corispondance with I have broke it aup intirely and they ar verry well satisfied and crop time is now heare and if Jim goes to maury he must be sent back to me for I have not time to go after him but I wante his servisis verry much indeade

Not long before Jim run away G More wanted him to make some gates and I sent him theire and he run away from him and cum home and then he left me withow a cause which if he goes backe I wante him sente to me Dear Sir you wante to now how I cum on the last month I have got all of my old ground broke aupe and my coten ground boded aup but about 40 acres I will have it all in tolerable good auder this weake but the olde newgrounde that lies on the creak that is nothing done to it yet On monday next I comence in it which I thinke that it will bringe good coten I thinke that I muste plante the rise of a hundred aceres in coten and the ballance of my olde grounde in corne and as for my newgrounde iS verry backwarde I do not thinke that I can get in more than 20 aceres at moste if that much but I shall get in as much as posiable loosinge Wally I hate it but he is oblige to go so walker sayes and to morrow I am a goinge to the alection and if I can hire a boy on reaseble terms I shall do it and if not I make the beter youce of the hands that I have for I am determened on makinge a crop to the hands that I worke I [know] that your lande is verry good for coten

I have sode 10 aceres in oats which they look verry fine and my corne is verry scearse my stock looks bad on the scarsity of corne my sheepe looks well and they is 9 lambs and as for my horses is undly tolerably the gray mare is intirely unfit for servise which I put my horse in her place and he works finely and I have got a firste rate set of runinge plowse and in fact I thinke that every thinge is moovinge on verry well at this time which I am glad to say so if you wante any thinge done let me no it nothing more but yours respectfully

Jack's next act of defiance came after Beanland wrote the letter just presented to the reader. It was the time he broke a stick over the head of his tormentor and got stabbed in return. It is described by Beanland in the following letter to Polk, April 1, 1834:

D EAR SIR:
We ar all well and have bin so since I rote the last letter and sir I can say to you that I thinke that I am getinge on tolerable well at this time I have all of the negroes at home and I did thinke that they all woulde of stayed but on munday last I took aup Jacke to corect him and he curste me verry much and run alf before my face which in runninge 2 hundred yards I caught him and I did not now that he had a stick in his hande and he broke it over my head the 3 lick which I stabed him 2 with my nife and I brought him backe to the house and chainde him and I have him in chaines yet in a fiew days he can go to worke ande he

furthermore swares that he will never stay with the Polk family any more   I can worke him and I intend to do it   I sente for Dr. Edwards and he examined the places where I stabed Jack and he sayes that are not dangeres by any meanes. . . . . .

The upshot of this matter was that Jack continued to run away until he was finally sold. When Polk sold the Fayette County plantation in 1834, Jim and Ben were sent back to Maury.

CHAPTER VI

Beanland and the Plantation Routine

AVING watched Ephraim Beanland safely past the crisis in farm management, with
particular reference to his ability to control the slaves under his charge, let us turn
to his work on the Fayette County plantation. There is no reason to believe that
he did not have ability in husbandry, as in planting, cultivating, and harvesting the crops. Dr. Caldwell, who showed
hostility against him on other grounds, did not raise ob-
jections on this point. The doctor's account of a visit to the
plantation, taken from a letter to Polk, March 18, 1834,
shows that he approved Beanland's farming and was satisfied with the way in which it was going. He said, dating
his letter at "Beanlands":

I arrived here[1] this evening and found your people all
well your negroes have been doing very bad Jim and Wally
both have been away two or three weeks I have Bot Wally
Jim got to Columbia was caught John Shaddon got here
with him this Evening Beanland thinks they will stay now
at least he is in hopes they will   he has got on with his business very well   agreeable to his chance   he will have all his
cotton land ready to plant by the first of next month   he is
now planting corn and will be able to get his old ground

[1] Dr. Caldwell dates this letter from "Beanlands," as he facetiously calls Polk's
farm in Fayette County. Some of Beanland's letters are dated from "Pleasant Grove
Plantation," others "On Muddy Creek," but most of them have it merely Somerville,
the nearest post office.

[69]

planted in fine time he wont be able to get in more than thirty acres of new ground he has about 60 acres fenced he thinks he will have in cultivation about 100 acres of cotton and that quantity in corn his horses and mules are in tolerable [condition] he will not have corn enough there is none in the neighborhood for sale at any price I expect to let him have what corn he may want your people has plenty of milk I think if the negros will stay at home Beanland will make you a good crop I think he is anxious to do so. . . . . .

Perhaps the doctor's phrase, "He has got on with his business very well agreeable to his chance," may be taken as a just summing up of Beanland's merit as a conductor of farming operations. The Fayette County plantation was a new one and he who conducted it had to clear away the forest year by year and increase the quantity of arable land as he went. If all went well the increase in the acreage cultivated stood for a growing return for the planter's efforts. But many things could happen on a Southern plantation to defeat the best made plans.

Beanland's operations in 1834 encountered impediments. In the first place rain and one thing after another made it impossible for him to clear as much land as he expected. Planting time was upon him before the clearing was accomplished. He put in as large an acreage as possible, a favorable season followed, and the cotton came up very well. Almost immediately came a cold snap with frost and the fine stand disappeared in a night. The long green rows of young cotton turned to a black streak of dead plants. Accepting the inevitable Beanland replanted. April 17 came a great storm and blew down many of the "deaded" trees in the corn and cotton fields, destroying the plants and making it impossible to plow. All the hands were now called out to remove the trees. In this process much time was consumed which was needed for other kinds of labor. Writing to Polk on May 1, 1834, the overseer described his troubles in the following manner:

DEAR SIR:

Wear all well at this time with the exceptions of ben havinge the rumatism but I thinke that he will be aboutt in a fiew dayes to geaut [get out] and on this day I will finish scrapinge out my cotten howsever finish scrapinge where is was wanste I thought that I had the best prospect for a crop that I ever had in my life but the froste cut it verry close I do shure you I never saw as great a destruction with frost in my life tho yet I think I can get a tolerable good stand provided there is no more fraust and there is no other axident to hapen to it my corne looks tolerable well and as for the new grounde I have got it broke aup wan way and on the 17th they caime a storm which it did throwe me back verry much I have got the timber all aup of my coten ground and on tomorowe I will comence a cleaninge aup my corne land beinge thrown back with the storme so much that it dose apear like I can not be able to get in any new grounde but if I can get in 25 or 30 acares I will be shore to do so if posiable takinge every thinge into consideration I believe that I can get in 35 acares my negroes all of them stayes with me and they apear like they are very well satisfied I make the moste buter and the moste butermilke that I ever saw and I have got the finest oats that I ever sawe in my life nothinge more by [y]ou most respectfully

The Plantation Overseer

Most planters lived on hope, and Beanland's optimism was only natural to the men of his class. A month later, June 1, he wrote again to Polk, by which it appears that ill luck still pursued him. The weather, which was the planter's most constant menace, continued adverse and the result was discouragement. Beanland described his situation in the following words:

DEAR SIR:

We ar all well and have bin since I last rote and I am sorry to informe you that I have got a bad stand of coten I have got a good stand on 50 acares it is ondly tolerable good and on the rest of the crop is verr indiferent which I planted over the second time and it came aup verry well and it all dyed which I have put it in corn 15 or 20 acares and my new grounde corn is come aup verry well I think I have got in 35 or 44 acares and my aolde ground corene is promising and I say it is cleane and the most of it looks well sum of it is as high as my head and I have the finest oats that I ever sawe 10 or 12 acares which I have been feeding my work horsis intirely on them for 3 weaks I have no corn to feede them on I have 6 bariles of corne that the DR Calwell let me have and he cant spare any more and I cant hear of any for saile under $3.75 per bariel[1] I am tolde that gavan [?] has corn to sell at $2.50 per bariel which I am goinge theire in the morninge to get my herd [?] some if I can the doctor disapointed me verry much for I engaged 40 bariles and I ondly got 10 My bakin holdes out verry well I thinke and I think that my crop is in good order and I shold like to see you verry much and when you come I want you to stay hear as longe as you can nothinge more at this time you moste respectfully

[1] A barrel of corn, by the count of Southern farmers, is five bushels.

Beanland and the Plantation Routine

This man Shelby that wants to buy your farme the information that I get about the man he is nothing more than awhim and a drunking man at that.

It was Polk's rule that his overseer must report to him the state of affairs on the plantation the first of each month. No letter survives for July 1, 1834; we have the following letter written by Beanland to Polk on August 2, in which it is seen that the writer was still hopeful:

DEAR SIR:

On yesterday yours caime to hand and you wanted to nowe howe I was a getting on and howe we all ware and what the prospects I have for a crop my corn is good and my cotten is promisin at this time I have seean grown boles in it yesterday nearly waste high I have sum good cotten and sum indifferent and to take the crop all to geather I am afraide it is two fine it is in the rite stage to make a firste rate crop or to make a sorry wan if we have a good dry season crops will be fine and mine is good I think tho my stand is not good tho I think I will make a fare crop if the season is dry and on to morowe I am a goinge to see Dr. Calwell and see what the chance for bagin and rope and make the arangements about it and as for the newe gin I never have seean the man nor heard from him and I am a goinge to see about it when I go down and as for the runing geares that is hear they ar no A count and I cant make out with them at tawl and I am sorry that you ar not cominge down for it is imposiable to make out with them and as for payinge for them I would not give a dam for them for I tore them all to peases to pick the last yeares crop the cogs was all wayes a workinge out and the runinge geares that is hear I cant under take to pick a crop with them and if the new gin is as indifferent he shant leave it in the gin house and I rite to you and let you nowe as soon as I get back we ar all well and I have sode 4 acares of turneps nothing more at this time you moste respectfully

If you please rite a note to my step fatheres peter williams Es livinge on Sillver creake and dyrect him to send my brother Edward to me as soone as posiable for I have got an openinge in Sumerville in A Le and Smithes store for him and I think it is a good place and I donte want him to delay send your note to Jim Bendens the firste opertunity please do this faveour and you will oblige your friend

In the following letter, dated August 3, 1834, Beanland was perhaps using the condition of the gin and the running gear that drove it as an excuse to remind Polk of his request of the previous day to have his brother sent to him. His writing is even more unusual than his spelling, but I do not think I have made a mistake in the name of this brother, who is Edward in the first letter and "gefson," or "gefsan," in the second, which, I take it, was intended for "Jefferson." I have been able to think of no plausible explanation of this contradiction, unless, indeed, the boy was named "Edward Jefferson." The letter, quite characteristic of the writer, is as follows:

DEAR SIR:

We ar all well without it is Casy she is verry lowe at this time and I have pict out 6000 weight of cotten and on yesterday I started my gin with the old running gear tho I can make out with them untill the newwuns is maid which I will have them as soon as posiable I got a letter from Silliman and he says that he cant repaire the running gear tho the is no repairinge to do for I will have new wuns maid and them is first rate Sir I shold like to see you hear before you sell out for I think that you have bin mistaken in your place I want you to hire a boy and rite a note to my step-father and dyrect him to send gefson hear forthwith as sone as posiable for I cant get A. Le and Smith to weight any longer then next friday weake. please do this and I will pay you when you come downe I am a goinge to baile cotten to night   Your verry respectful

Faile not if you please to let gefsan nowe of it[1]

Beanland's reference to Polk's sale of the Fayette County place shows that he had already heard of the plans being made by which he was destined to transfer his residence to Mississippi. It was a time of great adventure in the Southwest. After a long time the Cherokee, Creek, Chickasaw, and Choctaw Indians had been put in train for removal beyond The Mississippi River. The rich land they were giving up was eagerly grasped by the energetic men of the older part of the South. In the whole range of settlement offered to these adventurers there was no other land so attractive as the best tracts in Mississippi. The government offered the land at auction and sold what was left after the sale at a stated price of $1.25 an acre. Although the choicest tracts frequently brought fancy prices at the auction, many an excellent tract was taken up at the minimum price by some lucky man on the spot. Then came the tide of settlers, men who desired to come with slaves, establish plantations, and give themselves to cotton planting in a region which knew little of winter. Many a handsome fortune was founded in these "flush times" in this favored region. Land values went up rapidly as the prospectors

---

[1] This letter appears in vol. 18 of the Polk MSS., which is the wrong place.

sought out the good tracts and offered liberal advances on the first prices to those who had the lands for sale.

In 1834 the fever had broken out in Tennessee, and Polk and many others yielded to it. His Fayette County place produced cotton, but not so bountifully and of such long staple as the Mississippi lands produced. He decided to sell the place and buy in the South. Rumors of his intention reached Beanland, who became concerned at the effect such a move might have on his own affairs. In the letter of August 3, 1834, he tried, as we have seen, to dissuade his employer from selling. A few weeks later he heard enough to show that his efforts were useless and then he wrote the following letter, August 24, 1834, in which he came more directly to his own situation:

DEAR SIR:

Wear all well with the exception of Casy she is getinge better Jim and enykey all have had the congestif fever and I think shortly they will be able to go to worke on to morowe I shall go to picken out cotten and as for my crop I cant say any thinge about it Dr Calwell is hear and he has seean it all and he can tell you wheather it is a good wan or not Sir I understand that J Walker es shold of sayed that you ware a goinge to sell out your farme and if you are I would like to nowe it my reasones in this that I do expect to followe the busness for a liven that I nowe followe and I have got a good opertunity of makinge A ingagement for next yeare and do not think that it is rite for to make other ingagements untill I consulted you on the subject if you please rite me A fiew lines on this subject if you please I do not want you to think urge an ingagement for next year and if you cant cum I want to nowe wheather

you want to imploy any person for the next year   your
verry respectfully

with you ondly that I am had three applications for next
year

A month later Polk was at his Fayette County plantation
for the purpose of selling it. He found a purchaser in a man
named Booker. In a letter to his wife, dated September
26, 1834, he announced the completion of the transaction
and related some interesting information about affairs on
the place. He wrote:

DEAR SARAH:

Within an hour after I wrote to you on yesterday I
sold my land to Mr. Booker for $6,000, one half down and
at Christmas and the other half upon a year's credit. Today I have bought *Mariah's* husband, and have some expectations that I may be able to get *Caesar's* wife. My
crop is better than I expected; There is a fair prospect that
it will yield me including corne and cotton both, about
$2500. *Beanland* has done well, considering the trouble he
has had with the negroes. *Old Jack* is now gone without any
known cause, and has been away for near three weeks. No
account can be had of him. I fear he has taken another
trip to the Mississippi River.

I will send up *Jim* and *Ben* with olde Mr. *Moore*
(George's father) who will start on Monday. I will give
them a letter to *Mr. Harris* requesting him to deliver them
to their owners. I find negro clothing very high here, and
will write by them to Mr. Harris, requesting him to buy for
me, their clothing and send it down with old Mr. Moore, who
will be returning with a waggon. I am resolved to send my
hands to the South, have given money to *James Brown* to

buy a place and have employed *Beanland* as an overseer. I am determined to make more money or loose more one.

I have been kept exceedingly busy since I got here, have not been off the plantation except to a neighbour's house on business. I have received no letters from home, and have seen no newspaper, and of course know nothing of the character of the publication, which the editor of the Republican had promised to make before I left home. I determined not to pester [?] myself about it until I had done my business. I hope to be able to get off on tomorrow morning, or the next day; and I think I may have an opportunity to sell my land near Bolivar, and will probably be detained there for a day or two, and will then come directly home. I bought *Mariah's* husband, a very likely boy, about 22 years old, for $600 and paid for him with the notes I held on his master for land which I sold him several years ago

Your affectionate husband

P. S.   I will write to Mr. Harris giving him a statement of the articles I wish sent down for the plantation when old Mr. Moore returns. If he is not at home will you see to it and get *Samuel Walker* to buy them for me upon the lowest terms he can. I have written for enough to make two suits round. The negroes have no idea that they are going to be sent to the South, and I do not wish them to know it, and therefore it would be best to say nothing about it at home, for it might be carryed back to them.

The flight of Chunky Jack gave Polk much concern and he sent Beanland to find and bring him home. The overseer had shown his desire to master Jack on previous occasions, but he recoiled when he learned that Jack had taken refuge in Shawnee Town, a settlement of desperate men, mostly runaways, on the western side of the Mississippi. The swamps of the South offered safe asylum to such people, and such settlements existed, as in the Dismal Swamp, in North Carolina, in Scuffletown, on the border between the two Carolinas, and in the Everglades of Florida. Nothing less powerful than a military force was suitable to send against such a place if it was well stocked with desperate fugitives. No officer of the law could safely invade it and bring out one of the inhabitants. Beanland naturally recoiled before the task facing him. His letter to Polk, October 4, 1834, is as follows:

DEAR SIR:

On last nite I got home from the arkensis and I hearde of Jack but never cold get site of him and its seposed that he is in Shauney villege which I was advised to not go theire for they is a den of theives and to tell you the fact I donte think that you will ever git him. I sene John Bigerstaf in Memphis which I rote a letter to Jisco the sherif of philips county arkensis teritory that he was heare and as for Jack he has got alonge with them theives and I thinke that the chance is bad of getinge of him. . . . . .

It has bin a raininge for five dayes study   I am afraid that the cotten will turn alf but sorry I thinke if you and Booker can trade it would be best for you for I am afraide that it will be sorry   I shall make 6 bailes to day

Silaman caim hear and I sent the gin back and I also bought A negro boy from him for $600   the boy is 22 years olde and I told his [*sic*] that I would give $5 hundred dollars for the Boyes wife and 2 children   please rite to me and let me nowe sumpthing on on the subject   we ar all well at this time   Your very respectfully[1]

[1] This letter is filed in 1836 which is wrong.   It is found in vol. 23.

Beanland's supposition that Jack was safe beyond recovery in Shawnee Town was an error. A few days after
the preceding letter was written news came that the fugitive was taken and it was proposed to sell him. Beanland
acquiesced in the decision, although he protested that he
would work the "aolde scoundrel" if Polk decided to send
him back to the plantation. His letter to Polk of October
10, 1834, filled as usual with news of the people on the
place also gives us an idea of the influence of one bad slave
on the other slaves of the community. The letter is as follows:

Wear all well but Caasy and eny they aint able to go
picken out cotten yet and it has rained all moste everry day
since you left hear the weather in nowe fine for cotten for
the last 3 days I am glad to hear of Jack I say sell the
aolde scounderel tho if you wante him worked send him on
and I will take good care of him and secure him I am glad
to hear of you a byinge 5 negroes my cotten is a goinge to
turn out well I thinke if I can get it all out but I do ashore
you I cant get it out in time if I donte get more hands than
I nowe have got. I have sent 10 bales to Memphis and on
this morninge I have started my gin I cant get out my
crop in time if I donte get more help for when I run my gin
I have not got but 7 hands Please to send Jack to me and
I will ceape him if it is posiable and as for Bearneses boy
he will take $600 for him.

I nowe see parson reaves and he is hear and he says if
you sende Jacke heare he will cill him for he says that if his
boy fill would not runaway he would not take $1000 for
him for he is a right smarte blacksmith and A good shu
maker and a good huar [hewer] the boy fill will live with

you I would advise you to by him for he can be broke from runninge away this is the 2 time that he ever run away in his life and Jack went theire and got him alf. he will take $600 for him and I wante you to sell Jack and never let him come here no more for they is a greate meny of the neighbers is afraide for him to come hear Reeves will be theire in a few days and he wants to sell his boy which I have bargende for him at $600 and I thinke he is a verry cheape boy I bought him for you and if you are afraide to I am not. By him be shore he is such a handy boy[1]

Sir Silliman caime heare and I sente the gin back and I bought a negro man from him and the boy is 22 years olde weighing 180 to 185 pounds he is warented to be sounde healthy and a rite handy boy which I was to give him $600 for him and he was to send him on without faile and the boy has a wife and she can be got for $500 her and 2 children which I tolde him if I liked hear I would give it rite to me and let me nowe what to do I have paid the blacksmiths acounte withoute payinge out wan dollar in cash I got the receite in full ande I give the pony for the oxen which I have got a good teame nowe and I have loste wan milke cowe since you left Nothing more but your verry respectfully

Removal to Mississippi was now uppermost in the minds of owner and overseer, and every effort was bent to the completion of the work connected with harvesting the crop of 1834, so that an early start might be made at the new place. Polk's orders were to send the old and the infirm slaves to Maury County; for none but the most capable were fit for the work in the new country to which they were

[1] The upshot was that Phil was bought for $600 as is shown by a bill of sale dated October 18, 1834, and preserved in the Polk MSS.

[81]

going. By this time Beanland had been assured that he was to be retained as overseer and his letters are full of enthusiasm for the prospects before him. His pictures of plantation life continue rosy, although he was very apprehensive that they would not get the cotton out in time. It was on this account that he advised Polk to sell the crop as it stood to Booker, who had bought the place, leaving to that gentleman, who had slaves of his own, the task of completing the harvest. He was having trouble, also, with the running gear of the gin. Horses, or mules, were used as motive power, the day of the stationary engine had not arrived; and the crude gears made by local artisans were of uncertain service. In his letter to Polk of October 14, 1834, these things appear in his own terse language as follows:

DEAR SIR:

When we parted you said that I had better sende olde man Charly and Casy back to maury which I have got a good chance to sende them by Rily Johnson I was to find him corne and foder which he got it heare and I thoughte it beste to sende them on before the colde weather ande if he is pute to any trouble you will pay him for it Caasy and the olde man charly will note be of any servis heare and I sente them backe I gave him as much corne and foder as he woulde cary and he comes 12 miles oute of his waye with them you can settle it he cant aske much for his trouble please see peter R. Baaker ande get him to bringe my bed from Goodrumes for I am oblige to give the wan aup that I have got please faill not to get my bed and Bakers wagon and sende it to me and I will be under lastinge obligations to you I am pickinge oute cotten slolly at this time I thinke that I have got 18 or 20 bailes but I have got 11 bailes made and my runinge gear has broke and I cante stope from pickeinge oute cotten ande my cotten is a opninge verry well indeade ande I cante get it out in time to ge[t] away for I mus go to maury won time more any howe if posiable when bokers hands comes downe I wante to go backe if posiable tho I will note leave heare unduly when it is conveinante I am willinge to let it alfe a goinge to the laste but I do as I have [told] you that I mus come backe and see mother.

We ar all well at this time and I donte thinke that I am half done pickinge oute cotten   I would like for you to by a place that has good water if posiable   I thinke that seasers wife will go yet with him if he woulde preswade hear a little more   Verry respectfully

To get more slaves for the new venture was one of Polk's objects and he authorized Beanland to buy where he could obtain good bargains, which is evidence of the extent to which he trusted the overseer. In the preceding letters has appeared evidence that the commission was discharged with care and good sense. In the following letter dated October 26, 1834,[1] we may see at length with what spirit he carried on his negotiations:

DEAR SIR:

On yesterday I received yours and you wanted to nowe wheather Fill and Dicey had caime on they both got to the plantation on last friday and they ar verry well satisfied and you wish to nowe wheather I was to pay the rewarde or not   I was not   I was to give $600 and pay the Jaile fees   but as for the rewarde I had nothinge to do with it for I do ashore you that I would not pay it for Reaves

1 In the wrong place in the files.   It is in vol. 19.

may be ashor that if I had the payinge of it I would not do
it for my bargin was to pay the Jaile fees and he was to
make the bill of saile   and as for the rewarde Reaves mos
pay it himself for it is a matter of importance when I make
a trade to make wan at a time   I am Astonished to thinke
that [he] would think that I would make such a bargin
and donte you pay it a tawl for when I bought the boy fill
I was ofered $750 for him in wan hour after I hand [*sic*]
bought him   so I thinke that Reaves just cold as reasniable
expect the $150 that I was ofered more than I gave as for
me to pay the reward it is true that I have bin ofered $750
by 2 men for fill but I tolde them that I bought the boy for
you   and I was preswaided to take $750 but I would not
done such A thinge because I wanted you to owne the boy
and if you did not wante the boy I wold ceape him myself
for he cold be solde readily for $800 hear and as for Seasers
wife she cante be got

I went yesterday and ofered Carter $475 for Seasers
wife and she is not willinge to go with you so I tell Seaser
that she dose not care any thinge for him and he sayes that
is a fact Govan sayes that he would of give $800 for henry if
he would have thought that Carter would have solde him
so I thinke that we had beter go to negro tradinge   I have
been tryinge to trade the notes I hold on Durem and on
Bills for a boy 15 yeares olde which it will be a good trade
if I can and all of the notes is hear and I am agoinge to Sil-
limans today and I am ancious to come to maury and I do
ashore you I shold like to nowe wheather you have a wagin
a cominge down acristmust or not for I have 1000 pounds
to cover[1] [?] if I can make the arangements with you we

---

[1] Seems to refer to moving his personal effects.

ar all well and I am sorry that I sente Casy and Charles
aup you said to send them the firste

Dear sir I will see Silaman on this nite and amdetely I
will let you nowe what we do and on last friday I was at the
Doctors plantation and C. C. Jones will be in maury on the
4 of nexte month and he has a negro girl for saile and I ast
him if he would take his owne notes for the girle and he did
not say and if you will minde you can get a good bargin and
give him his own paper for the land that Gorge More solde
him if Booker will give you $1.25 per bariel for your corn
and gether it take it in cash or a credit of 12 monts $1.75
if you gether it or if he will gether it you take $1.50 per
bariel I have made 18 bailes of coten they has been a good
deale of wet and if Booker will give you $2500 for your crop
take it   when you see the doctor give him my beste respects and tell him that I shod as live go with him to the
Missippi as any other man I am ancious to nowe where I
am a going [?] I wante my bed sente down by Bookers
wagon olde mister more has brought all of your articles.

Polk did not trust entirely to Beanland's efforts to obtain
slaves in Tennessee, where they were scarce and comparatively high in price. While in Washington he met G. T.
Greenfield, one of his friends from Tennessee, as it seems,
who was trying to purchase slaves to take to Tennessee with
him. Polk asked him to buy for him also and Greenfield
agreed. The commission proved too difficult for execution.
The following letter from Greenfield, written in Washington, March 29, 1835, shows how hard it was to buy slaves.
It also shows that not all the slaves taken from the old sea-
board slave states to the new cotton states were carried by
negro traders. Greenfield wrote:

The Plantation Overseer

DEAR SIR:

Since you left here the weather has been very bad, and the snow is now falling and the roads in a desperate condition. I shall leave here as early as I possibly can. I promised to purchase you a couple of negro men, or a man and a boy, or a woman and a man. I have not as yet purchased any male negroes, as they are difficult to get. I will still endeavor to purchase if possible but do not wish to disappoint you. There are a great many traders here, and men and boys are very scarce, at any price. Should I succeed in getting all the negroes I want, you can have your choice of two, *and if you are supplied* before I get out, it will make no difference with me, as I wish to settle a plantation in Mississippi. The precise time I shall leave here depends upon circumstances. I sent out a man to purchase negroes of a certain description, he has failed. I shall set out as soon as the weather will permit. I am yours respy.

To these statements Greenfield added in another letter, dated June 10, 1835, the following information: "I regret to say it was out of my power to purchase you any negroes. Every exertion was made. I intended to let you have two of my negro men but they ran away and I sold them. I have no servants along, but family slaves, and those connected with them."

We have gone far enough into the plantation life as depicted in Beanland's letters to understand that slavery was just slavery. It was neither the thing of horror the abolitionists thought nor the benign institution its defenders depicted. It was a relation whereby men who had work to be done got workers to do it. From the stand point of the laborers it was a form of service in which men worked and

[86]

got the sustenance that their masters decided necessary for their wants. Beanland had no delusions about slavery. He seems to have had no idea that it was an institution. With him it was only a question of Jack, Ben, Caesar, and Gilbert. For them he did what good mastership demanded, made them obey, fed and clothed them, and tried to get them "to make a crop" for his employer, contending all the while against the uncertainties of season and health. His effort determined the success or failure of the operations on the plantation.

CHAPTER VII

The New Plantation in Mississippi

OR the first year of the Mississippi venture we have no letters from Beanland. He undoubtedly made the required monthly reports but they went to Dr. Caldwell, the more active of the two partners in the enterprise, who being nearer to the plantation than Polk, the other partner, had the task of direct supervision. Dr. Caldwell's correspondence is not preserved. The most definite information we have of this first year's operations is that twenty bales of cotton were raised. The expenses were heavy and the yield was not as great as was expected. Dr. Caldwell shows that he did not like the overseer and he went to Mississippi in September of this first year, 1835, with the avowed purpose of changing overseers. Arrived there he relieved his mind by telling Beanland that his services would not be needed for the following year. Whereupon Beanland, being a normal overseer, and suffering from chills and fever incident to a new clearing, lost interest in what he was doing. Caldwell later reported that Beanland did little work on the plantation from September to the end of his engagement. Dr. Caldwell made another visit about New Year's day and was greatly disappointed by what he saw. His account of what he found is rendered to Polk in the following letter dated at Yalobusha,[1] January 16, 1836:

[1] Later on the letters from the Yalobusha plantation were dated from, and postmarked at, Okachickima, Mississippi.

The New Plantation in Mississippi

DEAR SIR:

I arrived here last night from Mississippi I have not employed Beanland. I have got a man by the name of Mayo, from the district Beanland done very little good after I was there in the fall. he had not got out half of the cotton and we will make a light crop there I think fifteen or 20 bales after I left there he run off three of the negroes which cost between 50 and 60 Dollars to get them the worst loss was your boy Abram he started him the Post Office with some letters the Mule he rode threw him against a tree and killed him he Lived but a few hours after he was thrown I have sold the smith tools we made 43 Bales in Haywood; our expences in Miss. are very heavy indeed much greater than I anticipated I am going from here to Glass's I expect to be at Columbia by the first of next month then I will give you all the particulars in haste yours

One of Dr. Caldwell's duties was to have a final settlement with the overseer. The following receipt, dated without place and evidently dated back, shows with what terms the settlement was made. It runs: "Received January 1st, 1836, of Silas M. Caldwell five hundred and ninety Dollars it being for my wages as manager or overseer for Polk and Caldwell for the year 1835 and for Hire of a negro woman and articles Bot for the use of plantation in Mississippi. Ephraim Beanland." The articles bought for the use of the plantation probably included such things as were needed in emergency, as food for the sick, or tools, or repairs for which cash had to be paid. The receipt is of further interest because it shows that Beanland had become the owner of a slave woman, which meant that he was look-

[89]

ing to the day when he should become a planter himself.
This settlement was not mutually satisfactory as is shown
in a letter from Beanland to Polk written from Lagrange,
Tennessee, January 23, 1836, in the following language:

DEAR SIR:

Sin I have sen you I have had a serious spell of the
feiver but wear all well at this time Doct. Calwell has bin
down and we made a settlement with every thinge only the
shugar and coffy and he syas that they is a missunder-
standing be twean myself and you but I think differently
for I well now that you was to find me and to moove
[me] and family to the Mississippi and also to finde me
and family and you was to give me $400 and finde me and
family and pay me the hire of 1 hand the yousual price, the
extras [I] gave $75 for I wants and I throwed in 1 month
for the time I was sicke and I also bought 200 pounds of
beef and wich the Docter was verry willinge for me to pay
but as for the shugar and coffy he left it to stand untill you
wold come downe and I will say thet It is not rite for me to
finde the shugar and coffy for the youse of the plantation
we have had often 6 or 7 hands sick as long as 3 months
and I must finde them my that is out of the question The
shugar and coffy caust 26 dollars and if it was my bargin
to of payed it I wold of don it and also I bought 1 barel and
a half of flower which you will have to pay   I well recolect
that tolde me that you was a goinge to mateson county and
I wanted you and myself to drawe ritings and you wolld
put it olf untill another time you said as for a bariel of
flower or 2 you was willinge to by and as for the worke
me [n] that was bildinge the gin and the well digger I was to
finde them and consider that you will have it to pay for and

furthermore I payed 29 dollares and sum sence in the deas-
trict for you and the docter promised to pay me last cristmust and he failed in so doinge   Dear sir I want nothinge
but what is rite

YOUR FRIEDN

You will please to rite to the doctor or let this matter
ly over untill you come home   Yours very respectfully

This appeal did not produce satisfaction. Against a man
so highly placed as Polk in the affairs of the state the voice
of an overseer did not reach far when the affairs depended
on verbal evidence alone. Beanland continued to be an
overseer for the time being, with his eye set all the time on
the station of planter. Five years later his ambition was
accomplished. He had acquired possession of a section of
land and owned "three hands," which indicates that he had
worked and saved with good effect. These facts he revealed
in a letter to Polk dated at Panola, Mississippi, April 12,
1841, as follows:

DEAR SIR:
Necessity comples me to call on you for the small
amont you owe me which is ninety od dollars forty od dollars of the above amont was paid in Tennessee before you
and Caldwell entered into copartnership and the balance
was paid out by me in this state for you   both amounts and
the interest makes the amount first stated   I lent you and
Caldwell three hundred and fifty dollars for twelve months
I have received but five dollars Interes for the use of the
money. I refer you to Mr. Caldwell for the correctness of
the state of this lone and money.
I wish you to forward me the money by male directed to

Bellmont Panola County, as I am much in need of money. I wish you to do what you think is rite. Your attention to the foregoing business will confer a particular favour on
Your very obedient servt.,

P. S. I have quit overseaing and have gon to farming for myself I have one section of land and three hands and I wish to enter into copartnership with a steady and close calculating man If you know of any such person that would like to place some hands out to a benefit, I should like for them to join me for five or six years agreeable to the number of hands in profits and expenses. I will make sufficient quanty of corn this season to suppy the place I am living 4 miles from steamboat navigation, a good high road to the river you may safely calculate on us five Bales of cotton to the hand at the least calculation. It is in a healthy Reagion My land is good

Here we take our leave of Ephraim Beanland, the most interesting of all the overseers whose letters I have seen. He had many sterling qualities. He was a man of his word, he had good judgment in the conduct of the affairs of the plantation, and he met opposition with a stout heart. The worst Dr. Caldwell said about him was that he was too severe with the slaves under his care, which may have been true to some extent. But it was always hard to tell how severe was just severe enough. Some overseers had the art of managing slaves without punishment, saying little to them in condemnation or in praise, always watching, never irritating. Such an overseer Beanland was not. He gave his orders positively. He made it known that he was master, and having taken that position he stood ready to make his assertion effective. When a youngish man went single-handed into a new country, leading a band of slaves whom he had to direct and keep under discipline, he deserves some consideration from those who make appraisal of his conduct. On the spot he had a better opportunity to decide how an emergency was to be met than those who were not there. I do not ask approval for all he did. He may have been too harsh. On the other hand the situation may have demanded all he did. The only witness against him, besides the slaves whom he disciplined, was Dr. Caldwell, who was apt to form his opinions quickly and without taking all things into consideration.

Information relating to Ephraim Beanland's later life is scant; but it is learned that he lived on the section of land he took into possession until his death in 1855 or 1856. His wife, who was Sally McDonald, of Tennessee, long survived him. One of his five children, E. D. Beanland, became a physician, and others lived to be persons of importance in their communities. Letters received from surviving members of the family show that he had his desire, to rise above the station of overseer and to found a family of recognized standing. Many of the prosperous families of the South had an origin equally lowly.

The departure of Beanland made it necessary for Dr. Caldwell to stay many days at the plantation in order to get the new overseer, Mayo, installed and things running smoothly. There was much to discourage him and he was a man to let worry discourage him. Worse than all, someone — it is not evident who it was — spoke of buying the place for $20 an acre. which was double the price paid a year earlier. It became a haunting regret to Caldwell that he did not make a sale, and as the expenses of getting the place cleared and operations conducted smoothly proved larger than he had expected his regret became deeper. From that time until he withdrew from the partnership his letters were dismal. Writing to Polk from Columbia, January 31, 1836, he said:

DEAR SIR:

I got home yesterday after a long and Laborious trip of trouble and expence   the expences of the plantation in Mississippi are indeed very great   I have paid out at the two places not less than $1600. Our cotton crop will not make the payment on the land and other expences. I have recd. account of the sale of 25 Bales at 15¼ and 15 cts the Balance will not sell for that, being of inferior quality. 43 Bales we made in Haywood   I can form no Idea, what we will make at the other place   Beanland had not got out half the crop   he had done Very little after I was there in the fall. three of the negroes ran away which cost between fifty and sixty dollars   he was very extravagant in his expenditures   I give the man I employed there $325   the one in Haywood $250

I killed 95 Hogs at the two places which will I expect make our meat. We had made but three Bales of cotton when I left Missi. Our crop from there will be late getting to market   they will not get it out before the first of March   I don't think we will make more than 20 or 25 Bales. We owe Caruthers and Harris $4100. Both crops will not pay the debt. I collected the money of Glass $299, paid him $20 for charges   I come home by the way of Memphis found an account against you of $44.66 for Bagging Rope etc with Lawrence and Davis   also one at Somerville for $6.50 at A. L and Smith   Both of which I settled. I collected $420 of my own which I was compelled to use. Besides the $2933.33 for the Land I borrowed of Harris $1200 on account of our crop, which sum the crop will not near pay. I wrote in the other letter that your boy Abram got *killed*. I sold the smith Tools calculating we should not need them We have made corn enough in Mississippi and Haywood to do. . . . . .

It would have [been] well for us that we never had had anything to do with *Beanland*. I expect to plant at the two places 250 acres in cotton. Write me on the receipt of this. I am gratified at your success.

Very respectfully yours.

We are left in entire ignorance of Mayo's success or failure as an overseer. It is merely known that he remained on the Mississippi plantation only one year, which does not indicate that he was satisfactory to his employers. For this period we have no letter from him, and it is probable that he reported to Caldwell, who wrote to Polk at intervals. It is from these letters that we get such information as we have of plantation affairs in the year 1836. One of them, dated at Columbia, February 7, 1836, is as follows:

DEAR SIR:

Since I wrote you I have received an account of the sales of all our Haywood crop except 3 Bales. the whole crop will not amount to $2700 which will leave of the land debt about $300. The Mississippi crop will not pay the Balance of that debt and expences. I have drawn from Harris more than the amount of both crops and for want of funds have left our debts in Bolivar unpaid for shoes and clothing, etc., If you have any money in Mr. Harris's hands you will please authorise him to advance me what will be necessary. I collected between $300 and $400 of my money and paid it out. I have advanced considerably more money than you have my means are out and have to borrow money to send to Samuel at college Our expenses were much more than I anticipated. I mentioned in my last letter that Reuben was in Bad health if he is no better when I go down I think it would be prudent to bring him home he has been sick all summer and fall almost.

I will be obliged to send *Harbert* to the district he is doing very badly he is stealing Drinking and doing as bad as he can I should have sent him this morning with George Moore if I could have got him he is dodging about [so] that I have not been able to get him. I think Reuben had better be brought to Columbia and put another in his place the water or climate dont agree with him Write to me immediately as I shall start down towards the last of March what I will do with Reuben and Harbert, tho. Harbert I shall send to the district as soon as I can get him and meet with an opportunity to do so if he stays in Columbia I am of opinion he will be hung he is a very bad Boy indeed.

Very respectfully yours

Harbert was, in fact, a precious scamp, and he tried the good doctor sorely, so that I can hardly refrain from wishing that he had fallen for a brief space into the hands of Ephraim Beanland. He behaved so outrageously, he and Matilda, who was probably his wife, that the doctor washed his hands of him entirely. Then James Walker, another of Polk's brothers-in-law and a man of more direct action than the doctor, took him in hand. Walker's account of Harbert's doings is contained in a letter to Polk, dated at Columbia, March 18, 1836, and is as follows:

DEAR SIR:

Harbert has been acting badly for some time

past. William hired him to Mrs. Frazier. He was seldom there, generally at the grocery and places where he ought not to have been. When George Moore was here 1st of Feb. Dr. Caldwell concluded to send him to the District. Harbert and Matilda eluded the D. and he could not be found until Moore left. Two weeks ago the D. had another opportunity to send him, got hold of him, and put him in his room up stairs at your mother's. Whilst the D. was at breakfast Harbert jumped out of the window and cleared himself. It is strange he did not cripple himself. Upon this D. C. declared he would have nothing more to do with him. Not being able to prevail on D. C. to pay any further attention to him your mother hired him to Ament (a brick maker). To this Harbert and Matilda objected. On Monday last I heard that Harbert had gone off in the stage to Nashville. I immediately sent to have the stage overtaken and him brought back, put him in jail and kept him there until him and Matilda made such fair promises that I took him out and hired him to Ament at $5 pr. month. He has done very well since. . . . . .

From statements in these letters it will be seen that Polk and Caldwell were now operating two plantations as partners, one in Fayette County, Tennessee, and the other in Yalobusha County, Mississippi. They had bought the second place on credit, proposing to pay for it in three annual payments. The price was $8,800, and it appears by the letters of the doctor that they assumed that they would make enough money clear of operating expenses on the two places to pay the instalments on the debt incurred in purchasing the second place. They were expecting a great deal, under the circumstances, for the new plantation was entirely uncleared when it was purchased, and it was inevitable that it would not yield very much at first. When Dr. Caldwell realized that it would be impossible to meet the first deferred payment as expected he became discouraged, and being a temperamental man he began to think of withdrawing from the venture. Nothing could show better the rapid accumulation of value in such enterprises during these flush times in Mississippi than the fact that two men of normal good sense in cotton planting should have formed such expectations. In more sober days they would hardly have been disappointed if they had carried their undertaking to success in twice three years. In fact, Polk completed his payments in 1838, four years after the purchase, but it is not certain that the money came entirely from the place.

Dr. Caldwell's feeling of disappointment grew and he became more than ever anxious to withdraw from the partnership. February 22, 1836, he wrote to Polk from Columbia as follows:

DEAR SIR:

I recd a letter from the Overseer in Missi on yesterday stating that he had got his cotton out the letter was dated 3rd of this monthe he had only made Eight Bales owing to his not being able to procure Rope and Bagging until the time which he wrote, but that he should Bale and send off the Balance of the Cotton as soon as he could he dont state what he will make he writes he has commenced clearing land but I am afraid he will not be able to get land enough cleared he writes me the [sic] *Reuben* and Elizabeth have done no work since I left they were both sick when I left there. in fact *Reuben* has been sick the most of last year. I have not heard from the district since I left there. I have a strong disposition to sell out in Mississippi if I can get a good price. I could have sold when I was down at $20 pr. Acre I believe. I am afeard there is too much of our plantation too flat and wet. I can form a more correct opinion about that when I go down in the spring if that proves to be the fact I think we had better sell. I should have sold at $20 when I was down if you had been willing I find it very troublesome to carry on a farm at that distance it is so very difficult to get a man that will attend to and do their duty. I am clearly of Opinion it would be to Our Interest to sell and purchase again I am afraid our hands will be sickly owing to the Local Situation of our Farm.

All well.   Yours etc.

The season opened very wet on the Mississippi plantation. The industry of Mayo in clearing land is shown by the fact that he had 150 acres ready for planting in cotton, which was doing very well for the second crop on the place. But it was not possible to plant it all on account of the wet weather. Dr. Caldwell's letter to Polk, written from Columbia, April 28, 1836, gives us the following account of plantation affairs:

DEAR SIR:

I have a day or two since returned from Miss. and Haywood. I left Miss. about the 12th of April I had about half my Cotton planted the Balance I dont know when the Overseer will get planted owing to the season being very wet and part of the Land I intended planting in Cotton I am afraid will not be dry enough in time to plant. I calculated to plant 150 Acres in Cotton there I am fearful he will not be able to plant more than 100 I have

[99]

planted 125 Acres in Haywood I did not bring Reuben from Miss. he had got in tolerably good health, and was not willing to come and we needed him there I had to buy a Mule for the Haywood place. We made only 20 Bales of Cotton in Miss. I have recd. the amt. of the Sale of all the Cotton which is $3750 and the Bailing is to be taken out of that. Our expences last year was between 21 and 22 Hundred Dollars. Our crop will fall far short of paying the Land payment and Expences Our farming operations thus far have not been very flattering and I am afraid we will not be able to git in a full crop this year. I am very anxious to sell out in *Miss.* I am afraid that farm will not be profitable it is too far from home and too expensive to keep it up. I left the *Cook* note at Bolivar with Bills[1] and wrote to Cook where it was, and requested him to pay it.

Very respectfully yours,

Early in the autumn of 1836 Dr. Caldwell found his desired means of escape from the enterprise. He sold his one-half interest in the plantation to James K. Polk and William H. Polk, younger brother of the senior partner. William K. Polk gave Caldwell a tract of 330 acres on Carter's Creek, in Maury County, Tennessee, which the said William had inherited from his father, taking as part of the price of this place four of the doctor's slaves in Mississippi, intending it seems to leave them on the Yalobusha plantation. The memorandum of this transaction is in the Polk Correspondence, with date of September 12, 1836, although the deed as recorded is dated September 4, 1836. It was agreed that the new partners should take control on January 1, 1837.

---

[1] This letter is filed in vol. 18, Polk MSS., which is the wrong place.

The New Plantation in Mississippi

In the following letter from Caldwell to Polk, dated at Columbia, November 11, 1836, we may see with what success the operations of 1836 were carried on:

DEAR SIR:

I got here last night from Miss When I got down I found some of the negroes sick and the Overseer they had made a Tolerable good crop of Cotton but a very indifferent Crop of Corn the overseer had got out but about fifteen Bales of Cotton I discharged him and employed another I Bot $500 worth of corn It will require that amount besides what is made on the place. I had to pay $140 down which money I had to borrow the corn is to be paid for on the first of January you had better write to William to come prepared to pay for the corn you had better write to him as soon as you [get] this he ought to be at Bolivar by the 20th of next month He ought to start with the negroes from Haywood on the 22nd. It will take Eight days to move down.

Reuben is not well he has had chills and fever this fall he is willing to come to Tennessee I think you had better have him Brot up. We will make fifty Bales of Cotton in Miss. I think, perhaps some more our Bagging and Rope had got there. *Vanburen* Beat White 73 votes in this County, Got Beat 6 votes in *Fayette*. Other counties not heard from. I start today to Haywood.

Yours respectfully.

William H. Polk was a young man just arrived at his majority and was known in Columbia for his fondness for good company. His friends seem to have thought that he was no match in a trade for his more astute brother-in-law, the good Doctor Caldwell. James K. Polk went so far in the same direction as to give the young man very explicit instructions for the division of the moveable property on the plantation in Heywood County. Probably William went there to represent the elder brother, and it seems that the dissolution of the partnership in Mississippi was to go along with the dissolution of that in Heywood. William needed no such warning. He met the doctor in a positive manner, letting him know that he was not to be trifled with. His letter to Polk, dated at Bolivar, Tennessee, December 17, 1836, gives us to understand that he was fully protected. It runs as follows:

DEAR BROTHER:

I received your letter this morning, it having been forwarded to Bolivar. I have seen *Dr. Caldwell* and conversed with him concerning the division. it is my opinion that we will settle without any difficulty. He seems disposed to act upon equitable principles. I gave him to understand, in the outset, that he must toe the mark of justice, and that nothing else would satisfy me. I shewed him the directions which you gave me, which will I have no doubt influence him in the division.

George Moore and Mr. Walker, had employed a man to attend to our business, before I got down. He comes highly recommended, and Moore knows him personally, he having attended to business the present year for Natl. G. Smith who lives at Uncle Billy's old place. Moore says — and I trust somewhat to his judgment — that he has made Smith a fine crop, and he is a study man, on whom we can with safety rely.

Myself and Dr. will go into a division of the property on Monday next. The Negroes will all start on the day after

Christmas. I will start with the Dr. two days before the *hands,* so as to make the necessary arrangements for them by the time they get there. *Eve* will not be able to go with the ballance of the hands. I will leave her behind, and make some arrangement to have her carried down as soon as she is able. I will remain in Mississippi until I see everything properly under headway. I will take *Reuben* home with me and leave Julius, keeping him at Tenne. rates for *hire.* You may rest assured that I will do everything in my power to have things carried on in a proper manner. I am decidedly in favour of your getting Judge Yell,[1] to procure for us, a plantation if it can be done in a good *cotton region.* . . . . . .

George Moore's name has appeared several times in these letters whereby it appears that he was a friend of the Polks and that they looked upon him as one who would represent their interests on the spot. He watched the coming of William, younger member of a house that he liked, with some concern. The result met his entire approval and he could not refrain from writing the elder Polk to express his gratification, as is shown in the following letter postmarked at Bolivar, Tennessee, and dated January 10, 1837:

DEAR SIR:

After my Respects you and Lady I will in form you that Wm. H. Polk is now in Mississippi at your plantation he will be up in a few days. I never was more agreeable disappointed in a man in my Life than I hav bin in Bill I exspected he would be in sutch a hurry to get back to Columbia that he would hardly take time to attend to anything; but he has taken every thing quite patinly and was

---

[1] See note 1, p. 134, below.

vary perticlar in making the divission with *Caldwell* and appears to have his mind entirely devoted to his fairs [?] and will I hav no doubt devote a grate portion of his time on his plantation. I could not get C. C. Jones to go to *Mississippi* for you but employed a man by the name of G. W. Bratton, that has followed the business of overseeing for several years and has considerable standing as a planter and manager.

W. H. P. left my house a few days before Christmas for Missis. in order to attend to all the business down there by the time overseer and negroes got there. I started the negroes and overseer from my house on thursday 29th of Dec. I bought 3500 lbs. of Pork for you and Doctor Caldwell Let you have 1100 pounds in all 4600 pounds. William said he would if he needed buy the balance down there please inform me what disposition will be made of Texas, also of the aucapants in the District, etc. Our White friends is as cool as the senter sead of a cucummer. . . . .

CHAPTER VIII

The Overseership of George W. Bratton, 1837-1839

N the Polk Manuscripts are few records of the partnership between Polk and his brother. No doubt William Polk, living nearer to the plantation and his mind unoccupied by other matters, became the supervising partner and made visits to the place. Perhaps the overseer's reports about the state of affairs there were sent to him. William was a temperamental young man, given to pleasures and not likely to carry through by persistent effort a tedious and difficult enterprise. The long ride of more than 200 miles by buggy or on horseback was not attractive to him after he had taken it two or three times. A stronger reason for his becoming discouraged in the Mississippi venture was that he became embarrassed in his ventures at home and was in need of money there. In 1838 he purchased a farm near Columbia, promising to pay $8,000 for it in three annual payments. He said at the time that he could sell lands in the Western District of Tennessee and pay for it, but when the pinch came he preferred to take his money out of the Mississippi investment. It resulted, therefore, that November 3, 1838, he sold to his brother, James K. Polk, his one-fourth share in the plantation and several of his slaves placed in the partnership. It thus came about that James K. Polk became the sole owner of the enterprise.

The overseer through the period in which the younger

Polk was actively interested, and for nearly a year later, was George W. Bratton, whom William H. Polk took to Mississippi when the partnership was created. A letter survives from him to James K. Polk, dated May 13, 1837, in which can be seen a spirit of confidence and enthusiasm. It runs as follows:

> DEAR SIR:
> I received your letter in good time, which gave me a greate plasure to heare tha yo ar comming out here as yo wish to know the sise of the crop, I have one hundred an fifty acre in cotton and aty or ninty in corn and both corn and cotton are as likely as I ever saw and if I hav luck I will make corn an nough for the plantation and the rise of 1 hun Dred bales of cotton if health will admit I hav my crop in first rate order at this time   as for your plantation beleave it a firs rate one if well improved   my team ar vary weak an one av give out   i hav bin forst to by a horse for which yo will hav to pay for when you com   your negros ar all well and has bin well all but dissee [Dicey] she is better than when William was hear   I cant writ but work   com down and i will tell yo all about it

Few letters survive to show the course of operations on the plantation in 1837. Whatever reports William may have received from the overseer are lost to posterity. Late in November, however, he made a visit to Mississippi and he described what he found in the following letter to his brother dated at Columbia December 2, 1837. It runs:

> DEAR BROTHER:
> I reached home a day or two ago. I would have written to you from the plantation had I not thought it best to defer it until my arrival at home as I would be more proper-

ly able to give you a detailed account of the situation of the plantation. The crop was fairly represented to us, as the best in the neighborhood, it has proved itself so. We, it is true, had a better stand of cotton, being less injured by the late frost in the spring. We will make from seventy five to eighty Bales, averaging in weight about 450 lbs., with 100 Bls of corn to sell, over and above what will support the *farm,* and raise our Pork next year. We have about fifty shoats half grown, with an equal number proportioned in sise down to suckling pigs, all of which will answer for Pork *next year.*

The negroes are all well with the exception of Dicy who is very weakly, unable to do anything, and Phil who still attends to his business but has to be favoured on account of a weakness in the *Breast.* Barbary had a spell of fever in the summer, from which she has not entirely recovered. Her mother (LucY) says from her complaints of her breast, she fears she is going in the manner in which Alston, Hamp and Charity did, though it may be only the fears of a mother occasioned by solicitude for her welfare.

I have employed Mr. Bratton for the next year at $500. There was no Pork in market when I left Coffeeville. I left money, $500.00, with Abbert McNeal to purchase it for us. the probability is that it will sell from 6 to 6½ or 7 cts. It cannot sell for more, as I met a great quantity making for that market. I apprised A McNeal, from Bolivar by letter, of the number I had met so as to put him on his guard against purchasing too soon. From the quantity I met on the road making for that place, the market must be surfeited, and of consequence sell low. When I left the plantation they had made 42 Bales of Cotton, a part of which I had sent to the River and left word for them to haul it, as fast as it was bailed. . . . .

Myself and George Moore have settled our business relative to the negro. He attempted by soft words and professions of friendship to seduce me into his terms, which he saw were fruitless, and at last agreed to pay me my money.
. . . .

The reader should not fail to observe the significance of the last paragraph in this letter. It will be recalled that when William came down to the Western District to settle up the business of the Heywood County farm with Dr. Caldwell, it was from George Moore that we had a note of relish when the young man held his own and forced a favorable settlement out of the hands of the doctor. It now appears that George Moore himself had to have a settlement with this same young man, whom he tried to cajole, and, like Dr. Caldwell, found that his arts were in vain. William H. Polk was not a fool and he was not to be bullied. He was, also, sincerely attached to his brother, the future president, and the letters he wrote to him, abundantly preserved in the Polk Correspondence, witness his willingness to spend his efforts in behalf of his brother's political and business success. His letter of December 2, just presented, did not give James K. Polk as full information as Polk wished and William wrote, on February 5, 1838, the following letter:

DEAR BROTHER:

In your Letter, which I this evening received, you desire me to give you a statement of the expences of the plantation for the past year. It is not in my power to do so entirely, as the store accounts which are inconsiderate [*sic*] were not presented to me when down, and if they had been, I had no means to pay them, having to incur when down other expenses sufficient to consume all the means I possessed. The Doct Bill was not presented, of which I am unable to tell the amount. Exclusive of these and a ballance due Bratton of 250$, my expences, money laid out for our joint interest amts to $1385.07½ including the purchase of *three mules,* at $100.00 each, and another mule bought by George Moore last summer and sent to the plantation, at $125.00, and the Horse purchased by Bratton, at $72.00, and the $150.00 paid to Bratton in part for his services. Also $500.00 deposited with Albert McNeal to buy our *pork,* and other little expences not necessary to mention, which will make out the amount stated above. I have all the articles set down in my book. Albert McNeal has purchased our Pork at *seven cents.* As to the deed I ascertained in Coffiville, certainly, that Mr. Wilkerson was not at home,[1] and that it would be useless for me to make a trip to Manchester. I wrote to him on my return home and received an answer a fiew weeks since. He said he had not the calls, and could not make a deed until I sent them to him, which I intend doing. I have not been as yet able to make any collection for you. Messrs. Caruthers and Drake were off in the lower part of the state, or at least some distance from home, attending court and I was unable to see either of them. The debt in Fayette was not due when I was down and I could do nothing with it. The C. C. Jones note, I paid over to Mr. Walker for some money which I owed him, as you give me the privilege of using any of your money collected. The money for the rents had not been paid in, and McNeal could not pay me any. I told him when it was col-

---

[1] It was from Wilkerson that the Mississippi plantation was purchased.

lected to pay himself out of it, for the negro clothing which was purchased of him and sent to the plantation last fall. Your $125.00 debt on the estate of Gillespie can be saved without purchasing the negro. I will use every exertion to make collections for you.

I have purchased since you left Alfred Nicholson's place, near Town. I gave him $8000, payable in one, two and three years. There is in the tract 275 acres, 180 of which is woodland, which woodland is worth the money and more. I am at this time living on it, farming on a small scale. I had but one negro to hire. Doct. Dickinson furnished me with hands to work it, and a good cook. You I know will disapprove of it, and I have no excuse to offer except that *I wanted a home.* . . . . . .

Please write to me, your opinion about selling our plantation. I may be after this year constrained to do it, though it depends greatly upon circumstances. It may be our interest to sell, if landed property and Negroes should rise to their former fictitious value. You will ascribe my desire to sell, to my embarrassed situation, occasioned by the purchase of this place, on which I now live, but it is not the case. I can pay for it by selling my district land. You as I said above will disapprove of the purchase, and you are the only one to whom I acknowledge the right of disapproving. Write me on the reception of this concerning the propriety of selling.

William H. Polk was expected to visit the plantation twice a year, once in planting time and once near the end of the harvest. This practice had been followed by Dr. Caldwell and it was followed by Polk, in the main, after the retirement of his brother. But the young man was much interested in other things in the spring of 1838, made a long visit to Nashville, and put off his proposed visit to Mississippi. May 25 he wrote that he intended to set out on it in a few days; but he seems to have forgotten his promise. Polk then appealed to Albert F. McNeal, of Coffeeville, Mississippi, for information about the plantation. The result was that McNeal wrote him on June 15, 1838, the letter from which the following extract is taken:

COUSIN JAMES:

Your favour of the 21st ult. reached me a few days since. I visited the plantation the day after it was received and rode over the farm. In consequence of an unusually cold spring, it is generally thought the cotton crop in Mississippi will not be so good as it was last year, but it is difficult at present to say how that will be, much depending upon the fall season. The corn crop however will be better. Bratton has in cultivation one hundred and sixty or sixty five acres in cotton and one hundred acres in corn. he will evidently make a better crop of corn than he did last year, and I think the prospect fair for a good crop of cotton. the stand is equally as good as it was last year, but the cotton not so large and flourishing as it was this time last June. Bratton says he will make Eighty five or Ninety Bales of cotton. He is somewhat in the grass, but promises with fair weather, which we now have, to be out in two weeks. he seems to have the negroes completely under his control *now* and I was glad to hear him praising them for their good conduct. they were no doubt spoiled by the inefficient and trifling overseer who preceded him. There has been some sickness among them this spring (principally a kind of dysentry) and consequent loss of time. the girls Nancy

and Elizabeth have not yet sufficiently recovered to be able
to work. Bratton says he has a hundred barrels of corn
that he can spare for sale, that the hogs on the plantation
will furnish from three to four thousand weight of pork next
fall. this, I think, better than buying. It would certainly
be well for William to visit YalaBusha at least twice a year,
say in the spring and fall. Any advice or aid in my power,
will be most freely given to the overseer. You will do me a
favour by having the Democratic Review forwarded to me
at this office with the numbers back if they can be procured,
as I am very anxious to have the whole of them and I will
forward the money to the publishers the first Ala. Bill I can
get. . . . . . .

The letters from Bratton show that he was a hard working man and that he kept well forward with the work on the
plantation. References to his operations in letters from
Albert F. McNeal support the idea that Bratton was
an overseer of more than ordinary capacity. He cleared
the land in months when the crops did not occupy his efforts, with the result that the cotton acreage was increased
and the yield raised so that in good times it went to more
than one hundred bales. His career ended in death July
2, 1839. His place was taken by John I. Garner, who also
proved a good manager. Garner continued in the process
of clearing land and increasing the acreage, with the result
that in 1840 the place yielded 134 bales of cotton. Garner,
however, was accused of harsh treatment of the slaves, and
it was probably on that account that he was not kept on the
place after the end of the year 1840. Bratton and Garner
were both matter-of-fact men. They saw little around them
but plantation routine and they put little else into their

letters. Except for the letter of May 13, 1837, already
given, the first we have from Bratton to Polk was written
September 7, 1838, and it is as follows:

DEAR FREN:

after my best respects to yo I now will let yo now
that wear all well at this time your crop is indiferant i
shal not mak more than a half a crop i will not make more
than a half a crop of cotton but aplenty of corn i hav not
had any rane since the 20 of May untill the 19 of Augus
and i hav not had any since with boles a fauling of faster then
tha cum on the cotton crops in this naberhood ar now dead
i am now picken out coton barbry picks out one hundred
and seventy five the resn [reason] i did not wright mcneal
said that he woold wright evry 20 days I have the rise of
one hundred head of hogs and will be abile to kill three
thousand and one hundred pounds of pork i ad no more at
present[1]

September 13, 1838, Bratton sent Polk the following
equally brief and simple report on the state of affairs on the
plantation:

SIR:

i take the presant time to rite a few lines after my
respects to you i will inform you that myself and family is
well the negros is all well i understood from a letter to Mc-
Neil that you would be down the first of October i wish you
to not fail to come on last munday Gilbert left home and
we believe is aiming to git to Dr Caldwell i think you had
best come by thir for I have serct the neighberhood and
Cannot hear of him i do not no what took him of unles it
was becaus he had ben stealing i have not struck him one

---

[1] This letter is filed in vol. 40 which is the wrong place for it.

lick in a year nor yet thretend him i would advis you to not sell him for if you do henry carter will be sirten to foller i rite no more.

It was at this time that Polk bought his brother's one-fourth share as has been said. The agreement of sale, dated November 3, 1838, shows that William sold to his elder brother for the sum of $5,600, the receipt of which was duly acknowledged, the following eight slaves:

Gilbert, a man aged about	30	years,
Perry, a man aged about	20	"
Marina, a woman aged about	20	"
Cloe, a woman aged about	50	"
Caroline, a woman aged about	21	"
Manuel, a boy aged about	14	"
Fan, a girl aged about	10	"
Eliza, a girl aged about	8	"

It also shows that on the same day he sold to the said James K. Polk for the sum of $2,000 all his interest in the stock, hogs, corn fodder, and farming implements on the Mississippi plantation. No echo of this transaction appears in any of the few letters which Bratton wrote to Polk. To the overseer it seems to have made little difference whose man he was, James K. Polk's or William H. Polk's. His task was the same whoever owned the plantation, and his reports proceeded in the same unimaginative way. Writing to Polk on November 24, 1838, he said:

DEAR SIR:

we are all well at present   I shall soon be done gathering of my crop of cotten   I think that I shall make about seventy bales of cotten   I have made the arrange with James Minter and Chisolm agreeable to your request about your cotten.   There has not no cotten gone of yet   the riv-

er has not rise yet   I think I shall have my cotten all ready
for shipping by the first rise.

You rote me that you wanted a good crop made if I can
have seasones I shall make you as good a crop as you want
if health will permit and strength   If I can keep before I
can do putty well   I think I have keep before this year

I will make the exchange of negroes at the time appointed. Losa died the sixteenth of this month   I had good
atten[tion] paid to her I call in and other phisian to Loosa
she died with the brest complaint.

As it respect your cotten that was sunk on the river last
winter Minter sas he took the insurence polacy out leagally
and mailed it at vixburge to Harris and Careathers Co
Minter told me that they got out three or four bales of the
cotten and was sold for the benefit of insurence company
not for yours at all an your merchants are a swindled you.[1]

The collection of damages for Polk's cotton on a boat
that sank in the river gave Bratton much concern. The
allusions to the matter in his letters are not always very
clear; but it is always evident that he had his employer's
interests much at heart. This affair, with some other ordinary business, he explained at length in a letter to Polk,
dated December 24, 1838, but not in his own handwriting.
It seems that realizing his inability to describe the claim
for the damaged cotton he got someone who was more accustomed to writing to copy and, perhaps, enlarge upon the
letter which he had in mind to write, it is as follows:

DEAR SIR:

After my best respects to you I have the pleasure to
say to you that I and family are all well and also all the
negroes belonging to the plantation. I am almost most

---

[1] The letter is erroneously filed with 1839, vol. 41.

[*sic*] through with the cotton I have delivered 50 some odd bales at Troy I think I will get through in a week I expect to be able to ship Seventy some odd. The negro that you was to to send me I understand that Gee killed him, and Julius I sent him to Bolivar a week sooner than I was to send him by A. C. McNeel.

As to the cotton that was lost by the sinking of the boat Gladiator last fall was a year ago, I saw Minter a few days since he requested me to say to you that a protest was drawn up by A. C. Baine Esqr and served on the managers of the boat and qualified before Esqr Boon and made oath that your cotton was not damaged. the protest was then returned by Minter to the Insurance Company and its service by them acknowledged. the cotton then was re-shiped on the Gladiator belonging to the insurance company. after getting up some of the cotton it was then sold for the benefit of the Insurance Company. Esqr. Minter says that at any time that he is called on he will render any assistance necessary.

I now have further to say to you that I do earnestly and wishfully look for one or two negro men as my force is too weak for the place at best as one of the women will be of little or no service in April and May if you can in any way send your waiting boy here I have no doubt but he will make a good hand. If you cant get him here try and swap him with Wm for the one he took away. T. R. Reed has never wrote to me respecting the bill you sent him. I have made a punctual contract about the Insurance of the present crop please write immediately.

Yours Respectfully,[1]

The results of the year's operations were set forth in the

[1] This letter is filed in volume 42 which is incorrect.

following letter from Bratton to Polk, dated January 25, 1839:

DEAR SIR:

  I have received your letter dated the 23 of december i now inform you that wee are all well the negroes is all well i have finished the Cotton crop and has delivered it all at the river i made seventy four bailes i have killed thirty eight hundred pounds of pork i am better than half done making the Cross fence i have got my cotton land the half of it cleaned up and is running four plows i have marked you 38 bailes and the bail numbered 38 is your tole cotton i send you your bill of laden the mule that julis rode to hardaman i instructed alferd McNeil to sell it for one hundred dollars i have not saw McNeil since he returned but when I see him i will rite to you whare he left it thaire is five of your bailes that has not left troy yet

By "cleaning up" the cotton land was meant clearing it of the stalks left from the preceding year's crop. The common way was to knock the stalks down with bludgeons on winter mornings when the ground was frozen. At such times they broke off easily. If cold weather did not come they must be cut off with hoes or other implements. Where the previous growth was rank it was found advisable to burn the stalk after raking them into piles. Under ordinary conditions it was sufficient to plow them under.

Selling his cotton through a commission merchant at New Orleans, or elsewhere, was an interesting and important phase of the planter's business. In another place in this book[1] the subject will be presented with some degree of fullness. But at this place will be inserted the following

[1] See chapter XII.

extract from a letter from M. D. Cooper and Co., Polk's New Orleans agent, dated at that city February 12, 1839, in which we may get a useful glimpse of the relation between planter and commission merchant. The extract is as follows:

. . . . . We received 34 Bales of your cotton last week. Since its arrival the weather has been very unfavorable to outdoor business. a day or two before its arrival there had been very heavy transactions in the Cotton Market at prices in favour of the holders from ½ to ¾ cent, since which time the Market has been rather calmer. Upon Sampling your Cotton we find the Staple and Colour good, but it is rather trashy. We ask 14 cents for it, having great confidence in the firmness of present prices, and anticipating favourable accounts from Liverpool which we are daily expecting of a late date, we will not take less, although it is a fraction above the present market. The Yazoo and Yallobusha Rivers are now navigable, and we will look for the balance of your Cotton shortly. if we make a sale, in time for a letter to reach Washington by 1st March, we will forward you acct. sales there, if not to Columbia. Your Bill of Groceries shall receive due attention. . . . .

March 13, 1839, Bratton made a report to Polk in the following words:

DEAR SIR:

we are all well at present and at work as hard as we can drive I have commenced planting of corn on monday morning and I think that I shall get nearly done planting of corn this week if the weather holds good I can plant all of my crop in good time I am planting a good deal more land this year than I did last year with the calculation of them hands you promised to send me when you come home and you must not fail to bring them if you do I cannot tend my crop. the mule that Julius rode to tennesse is at James Walkers plantation the produce that he sent on all come safe but one plow mole.

I want you to buy me a negro woman young and likely and be sertin that she is sound on the best terms you can bring her down with you and I will work her on the plantation this year.

The second paragraph of this letter doubtless referred to a negro woman to be bought for his own property, to be hired out. The idea shows that he was looking forward to the time when he should be a planter on his own hook.

The next report made by the overseer to Polk is dated May 31, 1839, and it is in the following words:

SIR:
　　　i will inform you that we are all well at this time the negros is all well only maria she has bin in bad helth since the first of march and is likely not to be able to do any sirvice i have the promisingist Crop that i have had since i have bin in the miss i will finish in a few ours going over the cotton the first time and i am going over my corn the third time the mule that you sent me i can not sell it for what you give for it an i will keep it untill you come my negros and mules is all fat and you think go a hed and i say go a. hed and a good Crop i[s] the object
　　　Thir is a lot of negros to be sold in coffiville the first of August and for cash and i expect will be barganes to be bought and wish your assistance　　　Your friend

And June 4 we have this brief report in which echoes the

feeling of weariness which had come to pervade his being, the last he was to write. It ran as follows:

DEAR SIR:

Myself and family is only but tolarable well we have ben sick a grate [deal] all this year the negros is complaining a good many of them maria is down and is like to be elizabeth has done nothing since Crismas i do not think that [they] are dangerous i have a first rate cotton Crop and the corn is good but it is sufering seriously for rain rite to me when you will be down in this country

Then came the end: July 2, 1839, James Cowan, who owned a plantation near Polk's in Mississippi, wrote as follows:

DEAR SIR:

I have been here for some two months on my farm, and my place is entirely healthy, and the neighbourhood generally except the Bowel complaint, which has been very prevalent, and fatal in many instances. The Crops of Cotton are generally fine, the corn has suffered much for rain, but if we are blessed with it in a few days, it will be a fair crop.

The object of this short epistle, is to inform you that your manager, *Mr. Geo. Bratton,* died this morning with the Bowel Complaint, and perhaps the fever in addition. I learn that his wife is not expected to live. I also learn that your agent, Mr. McNeil, is absent on a visit to Tenn. Under all these circumstances, I regret, that I do not know how I could serve you agreeable to your wishes. Managers are scarce, and good ones not to be had, and bad ones worse than none. Upon the whole I would advise you to send some one from home, on receipt of this, for if you do not,

whoever takes your farm, *now*, will want your crop for pay.
I expect to leave for Mount Holyoke, Hy. County, Tenn.,[1]
in a few days, say two, after a long absence. If I was not
so situated, I do believe I would see and do what I thot
right for your Int. and that of Blk family and take the
Responsibility. please be assured of my good wishes for
your prosperity, here as well as elsewhere, and be assured
that nothing would afford me more pleasure than to serve
you or anyone else under similar circumstances. . . . .

I merely write you this hasty sketch as the stage will pass
in a few minutes. in the mean time I'll send my overseer
over this evng, to see how matters are, and may inform you
by next mail, which will reach you 4 days later than this.
MCneal being absent, I thot it a duty due you or any one
else to give you the earliest information.

The Mississippi neighbors were a friendly set and they
did not spare themselves in helping out in what was a dis-
tressing situation. S. Bell, another of these neighbors, added to the information given by Cowan. In a letter written
July 7, 1839, he describes the situation as follows:

Dr. sir:

A. T. McNeal being at this time from home on a visit
to Tennessee I deem it expedient to write you a few lines to
acquaint you of the situation of your affairs in Mississippi.
Your Overseer died a few days since. Dr. Towns living
near him was his attending physician. Seven or 8 of your
negroes have been quite sick with the same disease (Billious Dysentery), but all have recovered or are now con-
valescent save one (Caroline) and she I consider not at all
dangerous. Mr. McNeal being absent I took upon myself

---

[1] I can find no such place on the map of Tennessee. The county was perhaps
Haywood.—Editor.

the responsibility of riding down to your farm and employing a young man to take charge of your interest until Mr. [McN]'s return. The young man is recommended as one of steady and industrious habits.

You have a prospect for an abundant crop both of Corn and Cotton. The growth is large and in good order. If you wish any directions about the management of your farm, write to me and I will take great pleasure in attending to the same.

Respectfully, etc.

Another phase of the matter was taken up by J. T. Leigh, whose plantation adjoined Polk's. It related to Bratton's widow, who was left in a pitiable condition. She appealed to Leigh who, on August 13, 1839, wrote to Polk as follows:

Dr. Sir:

Mrs. Bratton (widow of your late Overseer Geo. Bratton) requests me to write you to inform you of her present situation. She has had to leave your place to make room for the overseer who succeeded her husband. She has removed some 8 or 10 miles off in the neighborhood of Coffeeville, is poor and in want of money to procure necessaries to live on, is anxious to know whether you will come down to your plantation this fall and at what time. She wishes to see you for the purpose of settling her husbands accounts and to obtain money to live on. She left with me a book containing some accounts, and some of her husbands papers (I reside adjoining your plantation). If you will inform me at what time you will be down I will send for her to my house, where I will be glad to see you.

Respectfully yours.

The Overseership of George *W. Bratton*

Your crop is very fine.   Direct to Oakachickama P. Office.

It was now necessary for Polk to have a new overseer.
Evidently he did not approve of the young man so readily
placed in charge by S. Bell until the return of McNeal. He
sought for a man in Tennessee, or in the adjacent parts of
Alabama. At last he made an offer to George W. Meek,
who wrote from Athens, Alabama, about sixty miles south
of Columbia, Tennessee, August 24, 1839, declining the
offer with a great deal of unwillingness. He said:

DEAR COL.:
        I hope you will not think the disapointment that oc-
cured between us last monday Evening as intentional on
my part. from the offer you made me, I enclined to live
with you had not Mr. Crofford considered me engauged to
him previous to our interview. If you do not engauge any
boddy for the next year and I can consistently get off from
Mr Crofford I will yet live with you. perhaps you can get
a man to gather the present crop that will not engauge for
the next yeare, or if you should get a man for boath the
ballance of this and the next year, and you should still desire it I will live for you the next year, that is if I should
not live with you in the year 40 (If I should live) that is I
will in 41 if I cannot get of from Mr. Crofford for the next
year. these things you need not mention to any body, and
you can write me at Charleston, Tallahatchie county Mis.
I came here on business and I think that I can let you know
as soon as I get down to Mis and time enough to make an
engaugment.   Respectfully yours

Billious dysentery, which proved fatal to Bratton, was a
common disease among the ignorant whites of the South.
It was due, no doubt, in a large degree to bad food and the

prevalence of malaria. The strong diet of bacon and corn-bread, persisted in throughout the winter months, broken with the coming of summer by fresh fruits, which were often eaten to an excess or before they were thoroughly ripe, made digestional diseases very common. Men like Bratton, who were not bred to control appetites, yielded to the habits that made life a series of formidable dangers. Once involved in illness they had little ability to right themselves. A man must have food and it was natural that he should go on eating what he had been accustomed to eat. The doctors might prescribe remedies. It was often impossible to give the patient what he needed most: well cooked and nourishing food.

CHAPTER IX

The Overseership of John I. Garner

FTER further searching Polk found a man to his like in John I. Garner whom he seems to have installed at the plantation early in September. He was a man of industry and he had a clear head. He was as illiterate as Bratton and his period of direction is not distinguished by any striking conduct. His letters are full of routine affairs, with a little more tendency to elaborate upon the ordinary news than Bratton's showed. In one respect we find a break in the routine. After he had been on the place a year, or more, we begin to read that there were runaway slaves. Such a statement meant, undoubtedly, that he was not very successful with the slaves. As the weeks passed it became clear that he faced a revolt against his authority, and along with this news went charges that he was whipping unmercifully. It was probably on this account that he was discharged after serving on the place a year and four months.

Garner's first report to Polk was dated September 10, 1839, and it ran as follows:

DEAR SIR:

I received a letter from you on yesterday giving mee some directions how to manage your bisiness on this place which I was glad to receive also to now what is wanting on the plantation there was when I came here 31 yeards of lincy cloth was all the cloth of any cind. I will want

one hundred yards of lincy and the same of cotton for shert-
ing twenty one pare of socks is wanting there is one pare
here only twenty two pare of shews three pare of No 10,
eight pare of 9, ten pare of 7, one pare for a little girl seven
or eight yers old if they are not a good lot of shews you
had beter send more than will shew them onst a round I
want some three or fore Barrels or sacks of salt for the next
year

Our crop of cotton are cut short from the drouth which
we have had to what it wold of bin when I came here there
was a prospect of a hevy crop I think it is ingerd a third a
beast on the ridges near half our corn crop I suppose is
something better than last yeare but the cuantity I cant
say yet not nowing the cuantty of acors in corn not so
mutch as last year. when I gether it I then can give you a
purty corect noledge of the cuantty I have thirty six thousand lbs. of cotton out and are gining at this time will bee
able to make some bales this weak I think owing to the
drouth I can get the crop saved in a reasnoble time with
the hands thats here it ought to bee saved in time to repare
the fencing a round the farm it is so indiferent that I am
pestered to ceep the stock from destroying the crop your negrows are at this time helthey withe the exception of the
girl Marier which has bin in bad helth for some time I
think here helth improving when I came here there was
some three or fore lying up without a cause though I have
not been pestered cence. it recuire a person to lern the disposition of a negrow to manage them. I will while in your
employ attend strictly to your instructions so far as I am
capible that is for you to judge of when you come down.

Yours respectfully,

The Overseership of John I. Garner

From a letter by William H. Polk to James K. Polk, then in Washington, we get evidence of Garner's quality as an overseer. It was dated at Columbia, October 28, 1839, and in part it is as follows:

DEAR BROTHER:

Mr. Trainum arrived here on yesterday. He is now with me. His account of your plantation is very encouraging. He says that thirty three Bales had been made when he arrived at the plantation, ninety one thousand pounds of cotton had been picked, inclusive of the 33 Bales. He said they commenced bailing again the morning he left, and according to his computation they have by this time 53 Bales. He thinks you will make 130 Bales, at the *least calculation* and your overseers opinion is, that there will be more than 130. Your overseer sends word that he will have by the 25th of December, 100 Bales at Troy ready for shipping. He says your overseer commenced in the right way, and has the negroes under fine command. Trainum is of the opinion that he will do you *full justice* he says that he is industrious, and attentive to his business. Trainum estimates your Pork, which will be made on the plantation, at 4500, and that six thousand pounds will be sufficient to furnish the whole plantation. According to that account you will have to provide 1500. The account which I give you, is the account which your overseer, gave Trainum, which accords with his own observations. He says you have sixty shoats, which will do for next years use, besides many small pigs. You will make 400 barrels of corn. Yours cows etc. are all in good order. Trainum says you were deceived in the whole negro property which you purchased of Harris. Allen he says is at least 45 years old, and says he cannot

perform a hands *labour*. West Harris is now in Philadelphia. he is at this time probably on his way home. . . .

Garner's report of November 3, 1839, gives us the evi-
ence that the plantation was prospering. It shows, also,
that his predecessor had made a good beginning of the crop,
which a favorable season had brought to successful ma-
turity. His letter runs as follows:

DEAR SIR:

I Take my pen in hand to say something of the af-
fares of your plantation in yalabusha county I shold have
written to you sooner had it not bin for a hurt that I receive in the wriste from the fawl of a mule. We are enjoying
the best of helth at presant bothe my famaly and the negrows are entirely helthey and I think we are getting along
verry wel a saving the crop I have seventy fore bales of cotton packed fifty fore of them delivered to Chisholm and
Winter and I think a nofe picked out to make something
about one hundred foour hundred pound bales, and I think
if the weather continues good until chrismos I can have 125
bales of cotton packed and delivered to troy your crop of
cotton is turning out fare better than I though when I came
here I will ceep your cotton halled off as fast as I pack it I
cant say how many bales you will make but I think the
wrise of 125 bales I have stoped picking at this time for the
purpose of gethering the corne Mr. Tranum and myself
thought perhaps it wold make fore hundred Barrels of
corne I have gethered a little part of it and think wil
hardley gow that mutch I can give you a purty corect
noledge in my next letter we also made an estimate of the
cuantaty of porke made we estimade it at 4500 lbs. we
thought 6000 lbs wold bee little a nuf to serv the plase there

is a fine chance of shoats here for the next yeare if they have any attention to them. The Boy charls you sent down last spring run away some fore weeks agow witheout any cause whatever I think he has goun back to tennessee where his wife is I am pestered withe mareners conduct stroling over the contery and corect her she goes to sqr Mcneal for protection with them exceptions we are dwoing wel the negrows you last sent down apere to dwo very wel the boy allen apere to bee weakly at this time he says caused from a mans stabing him before you bought him. I havent yet put my hogs up to fatten bin weighting for rain put them up they wold bee in a bed of dust if it donte rain soon I must tri them up as they are to fatten with corn entirely I will conclude by saying your directions shal bee punctialy attended two.

Yours respectfully

On November 23 Garner made further report of the progress of affairs on the plantation. A favorable season was permitting the steady gathering of the crops and both cotton and corn were coming out satisfactorily with the prospect that a fine store of bacon would be laid up for use the next year. The letter runs as follows:

DEAR SIR:

After my respects to you I wil inform you that we are all wel at presant bothe my famaly and the negrows Phil got his hand caught in the gin a few days after I wrote to you cut his hand very bad but has got very near wel I have not yet herd anything of charles I have cept a lookout for him and wil continue so to dwo the boy allen has aperently not bin able for hard servis sence he has bin here and I believe caused from the wond which he received in the side before he came here [I got] Mr. Walker to look at him a few days a gow and he thought with myself that it wold not dwo to put him to hard work yet

I have gethered the crop of corn and agreable to the waggon I hald the corn in there is three hundred and fifty barrels of corn fel shorter than myself and Mr Tranum estimated I have packed 102 bales of cotton them weighing 41,993 lbs, making 410 lbs. and something over to the bales, and I think there will bee thirty bales more, twenty five at least

N. B. I think if I have luck I shal make 4500 or 5000 lbs of pork I have forty hogs fatning and a plenty of young hogs for the next year. I have agreed with sqr Mcneel for the next year for this place and I shold like for you to bee at your plantation as soon as convenient after chrismos as I wold like to have your advise on sertin things. your friends here speak if this beeing a sickly place from some cause and speek of its beeing proper to moove the cabins to some other point convenient to the farm I have omited stating how many bales delivered to Troy 84 of them delivered and three days more I wil deliver the others

Yours respectfuly

December 25, 1839, Garner wrote again in a brief letter relating to the insurance of the cotton shipped to New Orleans, the renewal of his own contract for the next year, and the return of a runaway to the plantation. It runs as follows:

DEAR SIR:

I received your letter a few days agow dated the 14th of november my famaly was not in a condishun to live to gow to Troy to lern whather or not the inshurence was affected or not Mr. Chisolm and Minter agent in troy informed mee that all cotton is inshured unless a man says not inshured there is open polacy to that affect and they wrote to your comisheon merchant in new Orleans to inshure it as a speticial contract that it should bee inshured certain I intended saying to you in my last letter that myself and sqr Mcneel, had agreed for another yeare it was neglect in mee that I sayd nothing about it I persume you have received a letter from sqr Mcneel before this time to that affect N. B. Charles came in the 5th of December and the ballance of the negros ar wel and we have got 130 bales packed and I will get done in some fore or five days more picking I have kiled three thousand nine hundred lbs of pork and have nine hogs to cil yet nothing more at presant   Yors respectifuly

The escape of Charles to the woods had caused James K. Polk much concern, and he wrote to his brother, William H. Polk, to make inquiries for the man around Columbia and in the region where Charles had been born and brought up. William's reply gives us an idea of what migrations had been made by Charles in his brief existence. In connection with other letters in this collection it also has a bearing on that contention so often made by some Southerners that nobody sold his slaves unless they were "bad negroes." While these letters do not show that Polk sold his "good" slaves they do show that he was continually buying slaves, which means that someone else was selling them. The letter of William H. Polk to James K. Polk about Charles was written from Columbia, December 30, 1839, and runs as follows:

DEAR BROTHER:
    I have been delayed in answering your Letter, by not being able to see Mr. John L. Smith and obtain, the in-

formation which you requested in your letter, relative to
your negro Boy *Charles*. I this day, saw Mr. Smith, and
he informed me that your Boy, the year you bought him
was hired to Mr. Hatch Esq and would refer you to a Mr.
Dickerson the son-in-law of Capt. Jones as a person who is
well acquainted with the Negro. Also Matthew Rhea and
Mr. Fain. That the Mother and family connexion of
Charles belong to the family, of Cox's near Cornersville. I
will in the course of ten days, ride up to that Neighbourhood, and endeavour to catch him, if he is there, though
Smith is of opinion, that he is still in or about Somerville.

My circumstances are such at this time, that I cannot
afford to buy *Reuben* at any price for *cash*. But if it would
suit you I am willing to give the *last note* which you owe
me, which note amounts to one thousand and eighty three
dollars. That is more than your cash price and the interest,
which would amount to $1062. If you are willing to ac-
cept this proposition, you must let me know in a day or two.
Reuben informs me that you give him the privilege, if I do
not buy him, of being hired at this place, if he could find
anyone who would give a fair price for him. he informed
[me] late this evening, that Mr. Fisher the Druggist, was
willing to give $130 for him next year. That is a fair price
for him according to the rates at which negroes are hiring
here. I would like to have Reuben, and I think the price
which I offer is a very fair one, though it may not suit your
present necessities. . . . . .

These necessities had not been met a year later, and
William was again urged to sell one of Polk's slaves to get
money. The reply of William, December 4, 1840, in part
is as follows:

The Overseership of John I. Garner

DEAR SIR:

Having been unable to see Genl. Pillow until today, I could not answer your letter with the required information concerning Herbert at the time you requested. I conversed with him and Mr. Young today, they looked at Herbert, but would make no definite offer, further than that they would give six hundred dollars cash for him. I informed them that you would not under any circumstances take $600. They then informed me that they would probably give $650 cash. I of course refused it — though that is the price now given for likely negro fellows — until I could write to you and ascertain what you would do. For cash I do not think he can be sold for more, there being so fiew persons who desire to buy negroes. . . . .

Polk's Mississippi plantation was now paid for and it was yielding a fair income, sometimes more and sometimes less, as the seasons were good or bad, and as the price of cotton rose or fell. But he was deeply engrossed in politics, and he was heavily obligated to his party associates in the canvasses. In 1839 he brought to an end his fourteen years as a member of the national house of representatives, in two of which he had been speaker. In the same year he became governor of Tennessee after passing through a hot campaign. These activities had drawn on his purse heavily and he was in need of money. To sell a slave would give only temporary relief. James Walker, his brother-in-law, in a letter dated December 30, 1839, summed up Polk's situation as follows:

DEAR SIR:

William I presume has not written you respecting Reubin. He says he does not think he can buy him, unless

it is upon your two year note, Speaks of offering you $1000
for him on that note. This would be equal to about $700
cash as his hire certainly ought to be good for $150 pr. an-
num. I have told him if he would not take him as Cash
now, he ought at least to go down to the District and turn
Harry into money for you which can be done, I think, if
there was anyone to attend to it. He says he will go to
Cornersville to see if anything can be heard of your runaway negro, but I think this is uncertain unless you urge him
to it. I have thought a good deal about the aspect of your
Cash affairs. If you get what you expect from Yell[1] with
what bank accommodations you may get you can get on
and relieve yourself by degrees. The difficulty is that the
whole amount of your debts are pressing down upon you at
once. You ought, if practicable (and I think it is) to get
your debts so arranged that you could pay them in instalments, reducing about $2000 pr. an. Your plantation would
supply this, pay its own expenses, and supply I presume the
deficit of your expenses beyond your salary. . . . .

On the Mississippi plantation the work went on as usual,
Garner keeping the slaves steadily at work. Polk had sug-
gested that a grist mill might be set up using the horse
power that ran the gin in the ginning season. Garner
caught at the suggestion. Writing to Polk on December
31, 1839, he said:

DEAR SIR:

I received your letter of the fifth of this instant asking my opinion withe regard to a mill atacht to our gin for

[1] Archibald Yell of Fayetteville, Arkansas, judge, member of Congress and
eventually governor was an intimate friend of Polk's. Many letters in the Polk
MSS. witness his loyalty from early years. He resigned from Congress to become a
Colonel in the Mexican War and was killed leading his regiment against the enemy at
Buena Vista.

the purpose of our one grinding I was glad to lern that you was in favor of a mill there is but one thing we need as bad as a mill here and that a blacksmith I wold bee glad that we cold have boath I mad encurey what the coste of the work exclusive of the stones and irons wil bee one hundred dollars to attach it to the big whele of the gin I am entierly in favor of having a mill so soon as we lay by our crop I will have the timber to get and to season before the work can be done.

I went to see Mr. Chisholm and minter I cold not see them saw ther agent and he told mee to say to you that all cotton was enshured unless a man directed that it shold not bee enshured there was open policy to that affect and they had written to your comisheon merchant in New orleans as a spetical contract to enshure your cotton and I wil see them in a day or two there is a prospect of the waters wrising I can send 132 bales by the first boats and wil dwo sow unless you direct me otherwise by a letter I have but some 2 or 3 bales in the patch cold bin done before now but the wether is so very bad I cant pick when I can have a few days of good wether I wil pick out the ballence of the cotton Charles came hom the fifth day of december.

Yours with respect.

The time was unpropitious for any operations requiring cash, and it was cash that Polk needed. The panic of 1837 had laid credit low through out the Southwest and business had not yet passed beyond the period of hard times that follows every panic. Polk's efforts to sell some of his slaves led him to write to Albert T. McNeal of Coffeeville, Mississippi, whose reply, dated January 15, 1840, was filled with good sense and gives us an interesting view of this subject. It runs as follows:

[135]

The Plantation Overseer

DEAR SIR:

I acknowledge the receipt of your favour of the 1st inst. postmarked the 5th and also that of the 5th inst. which came to hand by last night's mail. I wrote to you from Holly Springs early in December, and on my return to Coffeeville from that place learned that Charles had come in. I did not advise you of his return learning that Garner had written about that time, and shortly afterwards I visited Bolivar, Te., and reached Home again on the 8th Inst. I fear I shall not be able to sell Charles. It is a very unfavourable time for a cash sale. Money is extremely scarce and I have never in my life witnessed "such screwing and twisting"[1] to get it. Charles ought to bring $750 or $800, cash. But few men have money and those who have it, will be disposed to hold on with the expectation of buying negroes low for cash at sheriffs sales before and at the Spring term of the approaching circuit courts. In consequence of low waters the planters have not been able to ship their cotton, nor have they found a merket at Home. I have not the least doubt that you might sell Charles for good Mississippi funds in Fayette Co., Te., at a better price than I can get here, and as it is probable I may fail to sell him here you might in the mean time sell him there to some one who may know the boy with the understanding that it shall be no contract in the event of a sale here, which is not probable. I saw Mr. Garner today.

[1] The state of the currency in Tennessee at this time is shown in the following memorandum, preserved in the Polk MSS., dated June 5, 1839, and signed by Wm. H. Polk.

"Due Richard B. Moore, one hundred and forty-five dollars, sixty Mobile, Ala., fifty Tuskaloosa, fifteen Decatur, five Montgomery, five Huntsville, and ten Tennessee, for value received.

"Recd. on this note by the hands of James Walker one hundred dollars in huntsville money. July the 2d, 1839."

The Overseership of John I. Garner

All are well at the plantation, Addison however in the woods. Garner, as instructed, is clearing more land. Your crop of cotton (136 bales) is at Troy, ready for the first rise in the river.

Carroll County lies immediately south of this county and I practice law there. The first time I visit that county I will see Mr. Hamon and get his note with security as desired. Mr. Hamon ought to give you about $400 a year for Harry, possibly I may be able to get more. A boy of his age and such as you describe ought I think to be worth $1200. The time has been when he would have sold for $2000 here. If Harry be the same blacksmith, who worked at the Caldwell place 5 miles from Columbia, then owned by Uncle Sam Polk, I remember him *well* (tall and muscular) though some 18 years have elapsed since I saw him, and my recollection admonishes me that I am fast growing an old bachelor. . . . . . .

P. S.   I will visit the plantation Sunday and probably we may determine to remove the buildings, etc.

January and February were important months on a cotton plantation and a good overseer was as busy then as in any other part of the year. It was the time for resetting the fences, digging ditches, building or repairing cabins, and clearing new ground for enlargement of the cultivated acreage. All this work went on this winter, and in addition the cabins were moved from their first location to what proved to be a healthier place. It was in this season that the rains usually came that raised the water in the Yalobusha River so that the light draft steamers could come up to the nearby landing and carry the year's crop to New Orleans. These activities drew heavily on the time of the overseer. In a letter to Polk dated March 2, 1840, Garner alluded to his labors in the following words:

DEAR SIR:

After my respects to you wil inform you that we have moved on the opposit side of the hill from whare the houses stood to my stables and cribs which wil bee out of my power to move until I lay my crop by or place myself backwards in my crop I have got a large potion of my cotton land ridged up and are getting along very wel I think. I have sowed some twelve or foreteen acors in oats on the ridges and have aded to the farm some forty five acors I think   I am aming to put about two hundred acors in cotton   N. B. I went to Troy yesterday and got a bill of lading for your cotton   it left Troy a few days cence all in good awder at the same time and in the same boat, 136 bales weying 57559 lbs., if I have not made a mistake in the calculation of them done in a hurry   I am trying to get a letter to you a mediately as you have fail to come   I would of written to you sooner had it not bin that I was looking for you every hour for some time   I wil now what to dwo in a case of this kind herafter write all the time   your cotton wil bee in new orleans in a few days from this time perhaps the last of the weak   it left here in a boat belonging to Minter for Williamses landing and wil bee [?] tode from there by a sterne boat which wil deliver it there very quick   I shal continue looking for you until you arrive here.   Yours Respectifuly

Shortly afterwards Polk made a visit to the Mississippi plantation. He found everything going well and his visit had a soothing effect on the overseer. Writing to him on May 3, 1840, Garner said:

The Overseership of John I. Garner

DEAR SIR:

After my respects to you I will inform you that we are all wel with the exception of the girl matilda   she had child some ten days a gow and is grunting yet, nothing serious   her child died after some ten or twelve hours, from what cause I dont now   she has not worked more than half her time cence you was here   N. B. we are getting along very wel with our crop taking the whether into consideration   it has been raining near half the time sence you left but I am in hopes from the presant apearence we wil have some good wether.   I believe I have as good a crop of cotton as I ever saw for the time a year.   I will git over hit with my hoes in a few days.   my fored [forward] corn is indiferent owing to the wrain it being on wet low land   I have to plow when the mules wold mier to the nees in places and of course it cant look wel.

Yours respectifuly

Garner's June report, dated June 1, 1840, was as follows:

DEAR SIR:

After my respects to you we are awl wel except marier and Evy   marier complaining as usul   she has spels onste a month very bad Doct Towns is giving her medicin   I dont think her helth ever will be restored entierly.   Evy has had the rheumatism so she was unable to gow about though mucth better at presant   she is gowing about at this time and I think getting wel fast   N. B. my crop on dry land is very fine on the lowest wet land it is very indiferent drownded from the unusial cuantaty of wrain we have had this spring.   I have bin trying to make arangements with a workman to start the mill and repare the big whele of the gin for instance new cogs, and a new band shaft. $100 is the lowest price I can get that work done for. I have bin talking to several workmen. I got a ginwright to look at the ginstand to see [?] the work hit needed and the price hit would cost. hit wants new saws the ribs fasing, new wheels, and a new brush, which cost wil bee $125 and perhaps a little more he says he can make hit as good if not better than when new

I wish you to write to mee whether to employ the work done or what to dwo as the prices apere hye. I wish to now a mediately, sow that I can make engagements of that cind in time to bwe sertain of the work I havent received a letter from your hand cence you left here they may bee one in the office, I havent bin to town in some time, I have bin cept very bisey. to ceep the grass down in my farm as hit has bin sow constantly wraining gras wold not die when cut up

Yours respectifuly

Six days later, on June 7, the overseer sent Polk the following long letter in which he dwelt upon several matters of interest to those who wish to know what was happening on the plantation. The letter runs as follows:

DEAR SIR:

I sent charles to town to mail a letter to you on thursday last and to make enquirey for the saws brought mee a letter from you dated the seventh of last month, in which I saw articles directed from new orleans for the use of the plantation. I went to Troy yesterday to see if they had come up. they had not, and had not got to Williamses landing ten days a gow, and the water is so low they cant come to Troy at this time. I am fearful I shal have to waggon them from Williames landing which is some forty miles from here, and my waggon is not sufisient to send that distance hawling. hit is getting crasy and [its] boddy very shacklin indeed. and now [mutilated] cloth. I had a notion to have made a cawl on you when here for a new waggon but thought as times was hard I cold save this crop with the old one though one waggon is not suficient on this plantation. for instance hawling away bales and cotton out of the farm at the same time which is a blidse to bee done.

My crop is very good considering the season except on the wet land there I could not get cotton nor corn to stand for the water standing on the land awl the spring though not mutch of that cind my crop of cotton on the dry land very good and the stand regular and not sufering for work though a little gras yet if the wether holds like at this time I wil have my crop in a beautiful fix in a few days I havent saw but one crop of cotton this spring my crop was far before that and Mr. Towns how [who] does bisiness not far from mee was over my crop a few days a gow and stated my cotton was a better averidge crop than his and I am enduce to belive there is none better in the contery the fact wil prove hit self in the fall though I have bin cept bisier this spring to cultivate the crop than ever before caused from the rain and some three neegroes out of the crop the best part of the spring. matilda had a child the day before I commenced scraping cotton her child died the next evening after born I believe caused from her one conduct not letting of mee now nothing of hit, until a few minets before the burth of the child. I cold not get the old woman there in time, her lying up at the same time. Evy has been aflicted with a rheumatism some time, was unable to walk about I had to have the doctor with her she has [now]

got purty wel over hit   she wil bee now [use] to mee any
more this spring   she wil have a child in some fore or five
weeks from what she says   I dont expect to put her in the
farm until after she has hit.

Mariers helth has not improved any that I can discover
she says she is worse of a spring   she is in a very bad con-
dishon every thre or fore weks   so very bad onst this spring
she was throne into fits of spasms in which I had to have
the Doct with her and he think hit very doubtful whether
her helf ever wil bee restored   though he wil if posable   I
think very wel of Doct Towns as a Physitian so far as I
have tride him   I wil take awl posable cear of your hogs
and stock of every cind.

Yours respectifuly.

I wrote you in my letter dated June the first concerning the
intended mill and the reparing of the gin stand   the reparing of the stand with new saws wheel and brush that hit
needs will cost $125 or perhaps something more   I wil as-
certain when I goin to granada   I did not see the bos workman is the reason I cant tel certain   the starting of the mill
and [filing] the big wheel of the gin making a band shaft
wil cost one hundred dollars   is the lowest I can get the
work done   write to mee what to dwo in those cases

A month later, July 5, 1840, he made further report of
his operations in the following manner:

Dear sir:

I received your letter of the 7th June on yesterday
the articles which you awderd from neworleans have a
rived at williams landing I lerned yesterday   I wil try and
make arangements to send my waggon down in a few days

The Overseership of John I. Garner

I wold like to send with some other waggon if I can swe one gowing down as the boy has now noledg of the rout

The negrows have bin very helthy except marier, matilda, Evy. Mariers helth has improved very mutch cence I wrote you before though she is better and worse the doct thinks I had better not put her in the farm until her helth is better Evy has I believe got over the rheumatism and wil make two of her self in a few days I cwep her out of the farm for fear of some accident Matilda is sick at this time though considerably on the mend I thought for some time I shold loose her something like the dropsey She tels mee that she had the dropsey last fawl sow that had to whip her feet and legs with holey busheys to let the water from them she is of now account she hasent posatively done mee as mutch servis cence she has bin hear as old Ben hasent worked more than half her time at best I think we will git her patched up again as she has bin before

my crop is something better than I cold of expected from the season it wrained hear awl the time until the last of may then cuit sudentley I havent had a good rain cence though shours they was a good rain last wensday in the settlement but did not retch mee Doct Towns rode over my cotton with mee some two weaks a gow stated he would give the preference to my crop of any a gentleman in our contery past threw the lain a few days a gow stated he had been over the contery a good deele, and threw Tallahatchey Cty and that part of my cotton was a little better than he had seen. my late corn is very good and if I can have a few more rains in time I shal make a good crop

my stock of hogs and catle apere to bwe dwoing wel. it was awl that I cold dwo to make the crop with the mules owing to the rain in the spring the hevy plowing and them

miering awl the while several of them give out in the
spring part of them two smawl for this contery

I am yours

Garner's report for October 4, 1840, was in an optimistic
spirit. He complained of the drought of the preceding
summer, which had cut off the crop to some extent. It gives
us a distinct view of plantation routine at that time. The
text is as follows:

DEAR SIR:

I take my pen in hand to write you a few lines. I
have nothing strange nor interesting more than I have had
the misfortune to loose Elizabeths youngest child I am
unable to say what was the matter with hit. hit was sick
some two months. Matilda is stil complaining yet, but is
able to spin she has not bin in the farm to work cence
early last spring I am fearful she never wil recover good
helth again. Marier aperes to enjoy as good helth at presant [as] any person Evy has recovered entierly from the
rheumatism and has got a very likely yong negroe with the
exceptions of them old standing deseses our place cold not
bwe beat in point of helth. We have had a cuantaty of rain
here in the last two weeks hit has defaced our cotton very
mutch. if hit dose not continue to rain by the last of this
month I shal bwe able to ship some sixty bales. I cant say
how maney bales I shal make but I think somewhere about
the last years crop My corn crop wil bwe short owing to
the drouth, but a supply for the place I think. I wil gowown
to ship your cotton in the same wey I did last year unles
you instruct mee other wise. I think you had better awder
your baling and rope earleyer in the season as our navigation is unsertain sow hit can come to Troy before the wa-

ter gets down in the spring hit gives mee mutch ilconven-
ience with some expence, having but one waggon, and
wanting that awl most constantly at home

I am fearful I wil bwe pestered to make my pork this
fawl owing to the dry sumer my hogs has not done as
wel as I wold wish grone very little I have fed them as
mutch as my corn wold bare I indevered to buy nothing
unles nesserly compeeled to have.

I am yours

Then enters again Dr. Silas M. Caldwell, whose complaints had been so stern against Ephraim Beanland. He
appears again as the protector of the slave against the reported cruelty of the overseer. In a letter to Polk written
at Dancyville, Haywood County, Tennessee, October 20,
1840, he said:

Dr. sir:

Your Boy Henry Carter as he [is] called came to
my House this morning. he is runaway his reason for doing so he says the Overseer threatened to shoot him he says
for nothing your Boy you got from William that he got of
Webster was shot the night before he left in the thigh by a
man he had with him by the name of *Lea* the Boy, *Perry*
that was shot could not walk Henry says. he says he is
afraid to go back I have concluded to let him stay hear
until I hear from you from what Henry says you have not
got a good crop of neither corn or cotton

Resply yours, etc.

Dr. Caldwell doubtless reported correctly the story told
him by Henry Carter the fugitive. He did not attempt to
decide how much truth was in it. In a letter from Garner
to Polk, dated October 1, 1840, we have the overseer's side

of the affair and it leaves us with the feeling that more was behind. The letter from Garner is as follows:

DEAR SIR:

I received your letter of the second of last month a few days cence and hav bin trying to find a waggon gowing to memphis to send for the box of shoes the negroes are needing them very mutch I am gowing to town to morrow and wil posably meet with an opportunity to send for them.

You wish to lern how the crop is turning out. I think from what I have gethered of boath cotton and corn, there wil bwe very little difference between this crop and last. I have gethered near half of my corn and have to weight until the ground dry some my waggon mier down in the field so that I had to stop I have got sixty bales made and wil ship them in a few days if the river is high a nuf. we had the dryest sumer I ever experienced and for the last 5 or 6 weks hit has bin wraining a gradeel wil make me more backward in getting the crop out. I have had the misfortune to loose the work of three of my negroes cence yesterday three weks rhunawey from mee Henry, Gilbert, and charls the same boy that was out last fawl so long I think they have taken another trip to Tennissee there was no difference in the world between myself and two of them Henry had become so indiferent about his duty I was compeld to corect him, he resisted and fought mee I awdered charls to take hold of him being the nearest but refused to dwo so. after Henry and myself [had been] combatting some time he got loose from mee and got into the swamp wile I was pursuing him Gilbert, Charls, and Perry was running the other wey. the only reason was becaus they did not take holt of the other boy when awderd I concluded that henry wold try to get his cloths while I was weying cotton at night got a cople of men to watch for him while watching for him Perry was slipping up and was awderd to stand but he broke and he shot him in the legs with smawl shot sow I got him, and he is at work. I have but very little doubt but what they have gone to tennessee likely trying for a free state I lern that charls told to the negroes that he cold of made his escape before if he had bin a mind to the ballance of them are wel Marier thinks henry wil gow to his old master near sumervill Ten.

I am yours

Here ends abruptly the letters from John I. Garner, overseer. Early in the next year we have the beginning of a series from Isaac H. Dismukes, now overseer at the Mississippi plantation. We are left to infer that Garner, whom Albert McNeal had recommended for reappointment for the ensuing year, was rejected because Polk believed that the stories of the slaves were true. He passed off the scene for the same reason that Ephraim Beanland passed, because he could not control the slaves without undue harshness.

CHAPTER X

The Overseership of Isaac H. Dismukes

ARNER'S successor, Isaac H. Dismukes, seems to have been selected by Albert T. McNeal. Where he came from is not stated. He was a man who wrote few and brief letters. His reports probably did himself little justice, for he was not skilled in setting forth ideas. No letters from him are preserved for the last years of his employment on the plantation. His discharge in January, 1845, was because he had too much company and neglected his duties on account of it. The first letter from him, dated January 21, 1841, runs as follows:

DEAR SIR:

I now take it upon my self to write you a fiew lines to inform you that your cotten left troy the 14 of this month for neworleans   I did not assertain it until the 19 of this month: the remaining part of your cotten is not yet pick out for the weathe has been so unfavourable that I could not have it pict unless picking it weat for wea have not had more than two fair dais since you left hear and they wase too could to pick cotten   I wil pick it as soon as the weather wil amit it I pick on it one day and the ground was so weat that the hands could scarcely walk through it   so if I had of pick it weat it would of bin hear yet for wea have had no sun to dry weat cotten: I have bin mostly engage in the new ground since you left hear when the weather

would amit it but there has bin several weat days and
snow togeather so wea could not work I think that if the
weather had not bin so very bad that I could of had it
cleard down to the bridge the pork that you bought when
down here lost 300 pounds and I saw baker after cilling it
and wanted him to refund something back but he would
not doo it: the hands work finely and keep will so far: the
best estimate that I can make of the hogs that wea wil have
to kill another year is between 60 and 70 head concludeing
pigs and all in and sum of them is very poor and I am
afraid that I shall loose sum of them as the corn is scarce
as you noe I paude thomas oliver $74 and there is a bal-
ance as yet of $12 for the reparing of the brush wheal after
the first work which you made nothing of the account was
presented to mea but I did not pay it as I ware not author-
ize to doo it: I am making arrangements to have some cloth
made as soon as I can: I am getting milk and butter more
than I myself make use of the children have some occa-
sionally wea have noe young calfs as yet nor wea wil not
have enny until spring I had to write about all these little
things to make out my letter Nowthing more but remain
your friend

For a time Dismukes wrote pretty regularly, dating his
letters about the first of the month and describing very
briefly, as though it bored him to write, the routine matter
of the plantation. Writing on February 1, 1841, he said:

DEAR SIR:

According to promise I wil now offer you a fiew lines
wea are all wel with the exception of some little complaining nouthing though very sereis: I am geting along very
smoothly with buisness I am now ready to starte my

ploughs as soon as the ground gets in order for the bisness and should of had a good deal of plough dun if the weathe had of bin enny more favourable but wea have had the wettest time since you left hear that I ever sean I believe I have got all the new ground in order for burning of as soon as it dries so it wil burn I have not had enny cloth made yet but are makeing evry nesesary arrangement and as soon as I can get sum purson to show one of the wimmin to weave I wil hav sum made: I have the balance of your crop of cotten hear yet but as soon as I can get what is due you from Mr. Minter I wil send it of immediately.

For learning the art of weaving Maria was finally selected. Her name has frequently been mentioned in this series of letters, usually indicating that she was on the sick list. She has never appeared as a slave distinguished for mental alertness. It is surprising therefore that she should so quickly pick up the art of weaving. Dismukes' statement in anticipation of her success in learning how to do it is so confidently made that we must conclude that the slave found weaving an easy thing. In a letter to Polk, dated March 9, 1841, he shows that Maria had made such progress with the weaving that she was about to get along without instruction. He wrote:

Dear sir:

According to promise I wil now writes you a fiew lines to let you hear from mea wea are all wel exsept lizabeth she has bin complaining now for three weaks or more but nuthing like daingers I have had 1 pease of cloth made the spining masheane has landit [landed] not many dais since in the neighbourhood I have not got it home as yet but intend to send for it soon marier sais she thinkes that she can put in a web now herself and weave it out with thout enny assistance: as for my plantation affairs I think I am geting aloung very smoothly I shall commence plantin now in a fiew daies nuthing more of consequence

Of all the overseers whose letters survive in the Polk Manuscripts Dismukes was the poorest letter writer. He did not know how to do justice to himself, being as it seems of that class of men whose thoughts congeal when they take pen in hand. The two letters that follow show the truth of this statement. The first was written by Dismukes to Polk, April 1, 1841, and the second, presented here in extract, was written by Major William Bobbitt, who was then acting as Polk's agent in Coffeeville. Dismuke's letter was as follows:

DEAR SIR:

I will now write you a fiew lines that you may hear from us wea are all well I have got all of my ould ground courn planted and it is cummin up but on the last saderday and sunday in this munth wea had a tremenderrous rain which overflowed and wash up a great deal of it and I expect to have most all of it to plant over again unless it cum-up better than I expect it will[1]

I am at a lost to noe what to write to you I have commence planting of cotten I commence today as it is the first of april I have noe diffeyculty with my boys. Mr. bobit was down to sea mea the other day for the first time and I have not heard from you since you left you must write nuthing more

---

[1] Although Dismukes now felt that the rain had done much damage to his crop he wrote to Polk on April 9, 1841, "Wea have had a fine time for bisness rain enuff and nun too much."

Major Bobbitt's letter, written on April 5, 1841, was as follows:

. . . . I was at your plantation a few days ago and am much pleased with the prospect for a crop. Dismukes is an energetic business man and I have no doubt if the season should be favourable and the health of your negroes good, you will make a better crop than has been made on the place with the same number of hands. The negroes and he are getting along smoothly and so far as I can ascertain they are well satisfied with the overseer. Health good except for one pregnant woman who has been grunting some time. . . . . . .

Dismukes' letters are not well preserved at this time. From one, written on June 1, 1841, the following is taken: "Sir I have not got my negrows cloths yet I have sent to troy too or three times to see wheather it had got there or noe but it has not cum." The clothing for the slaves should have been distributed in the early spring. A letter from Major Bobbitt, dated July 16, 1841, runs as follows:

DEAR SIR: 1841[1]

I wrote you in the spring and have received no reply, which will explain to you the reason of my seeming neglect. I must say to you in the outset that unless it rain in a few days we shall make nothing. We have had no rain for two months, and you must judge of the prospect. I was all over your farm on last friday and have no hesitation in saying Dismukes has done his part and with seasons would have made at least 130 bags of cotton and an abundance of corn, and even now with rain I think you will make more

---

[1] The letter is filed in the volume for 1844, July 16. The name of the writer is sometimes spelled "Bobbitt" and sometimes it is "Bobbit."

Cotton than was made last year and corn enough to do the farm.

I have received no more money of Ford than would lift the Garner note, for the balance I expect suit will have to be brought. Consequently only a part of your taxes have been paid. The Collector has agreed to wait 'till August for the balance

Dismukes thinks that in addition to a new Top you should have a new press altogether as you desire large Bails, and says that it will be impossible to do so with the old one. I think the charge very high, to wit $75, and concluded to consult you on the subject. if a press has to be put up the sooner the better, Dismukes says before cotton opens, please write me on this subject forthwith. Adison is in the woods and has been for three weeks and cannot be found. Dismukes informs me he has apprised you of the whole matter. upon the whole, I think, you would do well to sell him and supply his place with a better and you would have the most agreeable set of negroes with which I am acquainted. . . . .

Addison, the fugitive, betook himself straight to the house of refuge to which Polk's Mississippi slaves seemed sure to turn in their flights, the plantation of Dr. Silas M. Caldwell, near Dancyville, Haywood County, Tennessee. Here he received a fair welcome and told his story to attentive ears. The doctor forthwith wrote a letter to Polk, dated July 23, 1841, setting forth Addison's version of his wrongs in the following words:

DEAR SIR:

Your boy Addison has runaway from your farm and is at my house. From the wounds that are on his neck and arms it appears that the Overseer intended to kill him the wounds are well he says the Overseer says he will kill him and is afraid to stay there you will please write to me what to do with him he has been runaway about four weeks I have hired him in the neighbourhood until I hear from you Your prospects [political] are as good in this county as they were in '39. Saml. is sick

In the course of time Addison was sent back to the Mississippi plantation. But a year later he again took to the woods. Writing to Polk on August 24, 1842, Dismukes said: " Adderson kild a short [shoat] while I wass sick and thought I would whip him and hea has run of hea has bin gone three or 4 dais."

August 2, 1841, Dismukes described his ordinary troubles in a letter to Polk which runs as follows:

DEAR SIR:

I wil now offer you a fiew lines to inform you sumthing of our health and bisness I shall not bee very particular as I expect you down sum time in the course of this month[1] wea are all well at the preasent time my crop of cotten lookes very well my corn is sorrey my cattle have stop dying I lost nine of them thare is nuthing else of importance the money which you left with mea have given out sum time since for I had to pay freait on the bagen and rope to the amount of $42.62½ I have plied to magour bobit and hea has not got eny money by him I stand in neade of a niew waggon for this has past repairing

Addison's flight from the plantation mentioned by Dr. Caldwell in his letter of July 28 inspired Gilbert to flee also. He reached the neighborhood of Somerville where he

[1] Polk visited his Mississippi farm about December 1, 1841.

was arrested and put into jail. The watchful doctor sent
for him, took him to his own farm and sent him, with Addison, back to the Mississippi plantation. All of which is
described in the following letter from Mrs. Silas M. Caldwell to Mrs. James K. Polk, dated at Spring Hill, Tennessee, August 23, 1841:

MY DEAR SISTER:

I write you in haste as I am again in great trouble.
James is very ill of fever he went to stay with his Brother
took sick we heard that a Boy in jail at Sumerville said he
belonged to us Dr sent James and Wally to see it was as
we expected your *Boy* Gilbert the day was warm nineteen
miles to Sumerville and back the same day James took very
ill could scarcely reach home he is pretty much attacked like
he was at your house three years ago I am so uneasy about
him this is the fifth day no change for the better he took
Gilbert out of Jail and Dr. has sent him and *Addison* to
your farm from all accounts the overseer drinks and man-
ages badly we cant tell only from the negroes own tales. I
leave it with you as Negros *news*. . . . . . .

Brother James had better visit his place soon and get
another overseer. Mr. Allexander of our Neighbourhood
is willing to go he would Dr. says do first rate he is a very
study good farmer out farms all here he is very industrious
his motive for wishing to go is wifes health he thinks the
clymate would suit her better by all means you ought to
get him then you could rely on his as a man of entegrity
good morals and good manager he owns some six or eight
Slaves. . . . . . .

N. B. Gilbert has been out a month and in jail a week
Adison was hired here a month to the man that has now

taken them home that will defray the expense of taking them home partly[1]

In a letter to Polk, dated at Coffeeville, Mississippi, August 29, 1841, Polk's friend, Major William Bobbitt, gave advice about the suppression of the habit of running away and made interesting comments on affairs on the plantation. The letter runs as follows:

DEAR SIR:

Yours of the 13th instant came duly to hand. I was at the farm on yesterday and found that Addison had not arrived. Another *Fellow,* whose name I cannot at this time recollect, is out and I expect will endeavour to get to Tennessee, and I suppose without any just cause for running away whatever. I approve of your determination to put a stop to it, by making examples of the offenders in every instance, that is by correcting instead of selling. Mr. J. Leigh says no other course will correct the evil. The bagging, negro clothing, etc. have all been received, they had to be hauled from *Cocchuma* and Mr. Dismukes says he wrote to you on the subject and has not failed to write monthly agreeably to your request.

I was also at Mr. J. Leigh's on yesterday to ascertain if possible whether or not the *mill* had been delivered and Mr. Leigh informed me that it had not been delivered, neither his nor yours, that he had written twice to the gentleman with whom he made the engagement, and the third letter he directed to the *agent* in Memphis and had received no answer from either. If they are delivered in Memphis at all, Mr. Leigh says it will be out of his power to unite your *teams* as he has purchased a *Gin,* or rather contracted for one, and he will have a full load for his own team.

[1] The letter is signed L. E. Caldwell [Eliza]. The postmark is Hatchie, Tennessee.

The Overseership of Isaac H. Dismukes

Your waggon is worn out, and you will be under the necessity of getting one soon, the better way, I think, would be to get a *Substantial* one in Tennesee and ship it to Memphis, and if the mill is brought there it can be brought down in the waggon.

I had the Winter Clothing measured, and Mariah says there will be about 10 yds., perhaps 15 wanting, which, if wanting I can supply upon as good terms as it can be had for. Mr. Dismukes informed me that the Winter Shoes for the Negroes were all made.

Your crop of cotton surpasses any crop for the season that I have ever seen. It is decidedly the best that I have seen in the county. Mr. D. says, if the fall should be favourable, he will make as much as he can possibly save.

Mariah wished me to inform her mistress that she is worth at least $30 more than when she left Tennessee. She can spool, warp, and *weave* and with a little more practice thinks she will make a first rate weaver. . . . . .

Addison and Gilbert arrived safely at the plantation, but the spirit or revolt was high in Gilbert. He stayed only two nights and one day and then took the road for Tennessee. To Dismukes this was a source of regret. He did not like the instructions that came to him tending to restrain his dealings with the runaways and he laid his side of the case before Polk in the following letter dated September 1, 1841:

DEAR SIR:

I wil once more endeaver to write to you a fiew lines that you may hear from us   wea are all well at the preasent time hopeing that thes fiew lines may finde you and your family wel   I have nuthing of consequence to write to you   I am now goin own geatherin of the crop   I think that I shall make corn anuff to doo the fairm another year. I shall make as much or more I think than was made hear last year and my cotten crap cant bea beaten by the neighbour-hood Adderson and gilburt got hea a fiew dais since gilburt left mea about the last of July that new nuthing of hea got to tennessee the day that the doctor ware about starteing of adderson and hea stade there three dais and was sent back with adderson and when hea got hear hea stade hear two nights and one day and hea left again without one lik or a short word that ware not sent according to your request I should of whip them as soon as they landed had it not of bin your request that mr bobit should bea preasent though I think that if I had of taken them and of whip them as soon as they got hear that gilburt would not of run away again soon which I should of dun if I had not thought that you would of thought that I would of whip them too much though that is what I neaver have dun since I have bin dooing of binness and it is what I would not doo as to disenable them from work one our my fealings would not suffer mea to gone as fair as that you ware complaining in your letter to mr bobit of my not writeing to you though I have written to you the first or the second day of eavry month since hear I bin and started the letter to the post office wheather charles carried them or noe I am not able to say I dont expect hea did though had you would of got them I wrote to you about the thinges I got from neworleans I got the thinges the mill I have not got nor heard of since mr. pearse left hear mr lea has taken a gin and sum other thinges from memphis and wea cannot join in sending up as the understanding ware between you and him: I wrote you word that I neaded a new waggon hear and that soon if you would send a waggon down the river to memphis I could then send for the waggon and mill bourth at the same time.

Clothing for the negrows wea have anuff with the exception of a fiew yardes which mr. bobit sas his wife wil furnish on the best turms. I wil just say to you that I learned hear from the negroos that gilbert should say that doctor Caldwell wantes to buy him and I expect that hea is gone back to him again but do not sell him if you wish to brake them from running away for they had reather bea sould twise than to bea whip once if hea getes back thare have him iron and send him to mea if you please I wil not inger him by whiping him I beleave that they believe that tennessee is a place of parridise and the all want to gow back to tennessee so stop them by ironing tham and send them back again and they wil soon stop cumming to tennesee

In another letter to Polk the overseer unburdened himself about the same situation and with similar arguments. It was dated September 17, 1841, and runs as follows:

DEAR SIR:

I received your letter on the 23 of this month you requested mea to write to you as soon as I got your letter wea are All well at the present time I am goneen own geatheren the crop as fast as posible I have got 10 bails of cotten in troy I had my first thare the 14 of this month I should of had more pick and pack if the weather had not of bin so unfavourable wea hav had a great deal of rain hear this faul which has kep our cotton from opening

I saw majer bobit the other day hea had just received your letter hea said that you were very much perplext about your negrows runing away and goen to tennessee you will finde that you wil have to bea the man that wil have to stop that amoungst your negrows for you noe that you have had men hear of different ages and sises and the runaway from all I think though the plan that you have faulen on now will brake them if you wil keep it up for a time or too try it for an example though as I wrote you adderson ware not sent down accorden to your request had that of bin dun gilbert would not of left the second time send him as soon as you hear from him for I neade him hear for I have got my hands ful to save my crop as fast as it neades it. I do not noe wheather or not you want mea or noe for I have not heard for the next year and I should like to noe as places are filing up hear very fast indeed that I may have a chance to get sum of them if you doo not want mea and as I have lived hear for small wages this year I shall ask you $500 for the next let mea hear from you soon if you doo not cum down next month I expect that the mill is at memphis at this time and I want to noe wheather or not you are goen to send a waggon down to memphis or noe that I may send for boath under one you wil want sum plowes on the farm for another year and I think you had best get them in memphis too it wil take half dozen one horse ploughs

Yours respectfully.

The following characteristic letter from Dismukes, dated February 1, 1842, is the next survival from his correspondence. It runs as follows:

DEAR SIR:

I now write you a fiew lines to inform you sumthing of the bisiness of the plantation I am geting aloung as Comon wea are all well at the present and have bin evar

The Overseership of Isaac H. Dismukes

since you left I kild sum more porke about 700 P more and magoer got 3000.88 besides which makes a plenty. I have a fine lot of pigs and I shall feede them well if I have to buy a little corn to doo it if you say soe you must write mea. I am having 7 yardes of cloth wove ady [a day] nuthing more at the preaset.

Yours etc.

The letter which follows is the only scrap of writing I have seen from one of Polk's slaves. It is written in a very uncertain hand by Harry, the blacksmith, who was bequeathed by Samuel Polk, the elder, to his son Samuel P. Polk, for whom James K. Polk was guardian. Harry was sent to Mississippi, where blacksmiths received higher wages than in Tennessee, and was hired to planters near Carrolton, Mississippi, which was forty miles or more south of Coffeeville. This touching letter, dated May 10, 1842, runs as follows:

Dear Master:

As a servant I want to subscribe my freendship to you and famley as I am still in Carrollton yet and doing good Labour for my imploieer but tho I am filling [failing] in some degrees my Eyesite is falling of me I am well treated by my imploryer he feeds well and dont worke me Tow Hard I would wish to be remembered to all of my people old mistrs esphhirly Tell the old Lady Harry is hir servent untill dath I would be gld to see Hir one mor I Expect to come out a cristmust to see you the Hardness of Times and casness [scarceness] of money is Her[e] and will Reduce wages.

Dear master I Looked for you of Feburary but you never come up to Carrollton.

The Plantation Overseer

Dear master I have Eleven children I have been faithe-
ful over the anvill Block Evr cen 1811 and is still old Harry
my childrens names 1 Daniel 2 morcel [Marshal (?)] 3
ben 4 Elis 5 Carrell 6 Charles 7 Elushers 8 David 9 Moon-
rey [Monroe] 10 Carline 11 Opheeler Som Request from
you please to send me a Letter How all of the people are
doing in your country Dirrect your Letter to Mr. Edward
P. Davidson, Carrollton, Miss.

Harry your Servent

In the preceding fall Harry had made plans to hire his
own time and they were submitted to Polk in a letter from
Cothran and Neill of Carrollton in the following note dated
October 7, 1841: "Yr. Boy Harry has just applied to us to
exercise a sort of supervisory controll over him next year,
if he succeeds in procuring his time from you. Harry seems
to be a good boy and we have no objection to assume any
controll that you may suggest. If you make any such arrangement let us hear definitely what it is. A. T. McNeal
knows us well."

The reader will observe that when Harry was thus pronounced "a good boy" he had been a blacksmith thirty
years and was the father of at least ten, perhaps eleven,
children. His hire during 1841 was $350 and Major
Bobbitt writing to Polk August 29, 1841, said that he could
be hired for the next year for $450. Harry's efforts to hire
his own time did not succeed. Polk was receiving too fine
a return by the existing method. Later on he seems to have
been working at his trade on the Yalobusha plantation, for
Mairs wrote to Mrs. Polk January 26, 1852, as follows:
"Hary has requested me to let you nough what he is doughing for you I think he is a faithful servent he has Bucked

[booked] this year $487.76 besids your plantation act-count."

In another of his characteristic letters, dated May 17, 1842, Dismukes said "wea are still driveing own," which was quite in keeping with his spirit. The letter was as follows:

DEAR SIR:

I will now write you a fiew lines to inform you how times is with us hear wea are still driveing own wea are all well at the present time and has bin this season which I am glad to say as I have as much as I can doo for life I will soon bea over my crop again which is the second time: my stand of cotten is puty good if it gets noe worse and I expect it will not for the cotten is growen at the present time: my corn lookes very well: I have nuthing to write it will bea a tite squease for my corn to hold out: evry thing goes own smoothly soe foir

Yours in hast.

Under date of June 1, 1842, we have the following letter from Dismukes to Polk:

DEAR SIR:

I now write you a fiew lines about our health and crop wea are all well at the present time: our crop lookes very well I consider the stand of cotten puty good at least I thinke that it stands well unouf that if wea should have seasons that wea will make as much as wea can save my corn lokes very well at the present time at least my new-ground corn dont look soe well as I expected I have planted the highth of those wet places in corn annd will plant the others soon: I will get over my cotte[n] the third time this weak I have cotten squairs too and three on a stalk I lost

[163]

good menny of my piges though my piges and stock of hoges lookes very well I have nuthing to write I just had written to you when I received your letter and thought it would suffise I am in hopes this will give you sadiste faction for the present

The crop was pressing and the overseer was more than busy keeping it free from grass and stirring the soil in order to enable the young plants to do their best. The state of his crop depended upon the constancy with which he attended to it, and the letter of Dismukes to Polk, June 26, 1842, seems to indicate that he was most constant. It runs as follows:

DEAR SIR:
    I can say to you that wea are all well at the present time hopeing that these fiew lines may finde you and yours well our crop is still promising wea have a great deal of rain hear this season which keepes mea all the time in a push wea have intily too much for cotten or corn eather corn is overshooting and cotten is running too much to wead soe wea are hard to bea sooted: I am soe much push that I have not got time to goe to town to get my self a pare of breeches soe that you may noe that I am hard run but I am in hopes that the push will soon bea over you must cum down next month and bring your lady to sea the crop: my corn will hould out I am in hopes nuthing more worth your attention evry thing is goen on well at the present time Cum down   Yours etc.

As the season advanced the prospect for a good crop increased, which caused Dismukes much satisfaction, as we may see in his letter to Polk of August 16, 1842, which runs as follows:

[164]

The Overseership of Isaac H. Dismukes

DEAR SIR:

I will once more write you a fiew lines to inform you something of our health and crop our health has bin generly good though I have bin very sick for the last three or four dais but I have got about again clary is a little sick all well ecept her my crop of cotten cant bea beten by the neighbourhood all of my early corn is very good the drouth hurt my late corn very much. you must be-shore to cum down as soon as possible doctor colwell was hear about too or three weakes ago hea told mea that he would write you and that hea would write you that I had a fine crop which you will considder so when you sea it if I save it in time you will have to send me a four or five more handes that is a shore case for I am confident that I cant save it as easy as I have made it wea have fine seasons hear now though wea ware very dry hear when the doctor was down and evry thing showd badly if you wish to sell your land bring the man that wantes to by down with you when you cum and I think it is likely that hea will buy from the crop that is now grown on it

September 13, 1842, Dismukes made a longer report than usual. Polk had evidently complained of the quality of the cotton shipped from the plantation, citing the allegations of his agents, and the resentment of the overseer was aroused, so that he struck back as he could. His letter is as follows:

DEAR SIR:

I received your letters on the 10 of september which disaponted mea some what for I was looking for you down evry day though I shall not look for you now untill i seaure [see you]: Iam induse to believe that your cotten sould

[165]

very low from the last three letters which I have received from you: you did not write me word what your cotten sould for though I should like for you to of written what it did sell for: cotten from this neighbourhood sum sould for 6¼ to 9 cents a pound was the highest and I say yet that the first 40 or 50 bails was very nice *coten* and when you wass down hear in november you saw sum of the worst of it: if you write to mea again before you cum down write to mea what your cotten did sell for and you will oblige mea very much indeed it surtenly was sheld up too long or sould at a bad time for I have never heard such complaintes from noe crop that I have ever geathered before commisheon merchants all wais have sum excuse for bad sails of cotten and the ould saying is sum excuse is better than nun

I am goen ahead in geatherin the crop the crop will turn out well but I dount think that it will turn out all to geather as well as I once thought it would though I will put it against enny crop in five or ten miles of this plase: wea have bin very dry hear ever since the middle of August which has cause all of the top bouls to bea very small though wea have rain aplenty now and to much too: my cotten sead have soe near run out that it is imposible for mea to have the cotten as nise as it mout bea if wea had a niew supply of sead though I am trying to have it save very nise indeed and the gin dos not doo good work it draws too many motes through I am trying to have it alterd I am in hopes that you will bea down soon then you can sea and noe for your self about all of the bisness: I dount think that you had received the last letter I wrote to you I have a very puty stock of young hoges I have not got more than 32 or three hoges of the large sise we can make our meat hear at hom I think though the hoges apart of them will bea very small and I think that it will bea best for you to by about 2000 or 3000 poundes of pourk for the next year and then you will have a fine stock of young hoges on hand I could say a good deal more but I must close the letter at the present

Bad seasons had dogged the steps of hard working men in Mississippi for many months and they were left very low spirited; but in 1842 came a change. The weather changed as it always will change if we but wait long enough. Dismukes had a fine crop at last and he got John T. Leigh to send the good news to Polk, as though he distrusted his crude style of writing to present it effectively. Leigh's letter, dated September 28, 1842, is as follows:

DEAR SIR:

A day or two ago I rode over your crop, and at the request of Mr. Dismukes, I write you an account of it. It is I think the best crop of cotton I have seen this year, is now opening most rapidly, and Mr. D. appears to be exerting himself to save it nicely, tho I do not think the gin motes it well. he is opinion to save it as nicely as he wishes thał he will not be able to gather it all in time, tho I think that will depend altogether upon the season; if it is not favourable he cannot: he requests if you have any spare hands to aid him you will do so. I have no doubt that by gathering the crop as early as possible it will be of much better quality and will command a better price. The greater part of the corncrop is *very good*. some of his late corn particularly the new ground is not good it suffered too much by the dry weather during the month of July we had no rain during that month. Your hands have been very healthy. I do not think the Doctor has visited them but once until yesterday one of your men Adison (I believe) came over to see the Doct complaining of being sick. The doct prescribed for him and has I believe visited him today. The whole neighborhood has been very healthy. Corn crops the best I ever saw and cotton crops generally good. My own cotton crop is not I think as good as my neighbors. my corn *very fine*. my family have enjoyed good health white as well as black. County people quiet and easy. I believe as little disturbed by debt as any part of country. Some debts paid by the Bankrupt law, many by going to Texas. By both combined the greater part of the heavy debts have been settled. . . . .

After Leigh had broken the way Dismukes wrote also, adding what he thought necessary, and on the whole toning down the most optimistic parts of Leigh's communication. His letter is dated October 4, 1842, and runs as follows:

DEAR SIR:

I will [write] you a fiew lines to inform you something about our health and crop wea still have sum little sickness adderson have bin puty sick but is on the mend I shall loose more than three or four weakes with him the have bin more sickness hear in the cuntry than last year the fositions has bin bissey hear this season. I am still dooing all I can in geatherin the crop I nead sum six or eigth more handes to help geather it than I have made it with that is to save it in time the highth of the crop is now open and you noe they will a great deal of it faul out before I can save it with what handes there is hear though I am inhopes you will let goe evrything and cum down soon I should like very much if you could sea the crop at this time

though you must not let what nuse you hear about the crop
rais your expectations too high and when you get hear bea
disappointed in the crop adderson wass gone two weakes
to a day nuthing more at the present time.

When this you sea remember mea though many miles
between us bea

The final touch of sentiment in the preceding letter at-
tracts our attention. Aside from the uncouth method of
expression the form used by the overseer was what in
ordinary cases would be considered presumption. At this
time Polk had been long a member of congress and for
two years he had been governor of Tennessee. He was
fairly entitled to be ranked with the most respected men in
the country. Yet here was an illiterate man, his overseer,
closing a letter which should have been a respectful report
of affairs on the plantation by putting in a sentimental fling
as he might have done in writing to a silly girl in his own
rank of life.

It is to be explained only by recalling the utter lack
of a sense of inferiority in the poorer whites of the Old
South. These people had very little class consciousness.
They were not afflicted with an inferiority complex. Each
of them, if not crushed by some specific personal weakness,
was confident that he was as good as the best, and he was
not above showing his belief. He did not recognize that the
lack of property or education implied the lack of respect
by other people. To Dismukes the little sally was not presumption. He felt as good in his way as Polk in his way.
His next letter, dated October 12, 1842, returns to plantation routine and indicates that he was still on the best terms
with his employer. It runs as follows:

The Plantation Overseer

DEAR SIR:

I will write you a fiew lines to inform you sumthing about the bisness of the plantation adderson is still sick all the rest of the negrows are well at the present time you must cum down shortly though I am inhopes that you are own your way to the plantation I [am] still youseing evry effort to save the crop though unless I have more help I cannot get through it untill march unless evry day is good: I have 26 bages pack and 20 or 30 thousand pickout not gin I had to have the gin work on which have through mea back in jining I have geathered my newground corn evry thing is goen on well at the present

On December 25, 1842, Dismukes made the following report of affairs on the plantation:

DEAR SIR:

I write you a fiew lines today wea are all well but ould charles nuthing much to mader with him wea are dooing all wea can in saveing of the cotten but impossible to save all I am now goen on in saveing the cleanest and the best for it is impossible for us to save it as it should bea wea have pick and pach 27 bages besides some 4 or 5 bages in the pick room I received your letter on the 24 of this you said that you did not wish mea to buy a horse I think it alittle hard after I have made you shuch a crop and now cant bea allowed to have a horse that is fitten to ride in company I am inhopes that when you write again that you will write to mea to get one that will soot mea you said in your letter that you did not wish to assist in bying a barl of licker and that you did not want eny on the plase I am inhopese that you did not mean that I ware not to keep it for my self at my own expense.

[170]

December th 25 1842   Pokuebieh P
Gau
                    J K Polk

I write you afiew lines to day
wea are all well but ould charles
nuthing much to meaolor with him
wea are doaing all wea can in sarceing
of the cotten but inposiblee to saive
all I am now goein on in sarceing the
cleanest and the but for it is imposible
for us to save it as it should bea
wea have picke and packe 27 bages
besides some 4 or 5 bayes in the picke
rorm I received your letter on the 24 of
this sou said that you did not whish
mea to buy a horse I thinta it alitter
hard after I have made you shuch a crap
and now cant bea allound to have a horse
that is fitten to ride in company I am
inhapes that when you write again
that you will write us mea to get one
that will soot mea you said in your
letter that you did not whish to assist
in bying a barl of licker and that
you did not want eny on the plase
I am inhapese that you did not
mean that I ware not to keep it for
my self ats my one expense
            Isaac H Dismukes

The Overseership of Isaac H. Dismukes

January 14, 1843, Dismukes wrote Polk the following characteristic letter relating to the petty problems that engaged the attention of an overseer. It runs as follows:

DEAR SIR:

wea are all well except henry   hea has bin complaining for one or too dais but hea is getting better fast   I have kild pork   that is I have kild 34 four of the hoges that made five thousand 400.78[1] P and have 29 more to kill   I shall make pork aplenty for the plase this year for the first time that it ever has bin dun of the plase and have avery puty stock of hoges for another year for the plase   I have put up only 8 bails of cotten since I wrote to you   I wass baleing the other day and boath of the topes[2] [?] commense splitting so that I had to stop bailing though I think that I can clampit so it will doo to pack this crop and many longer   I have but one boult of baging at the present time and mr bobit is not at home nor I have noe money to get enny more so what shall I doo   you say I must not buy enny thing on a credit   write to mea what to doo

I have all above the cross fence next to sulliventcs field to pick now   I have now at this time about 14 or 16 bages to put up and but this one boult of 60 yardes   and I think thare is betwean 30 and 40 bages now to pick   wea have had a bad time hear for about two weakes for picking.

[P. S.]

I wan a jinban [gin band] very bad indeed for I cant get long well with this   your cotten had not gone the other day from troy   this is the weightes of the last bages   469: 535: 514: 462: 566: 515: 481: 510.

[1] Probably 5,478 pounds.

[2] Probably "tops," referring to the parts that came down on the cotton at the end of the screw and pressed the side of the bale.

The Plantation Overseer

The following letter is the last we have from Dismukes. He remained two years longer on Polk's plantation, but the later reports he made on affairs there have not been preserved. In fact, there is evidence that he was not always a faithful reporter, for we have information in letters written by other men that Polk complained that he did not hear from his overseer for long periods. This final letter in the series was written January 26, 1843, and runs as follows:

DEAR SIR:

I will write to you again wea are all well at the present time wea are still trying to get out our cotten and I think we shall get it out now in about 12 or 14 dais I shall not write to you enny more untill dun picking wea have had a puty spell hear now for the last eight or ten dais for picking of cotten and I have had all handes at it the giner and all so that I have dun noe gining for that length of time I think I shall save betwene 170 and 180 bails that is 400 P to a bail you wrote to mea to pick the second years ground to itself and to let you noe how much it made to the acre but while I was gone to tennessee the handes pick a part of it and it is so that I cant comply with your request: I have made the last killing of pourk I kill this time 3451 P of pourk and I wrote you word how much I kill before I have three barrels of lard and too of soap I am in hopes that this will please you and Mistress Polk

The following letter from Samuel P. Caldwell to James K. Polk, dated at Memphis, Tennessee, May 21, 1844, shows what trouble a planter was put to at that time to get a cotton gin that he considered reliable. It runs:

DEAR SIR:

I received your letter a few days since in which you

requested me to order a cotton gin at Gen. Farrington's Shop. I had a conversation with Farrington himself upon the subject. He is anxious to make it for you, but will not deliver it in Mississippi, nor will he credit you until you can try the gin. But he will warrant it to do well. He says he has a rule from which he never departs, and that rule is never to deliver a gin until it is paid for unless he receives interest while it is being tried at the rate of the interest which he exacts when he credits for work. I told him to make the gin or at least commence it, and that I would inform you of his terms immediately, requesting you to make a prompt reply, whether or not you would agree to the same. If you will not take it, write so much and it will not make any difference with him, as he can sell the gin as his own, absolving you from all and every obligation. His price is the same as it was when he talked with you. He will make you a *first rate* gin by the time specified in your letter. You had better address your reply *to* (Gen. Jacob F. Farrington, Memphis, Tenn.), as it is not probable that I will be here by the time your reply arrives, as I expect to visit the northwestern cities this summer, and may possibly touch at Columbia as I go on. . . . .

In the interval during which no letters are extant from Dismukes we have one interesting bit of information. It is the bare statement that in 1843 Dismukes bought a slave belonging to General Pillow, perhaps a runaway, and had to send him to Tennessee to escape a lawsuit. Of his final departure from the plantation and the source of dissatisfaction with him we have only the following extract to throw light on the subject. It is taken from a letter from Samuel P. Walker to Polk, dated January 3, 1845, and is as follows :-

The Plantation Overseer

I staid all night at your plantation with Col. Campbell
on the night of the 27th Dec. Your people are all well.
Dismukes has shipped 101 Bales cotton and thinks he will
make in all 130 to 140 Bales. I presume that James Brown
has written you that he has employed James Mairs for you
for the next year. He reached the plantation on the day I
left there. Brown recommends him very highly. I staid
with Col. Fly as I came up. he knows him well and agrees
with Brown in the opinion, that there is no better planter
in Miss., that he is honest *very economical* and industrious.
It was very well that Brown had made the engagement as
Campbell would have dismissed Dismukes anyhow. he has
to much company about him. I advanced Col. Campbell
$150 to pay some accounts in the neighbourhood which will
be charged to your account at New Orleans. . . . .

The departure of Dismukes fell in the same year that
Polk became president of the United States. For the four
years previous to it he had lived in Columbia a busy lawyer
and a much sought after politician. So many things had
crowded into his life that he naturally lost much of his interest in the plantation, which now and again interrupted
his course of living by making it necessary to take a long
and tedious journey into Mississippi. The result was a
growing desire to be rid of the whole enterprise. Mrs. Polk,
however, did not share this feeling. She looked upon the
Mississippi plantation as a stay during old age, as in fact
it became for her throughout a long period of widowhood.

Polk was apt to think most of selling when he found it
necessary to visit the place. It was a tedious journey and he
was not the kind of man who loved to ride in a buggy. It
was in that kind of a vehicle that he started in October,
1843, to drive to the plantation. For three days before he

reached Bolivar, which was 125 miles from Columbia, he drove through the rain, and the roads became so muddy that he was tempted to complete his journey on horseback, which would be 75 miles more. Naturally an ex-governor who had to travel under these conditions was inclined to think that it was not worth while to conduct a farm at such a long distance from home. He went on, however, for he had with him Mr. James Armstrong to whom he hoped to sell the plantation, and he expected to be joined after his arrival by General Gideon Pillow, whom he also regarded as a prospective purchaser. Writing to his wife from Bolivar, October 26, 1843, he said:

Mr. James Armstrong will go with me directly to my place, and if he is pleased with it, I think it probable I will sell him half my land. *Genl. Pillow* goes from here to Memphis, and will be at my plantation on next Saturday or Sunday week unless he buys some [?]. If I do not trade with Armstrong, I think Pillow is strongly inclined to buy it.

Mr. Armstrong requests that you will let *Wm. Cooper* know *where he is etc.* and request him to send word *to his wife.* Armstrong seemes to have *special reasons* for being very affectionate towards his *young-wife* just now. You will of course say nothing about the probabilities of my selling him half my land. I think the chances are that I will sell to him. This I know will suit your views better than to sell the whole plantation.

These hopes were not realized, for what reason I have not been able to discover. Polk retained possession of the plantation and Mrs. Polk had the satisfaction of knowing that the future was arranged as she wished.

[175]

CHAPTER XI

The Overseership of John A. Mairs

ISMUKES was succeeded by John A. Mairs, who was obtained for Polk by James Brown. He reached the plantation December 28, 1844, and was still there when our series of overseer letters ended in 1858. So far as his letters are evidence he was not superior to his predecessors. Probably he was the most illiterate of the group and there is no reason to think that he worked harder or had more ability in managing the slaves. His long and uninterrupted stay on the plantation may have been due to a certain abatement of Polk's interest in the venture. Mairs took charge as Polk was about to become president. He was left mostly to his own devices for the next four years, and on June 15, 1849, Polk died, within a few months after retiring to private life. Mairs then found Mrs. Polk his employer. She was a considerate mistress, and she looked to him for the ability that was necessary to carry on the place. Mairs's wages were $500 a year at first and later were raised to $550.

Probably another reason for Polk's less vigilant direction of the overseer was the increased easiness of his financial affairs. Memoranda preserved in his correspondence indicate that he was financially embarrassed when he became president. During the first year of his term of office he paid off old debts, mostly notes, to the amount of $17,747.26, from which we should probably take $5000 in cash which he carried with him for initial expenses when he went to Washington to be inaugurated as president. The second year in office he began to invest money and when he retired from the presidency he had placed aside $25,498.49. In this amount was $12,615.80 paid for the Grundy place in Nashville on which he built a fine new house at a cost of $6044.44. It is impossible to say how much of the money involved in these transactions came from his salary as president and how much came from other sources, as, for example, the sale of his home in Columbia and the returns from the Mississippi plantation. Such information as is available goes to show that these returns were rarely more than $3750 a year, and in some years as low as $3250, when the price of cotton fell, and from them was to be taken the expenses of the plantation: as clothing bought for the slaves, bagging and ties for putting up the cotton.

During this period Polk's agent in Tennessee was Robert Campbell, Jr., of Columbia. Memoranda preserved in his correspondence show that he bought while president several slaves through Campbell as agent. One transaction was the purchase in 1846 from General Pillow, of Columbia, of the obstreperous Harbert, his wife and child of nine years for the sum of $1436. In 1847 he bought a negro "boy," Jo. by name, for $650, a negro girl for $525, and from his mother a negro man named Garrison for $500. In 1846 he placed $3000 in the hands of Robert Campbell "to buy property for me," but the kind of property is not indicated.

During this period we have no letters from his overseer in Mississippi to show what was going on at the plantation. It is possible that Mairs, who continued to be overseer, made his reports to Campbell who did not preserve the letters.

Through this period we know he received his wages of $500 a year, but Mrs. Polk paid him $550 a year.

It is not until 1849, after the death of Polk, that we come again to the regular letters from the overseer, and now they are addressed to Mrs. Polk. They are relatively brief, for Mairs was a man of few words, but they are quite regular until 1858. The first we have is dated August 19, 1849, two months after Polk's death, and is as follows:

I receved a leter a fewdays Ago writen by youre Request of Col Robert CampBell of Columbia Tennessee

We have some sickness at this time But not dangerus the crop is doing well at this time we have had a fine spell of wether on the coten crop the corn crop is good if we have nomis for tune we will Ras a plenty of hogs to sloughter for the Plantation we are nough clearing more Land making the servants winter clothing Giting Redy for the coten so soon as it opens the Stock all Lucks as well as could be exspected the Death of my employure was veery unexpected and distresing to me the negrose seammed to be much troubled A Bout there Master But sense they have heard the be Long to you the are somthing beter Reconciled the negros have behaved veery will this year. I have nothing more of intrust

Your most obedient

September 20, 1849, Mairs wrote as follows:

MARM

Receved youre Leter of the 4th of Sept We have had some sickness chills and Feavors But the Casis has bin mild the are all on the mend won or Tow in the hous but clear of feavor the crop of corn is good But sense I rought you Last the coten will not be as good as I thorte as the Bold worm

[178]

has bin oppirating against it   But I still think it is a far
crop with the naberhood   I think we will make the winter
clothing for the negros in time   we are getherring the coten
and gining it   you have not givin me enny dy Recttions
About your coten the President Dy Recttions was this   mark
the coten in his name way it send me the numbers and wats
take the coten to Troy put it in the ceere of Thomas W.
Beal [?] I got Mr. J. T. Leigh To ship it to Pickett Perkins
and Co New Orleans   You will please give me some Dy
Recttions about the coten or eny thing els you want don
We have Packed 22 Bals of coten   I will sen you the wats
and numbers   no name have bin put on it yet   the calculation with me is to stay heare another year

Respectfully

Mair's next letter was dated October 29, 1849.   It informed his employer that "youre servents are all well except wone or two have chills And feaver," that they were
then making the winter clothing for the negroes, that they
made plenty of corn and pork "for the youse of the plantation," and that he had baled seventy-two bales of cotton.
December 12, 1849, he sent a more explicit report.   It runs
as follows:

I nough right you a few lines concerning your plantation
and people   your people are all well at present we have not
yet finished the Crop But nearly don it   we have packed
112 Bags and hald them to the river   I think 10 or 12 more
bags will be [all] we shall make we have 6 of them out in
the gin house   we are don gethering corn   we shall make a
plenty for the youse of the plantation   we have had a cold
spell of wether   And have sloughtered som of the Pork hogs
7000 lbs pounds or a part of them   I think we will Rase a

plenty for the youse of the place The stock all Lucks as well as could be exspected the negros are all behaving very well so far we are in cold wether clearing making cloath for summer clothing and finish picking out coten I am man[ag]ing to the best of my nolage and to the intrust of the plantation

Yours veary respectfuly

Although Mairs's sentences are short and to the point they convey much meaning. Into one brief letter he compressed a large amount of information. The following letter dated January 12, 1850, not only reveals the size of the crop, but gives us a very interesting glimpse of the supplies needed for the plantation in a year's operations. It runs as follows:

MARM

Receved your leter Dayted 11th of December I had Riten to you I am in hopes you got it soon after yours was writen I would of writen this leter suner but I was wating To finish getherring the crop your people are all well except Joe and pompy the have bin sick but are nough mending thare wore 112 Bags of your coten shiped and I surpose got to new orleans the 10 or 15 of December I dough not nough the date thare is 13 bags mor will be shiped in a day or two as the bote is nough oup we only made 125 Bags saved spining coten we have had some cold wither fine tim to save the pork we are nough clearing Land or making clothing

I was thinking I had beter say somthing aboute the Rope and bagin Say 1000 yds of Bagin 900 lbs of Rope 20 lbs of Twine the forse and stock has incresed 12 Sacks of salte 3 dosens pair of negros shoes 1 Dos No 12 and 1 Dos 13 and 1 Dos of smaler sise   As for hats and Blankets the had Las Winter you nough Best   I leave it youre self   I was thinking the would be cheaper in new orleons

Yours Respectfully

February 1, 1850, Mairs wrote as follows:

MARM

I nough write you a Few lines concerning your plantation and people   the are will except some chills an fefor among them   I am sorry that I have to inform you that Mr. J. T. Leigh dyied the 20 of last month   I think he was a fine clever man   he has bin verry kind in advising with me in enny thing that I Asked him to the intrust of the plantation I am trying to manage to the best of my Nolage   We are clearing land preparing to plant as soon as the season will Admit   making the clothing for the Negrose   the Stock all Lucks well as could be exspected   I have writen to you sense I have receved word frome your Maj Daniel Graham But we have received no male for 12 or 15 days on the ectcount of high water

Yours vary respectfully

Mrs. Polk was a woman of unusual business capacity. Her close oversight of the plantation is worthy of commendation. Early in the year she decided to visit it herself and so informed the overseer. His reply to this announcement is contained in the following letter dated March 15, 1850:

MARM

I have Received your Leter Dayted feb the 22   the Negros is behaving varry well   the Negros was muched pleased to hear that you was coming doune to sey them the are all well at this tim though wone of them has dyed sense I rought to you Last By the name of Carline Davis won that Mr. Samuel P Walker sent hear Las april frome Memphis   this negro was Diseased   she come her sick and has bin complayming of and on ever sens she has bin heare she dyed 21th of febuary   Bilous pneumonia

we ar going on with the plantation Bisness as well as as we can   planting corn   preparing to plant coten   making the sume[r] clothing for the Negros   the Stock all Luck as well as could be exspected   the artickles you ordered up from New orleans have not arrived yet   so soon as the doug I will Let you nough

Varry Respectfully yours

Mairs's letters throughout this year are devoted to plantation routine. They present in terse language a picture of the life that was lived on the plantation. And it will be strange if the reader does not find a source of continuous amusement in discovering the meaning of many of his curiously misspelt words.   In the letters which follow for the year 1850 I shall leave the reader without suggestions on my part, believing that he needs no aid of that kind to get the meaning. The first of these letters is dated April 12, 1850, and it runs as follows:

MARM

I nough right you a few Lins   youre people are all well except colds   the wether continues cold   the spring is late   we are planting coten   And planting corn instead   I had some 25 acres to plant over it was planted veary early making clothing for the negros clothes the Stock all Lucks as well as could be exspected   All youre artickls has arrived you ordered from New orleans   10 pieces Baging about

103 yds in each peace or about [?] 8 coils of Rope   125 lbs
or the rise in each coil   1 Bale Twine   2 Boxes of mer-
chandis   1 Box have 4 dosin hats, 1 Box   Box 3 dzin par
shoes   10 Sacks of coars salt   2 sacks of fine salt

Vary Respectfully yours

May 6, 1850, Mairs wrote as follows:

MARM

 I nough right you a few lins concerning youre plan-
tatibn and people   your servents are all well except won or
two   litle complayning   wone of the Gurls mannels wife
misscaired a few days ago   But is as well as could be exspected by the name of Jane   I got a leter today from
Maj. Graham dayted the 17th of April   in it and order to
pickett perkins & Co in favor of me for $560   I have not
yet receved the Last artickls you ordered up from Neworleans.

 this has bin the coldest and Backwardest spring that has
bin sense I have bin on the farm and we have had rans in
floods   Idount think I evr sough the like at this time of
the year   we have got a good stand of coten on all But 40
acres   we hade to plant over so cold and wet it dying and
we trying to work it   the corn is a good stand but 10 or 12
acres I had to plant over

 We are trying to get on for the Best   the Negros all seem
to behave vary well   the stock all Lucks as well as could be
exspected   Varry Respectfully yours

June 7, 1850, Mairs wrote the following letter to Mrs.
Polk:

MARM

 I nough write you a few lins concerning your plantation an people   youre people are all well at present ma-

riar has bin sick But has got about   Daphney has a child
Born the 15 of May   she cals him Silas Mac Gomry [Mont-
gomery] the spring has bin vary unfavorable on the farmers   we have sufferred from the fluds of rane and nough for
the want of some   we turned about and Replanted coten
and got a tolerable stand   About the 18 of May we hade a
little rane and it turned of cold an the coten has bin dying
ever sens we have bin trying to save a stand but I cant save
a good stand and I dount beleave thare are a good stand of
coten in this naburhood and apon the whole the prospect is
unfavorable   I am trying to manage for the best   the Negros behave vary well so fare and the Stock all Lucks as
well as cold be exspected

Yours vary respectfully

the las artickles you had shiped to troy from Neworleans
has arrived at troy I have got the bad toes [?][1] and will in
a few days goan get them all   I surpose thare are all safe I
will wright you in the next leter.

Vary Respectfully yours

July 6, 1850, the overseer wrote the following letter to
Mrs. Polk:

MARM
I have a few days ago Received a leter from you dayted the 19 of June stating that you had not Received a leter
from me sens the 6 of May   I have writen to you the 7 of
June

we have had some sickness but the casis has bin mild
childs and fevurs We have won or two a little poly at this
tim the crop of corn is good at this tim and if it should be

---

[1] Probably refers to the "toe itch," due to excessive rain.

seasonable from this tim out we will make a fine crop of corn we have had good seasons and the coten crop has improved vary much and if it shold be seasonable for coten from this tim out I am in hopes we will make a good crop yet the stand is not first rate but as good as enny I have seen in the setlement the stock all Lucks as well as cold be exspected I have receved the Las artickles you ordered from New orleons say 9 par of Blanket of Large sise 5 par of smaller sise 18 hand hoes the weovous sicle hasnt come to hand. Daphny has a child bourne the 15 the of May she caulds him by the name of Silas Mac gumry. I shall be able to spare some of the hands out of the crop. I have stables to build a good deal of diching to doug and making clothing for the Negros I have the coten press to Repar I am in hopes a part of it will doug the gin stand ought to have some Reparing too Nothing more worth atention only Remain marm yours vary Respectfully

The next report is dated August 10, 1850, and runs as follows:

Marm
     I nough write you a few lins concerning your plantation and people your servents are all in seasonable helth at present the helth of this nabohood has bin good so far this season we are needing Rain at this tim vary much Late Corn is sufferring urly corn is good fored planting the coten crop the coten is small But seoms to be full of forms Blossoms and Bols it begins to need Rain evy increased hir family the first of August had 2 children she cauld them by the name of urvin and Mary An
     the last Leter I receved from you was dated the 18 of June Your servents all behave vary well except Joe has

left me wonst this year But Return home in a few days o
his on actcord we have put up a coten press making th
negro clothing puling foder cleaning the ditches out th
stock all Lucks as well as comon

Yours most obedient servent

On September 8, 1850, Mairs reported as follows:

MARM

I have receved your Leter of the 18 of August
nough write you a few lins to inform you that your servent
are all in Reasonable helth at present we are nough pick
ing out coten the coten crop is a far crop for this year
think if the fall is favorable from this tim out we will mal
as much as we made Last year and more I think we wil
make a plenty of corn to surply the plantation Your serv
ents are all behaving well at this time the stock all Luck
as well as could be exspected Am in hops we will Ra
enough Pork for the youse of the place I am a man[ag]in;
to the best of my knowledge

Yours very Respectfully

October 8, 1850, Mairs reported as follows:

MARM

I nough write you a few lins concerning your plan
tation and people Your servents is in reasonable helth a
this time Betsia Lost hir youngest child by the name o
Fanny we are nough gethering coten the wether has bir
fine sense we commensed we have packed 39 Bags I thinl
if the fall should continue favorable we will make over [?]
180 Bales waing 400 lbs each or more. I am in hopes you
will get a good price for it I think we will make a plenty
of corn to surply the place I think we will slaughter a

plenty of Pork for the youse of the place the stock all Lucks as well as could be exspected we are nough trying to Gether the crops the hands all work find and behave them selves

Yours most obedent servent.

The next letter in the series is dated November 6, 1850. It contains definite information touching the habit of allowing the slaves to cultivate bits of land for themselves, working these allotments on holidays or at times allowed them by the master. In this particular case the yield of 8400 pounds was large for slaves' cotton. The usual thing was to count ginned cotton as one-third in weight of the seed cotton so that in this case the slaves on this plantation would have raised and disposed of 2800 pounds of ginned cotton, or seven bales at 400 pounds to the bale.[1] The letter runs as follows:

MARM

I have just Receved a leter from Maj Daniel Graham stating that he exspected To visit your farm some time in december Next. He wishes to nough whether or not I have muls anof to surply the plantation I purchased a mule last May Give $95 for him we have a plenty of mules at present But 3 or 4 of them are giting old And Jaded and mules are seling high at present and I nough leave it with you to say whether or not it wold be beter to part with the old wons and by more or not I will wate for and ancer from you Youre servents crope of coten in 1849 was about 8400 lbs of sead coten youre people are all well at present Evy has Lost Both of hir youngest children We are nough gethering the crop of coten have packed 67 Bags and have

---

[1] This year Mrs. Polk's cotton sold at 7 and 7½ cents a pound for the poor cotton and at 10¾ and 11½ for the good cotton.

90 or 95 Bags out   I think we will make a 175 Bals waing 400 lbs each   We have getherred a part of the corn   I think we will make a plenty for the youse of the plase   we have 75 head of hogs to slaughter   I think will surply the plase plentyfully

To Mrs. Sarah Polk, Marm, I dough not Recol Lect being imploy by you or eny agent of yours for another yeare though the way Mager Graham Rits he exspects me to remane as I surpose   I would of writen to you before nough but exspected Maj Graham heare by this time   I am wiling to Remane in youre bisness if it is satisfactory   But I think the present prises of coten will justyfy me to cal on you to Ras my salary   Allso I have receved 6 adishalnal hands and the Blacksmith   sens my wages was raseed.   I wold of made this request last year but things seam to be in confusion   I will be satisfide with youre oppinion or Maj Graham

Yours most obedient.

January 13, 1851, Mairs wrote to Mrs. Polk as follows:

MARM

       i nough rite you a few lins   i would of writen to you before nough   But i thort youre coten would of bin shiped before nough   but thare has not bin a boate up sens i got orders to have it shipped   indead thare has not bin but won bote oup this season   we have 125 bags at the River   we have finished picking out of the field   but have not finished Gining of it yet i think we will have 10 more bags only[1]   I will write to you so soon as it is shiped to new orleans Your servents are all well at present   some of them have behaved vary badly   Some of them Are in the woods nough   the

---

[1] On the next page Mairs set down the numbers and weights of 132 bales of coten with weights of 7 bales wanting.

stock all lucks as well as could be exspected   we are making
the somer clothing and Preparing for a crop
Yours most obedient

Mairm, if you can make it convenient i would like to
have the mony due me as I have made arrangement to
youse it.

Writing to Mrs. Polk February 10, 1851, Mairs said:

MARM
I have receved yore Lete of the 27 of January   I
nough write you a few lins   youre people are all well   Gil-
Bert has ran Away   left 5th of January   I have not hurd
any thing frome him sens he left   thare has bin shipped Today 75 Bags of youre coten to N orleans And I will try and
git the balans as soon as i can   this is the 3 bote   we make
136 Bags of coten   we are nough preparing for a crop   the
negros are nough working vary well   the stock all lucks as
well as could be exspected.   List of articles for the plantation of Mrs Sarah Polk
1   1100 yards Coten bagginge
2   1000 lbs baling rope
3   12 lbs Twine
4   12 Sacks salte
5   100 lbs of six penny Nals
6   3 Dosin par of negroshoes of which 1 Dosin No. 12,
    1 Dosin No 10, 1 Dosin No. 7
7   Some hats for the Negros
the blankets you ordered has not yet come to hand
Yours respectfuly

Mairs's letter of March 5, 1851, shows that he still had
trouble with the slaves through their running away, and

that he had further trouble with the transportation com
panies in shipping the cotton. His letter is as follows:

MARM

i nough write you a few lins concerning your planta
tion and servents youre people are all well at present thoug
Gilbert left heare 5th of January last and i have not hur
from him sense he left i expect he is up in haywood count
tennessee Joe is all so ranaway the balanse is at presen
working vary well i have receved 6 par m naugh [?]
Blankets you ordered oup frome New orleans thare has bi
shiped 45 bags of youre coten to new orleans on the steam
er Monroe 75 bags before making in all 120 bags we hav
had a rise in the yellowbusha river and thare ware 17 bag
of your coten got wet I went to sey about it and found i
vary wet and finding the had a Great many more had go
wet and thinking it doubtful wheth[er] the would be able to
pay damagees if the ware willing imade a bargain wit
them that imite take the coten home and dough as i thor
for the best it would not release them the would be a
legally bound as the ware before before witnessis i hav
picked the white coten of that dyed not git wet and packed
it 9 bags of it the balanse is not all dry it is a little stained
ithink tha ought to pay damages on it counting in the trouble allso. isurpose you will not nough untwel youre merchant sels it Some say the can be made to pay and some
say not the river has bin higher and tha has shiped coten
that has bin hald to them sens you give orders to ship yours
while i was in troy isough a bag of mote coten we hade a
rany day and igined the mots over and made a bag No 137,
waing 420 lbs

Wone of youre servents by the name of sally has increased her family and calds her child Burrel we are pre-

paring to try and make a crop   i shel indever to dough to the best of my noledge the Stock all looks as well as could be exspected ihave setled the taxes and all clams aganse the plantation that inough of

> Veery respeckfully yours

Major Daniel Graham and Major John W. Childress, the latter being her brother, seem now to have been acting as Mrs. Polk's advisers in business matters. Nevertheless she herself kept a keen eye on plantation affairs and it was to her that the overseer made his monthly reports. On March 18, 1851, he sent her the following letter:

MAIRM

received A Leter from Mag Daniel Graham dated 6th of March Received 16th I nough comply withe his Request Marme youre servents are all well at present Joe and Gilbert is still out of plase

We are giting on vary well with the farm and will finish planting corn in a few days making the summer clothing preparing the land for coten the stock all lucks as well As Could be exspected I have dryed the wet coten that I mentioned to you in my last leter 17 bags thare was 9 bags we picked of the wet that never got wet the 8 bags was staned some it is all dry and packed and we are nough haling it to Troy and i think it will be shiped to Neworleons shortly I attended to it to the best of my judgment

The 2 day after I got Maj John W Childress Leter to ship your Coten I got Doctor Towns to rite to Cols and Mc swine to ship your coten on the first steambote that he thort a safe bote move it [?] in short not put it on a ceal bote [keel boat] for the Ginerly reshiped and some tims it is exsposed to the wether it certainly have bin an unusual

season about giting coten of   as the river in the urly part
of the season was vary Lough   I receved your leter stating
you regreeted to hear your coten was not shiped   I hurd
that thar would be a bote oup in a few days   I went to troy
and asked cols to ship youre coten   he told me he would
dough the best he could   he would ship a part   insisted he
would ship it all   he said he had to Go by the first that Give
orders to ship   he shiped 75 bags on that steambote Col
Monroe   he has I lurn shiped 1 small Lot on the same bote
that was hald in sense you give orders   thare i think he was
ronge i surpose thar ware over 100 bags got wet in troy the
sayed the ware not agoing to pay damageis   the most all
shiped it of wet to Neworleons   I thort it best to hal yours
home and pick as to have it picked at Neworleons or sell it
at a [?] an coten on the decline at that time   I think he
ought to pay some damages   it was a right smart troble
haling it home and picking it over   i am in hops you will
not Lose much on the prise of it   i will nough give you the
nombers   thou thar was won or two was hed so that I dough
not nough   the are the same nombur the ware before   136
bags coten, 1 bag of mots, 120 shiped[1]

 Vary respectfuly Yours

The progress of plantation affairs during the spring of
1851 is described in a letter from Mairs to Mrs. Polk, dated
April 16, 1851, and it runs as follows:

MARM

I have receve your Leter dated 3th of this month
Youre people are all well And behaving well at this tim
Gilbert is still out of plase   I got him home and he Ran of

---

[1] Here follows the several numbers of the repacked bales. The fate of this hand
dried cotton may be seen below, p. 231.

the next day Pompy Left about 4 weaks ago and I have not hired a word from him sens he left he rana way from him self Barbra has increased hir family has a daughter and calls it By the name of Marthy Born 20th of March last

We are giting on vary well farming I have prepared the Land well this season we have a find stand of corn all to about 8 acres yet not planted subject to over flough planting coton sloly nerly done

I have received the supplise you had sent oup for your plantation and examined it thare ware 1 bolt of baging a little wet but not ingered I dryed it To 11 bolts of baging 100 y. each bolte To 10 coils of rope 119, 114, 122, 110, 116, 115, 126, 117, 118, 120 the Rope waing in all 1177 lbs. 1 Keg of nals wa 100 lbs 12 sacks of salte 1 Box of shoes and hats 2 dosin wol hats 3 dosin par shoes 1 Bale of Twine 12 hanks of it the blankets I have Riten to you before 1 Bal Blankets 6 par

Youre coten has bin all shiped from Troy Febuary 10th shiped 75 bals shiped March 5th 45 Bals shiped March 18th 8 Bals shiped March 25th 9 Bals, makin in all 136 Bags coten 1 Bag of mots in all 137 if I understand you thar ware 20 bals of youre coten that was shiped first injured and staned that it commanded but a vary low prise which I am vary sorry to heare The last picking was in the first lot shiped I surpose it being most convenient to git to when shiped I thort I had taken as much pains with the crop as i ever had taken with a crop and the coten was handled nise it is true thar ware more yellow coten this last yeare than usual oing to the spring we had to replante a good deal to git a stand I picked it clere out of the pach I mix some white with the last picking to try to make it sample well it dyed not mature well if ingerd otherwise it got so After it left your plantation I halded it to the river in good wether and all the Recets say Receved it in good order I would like to nough hough your coten sample all round and when sold what sort of prise it brings I will indever to manag to youre intrust as it has bin all ways my wish

Yours most obedente

Mairs seems to have been little more successful than his predecessors in keeping the slaves on the plantation. Gilbert was an habitual runaway and Harbert was often in the woods, while others followed their example. In this spring Mairs had 340 acres in cotton, 180 in corn, 40 in oats, and there were six that were not in cultivation, a total of 566 acres of cleared land. In 1839 the total cleared acreage was 271 and in 1842 it was 374, which shows that the plantation was being made more effective steadily. Another thing that appears from the short letters of the overseer at this time is the fatality among the children of the slaves. May 18, 1851, he reported that "Daphny has lost hire child by the name of Silas" and July 8, 1851, he wrote "barbara has lost hir child by the name of Eliza an was not a helthy child from the first."

Through the summer of this year Mairs's letters are very brief and concise. The following, dated July 25, 1851, is a fair sample:

MAIRM

I nough write you a few lins concerning youre Plantation and bisness your servents are all well at present the wether has bin vary dry sens I rought to you last and the corn crop has suffered for the want of rane but I think we shal make anof for to surply the plas the Coten crop is yet vary good and if the season is favorable from this out we will make a fine crop of coten

Your servents ar behaving vary well at present we ar giting on vary well bilding stables and corn crib clening and ditching the wet spots in the field making clothing for the negros I have not Received a leter from Maj John W. Childress for some time   Respectfully

August 15 Mairs wrote that he had begun to pick out cotton, but the crop was short on account of the drought. September 29, 1851, he continued his story in the following letter:

MAIRM

I have just Received youre Leter dated 17th of the present month I nough write you a few lins youre black people are All well at present and behaving well we have suffered vary much from the drought I think we will make a plenty of corn to surply the plase as much or more than we made last year the coten crop has suffered vary much from drought I dough not think we will make as much coten As we made last year by 10 bags though it is turning out beter than I wonst thought it would of don we have had so far a fin season for gethering coten we have at this time A Bout 100 Bals picked out of the field but we have only packed 20 bags yet I have got the new gin that your Brother ordered and it is superer to enny Gin I have ever sean I am trying to Put oup a nise artickle of coten for market this season I think we will have 75 or 80 Hogs to sloughter
                    Vary Respectfully

Despite the overseer's forebodings the plantation yielded more cotton this year than the year before, as appears from the following letter dated January 26, 1852:

The Plantation Overseer

MAIRM

I have receved youre leter of the 8 of this month I nough rite you a few lins concerning youre plantation and people youre people are all well and behaving themselves well the wether has bin vary cold more so than usual the stemer Monroe which took your coten the 7 of this month dyed not git out of the rivir for the want of water we have had a little rane and I am in hops she will be able to git out of yellowbushia river I have sent you a bill of artickles needed for the plantation I dyed not like to call on you for bakin but i have done my beste to Ras it and faleed but i will still try to Ras it Hary has requested me to let you nough what he is doughing for you I think he is A faithful servent he has Bucked [booked] this year $478.76 besids your plantation actcount we have packed 138 bags of coten and have 5 or six more to gin   Vary Respectful

   [P. S.]

List of articles

1 1200 yards coten bagging
2 1200 lbs of baling Rope
3 12 lbs Twine
4 12 sacks of salte
5 3 Dosin par negros shoes of which 2 dozin To be of large sise No 12 and I Dos of smaler sises
6 1 dozen hand hoes 8 inches wide
7 1200 lbs of bakin or pickkle pork
8 400 lbs of slab iron $\frac{1}{2}$ in thick 7 inches wide
9 50 lbs of blistered steal
10 200 lbs of bar iron $\frac{1}{2}$ inch thick 2 inches wide

Into this series of letters dealing with overseers and plantation affairs I insert the following dealing with one side of slavery. It was written by John H. Bills to Mrs. Sarah C. Polk and is dated at Bolivar, Tennessee, January 28, 1852. It runs as follows:

DEAR MADAM:

I am advised by our mutual friend James Walker, Eqr., that by the lamented death of your good old mother-in-law, Mrs. Jane Polk, my ward, Marshall T. Polk, is entitled to "two negroes, a man and woman and perhaps children," which he says are at your plantation in Mississippi.

My object in addressing you is to know your wishes on the subject of retaining them for the present year and if so to settle the amount of hire. If (as in the case of Bob) you do not desire the use of them, you will send me an order for them that I may have them removed to this place.

With my best wishes for your health and happiness I am
Very truly your obedt servt

Mrs. Polk replied proposing to exchange the said slaves, Charles, his wife Lucy, and their two children, so that they might remain with their friends in Mississippi. Marshall T. Polk, then a cadet at West Point, wrote that he would do what seemed best for humanity's sake. This suggestion did not materialize and the slaves were taken to Bolivar in April. Bills wrote that they seemed in distress over their separation from their family and friends in Mississippi and said he would try to arrange the matter when Marshall T. Polk returned to Tennessee in such a way that the feelings of the slaves should be satisfied.

The total yield of the plantation in 1851 was 154 bales, which was very satisfactory. Mairs turned to the new crop with much earnestness. Writing to Mrs. Polk on April 3, 1852, he said:

The Plantation Overseer

MAIRM

I nough write you a few lins About your plantation
and People Your people are all well and behaving vary
well we have a find stand of corn and are nough Planting
coten and making cloth for the summer Daphny has increas hir family has a daughter and calls it by the name of
Mary An youre surplise for the plantation has got to troy
and I have got a part of them home I have payed the frate
and have got a bill of the artickls thar is won coil of rope
missing your shiping merchant at troy says he will make it
rite he says that is all that is missing by the bill of Lading
I was thinking that the iron was short 3 larg bals bagging
= Twine 6 Barls Pork 1 bunch hoes = 1 box merchandyse
2 Bars iron and 1 Bar steel 2 Bolts Baging 8 coils Rope
and 12 sacks salt

When your last lot of coten was shiped thar was wone
bale could not be found Ro Martin has found it and shiped
it 2th of april on the steamer Monroe I have receved your
leter da 27th of Febuary last when your brother coms down
it will sut for him to setle with me

Vary Respectfully

April 24, 1852, he wrote further on the same subject and
expressed himself as follows:

MAIRM

I nough write you a few lins to inform you that your
people are all well and behaving well the last Leter I
rought you I thort thare ware a misstake in the iron you
had sent oup frome neworleons I have nough got it home
and R. Mullin sent me mor than the frate bill I pad cald
for R Mulin fiels himself responsible to dough rite I think
your surplis for the plontation is all rite to the best of my

[198]

nolage Please send me A list of the artickles frome your
bill the iron that I have receved is this 2 bars wats 115 lbs
1 bar steal 30 lbs   2 bars slb [slab] 290 lbs   I am doughing
to the best of my Nolage we have a fine stand of corn and
some of the coten is com oup iam in hops we will get a good
stand of coten   Vary respectfuly

During the summer a severe type of whooping cough appeared in this part of Yalobusha County. Mairs, writing to
Mrs. Polk on August 3, 1852, said in his usual optimistic
way: "We have had some sickness won of the little boys
by the name of William dyed the 18 of July some of the
children have the whopin colf at this time the Doct sayed
william dyed with pneumonia." As the days passed the
disease became more violent and August 18 Mairs wrote
Mrs. Polk the following letter to let her know the extent of
its ravages:

MAIRM
        i nough write you a few lins concerning youre plan-
tation and people we had some sickness and have lost
2 of the children sens i rote you last Daphny youngist child
by the name of Mary an and Marier davis is youngist child
by the name of Judy an dyed with whoping cough seams
to have a sor thote with it the whoping cough has bin vary
destrucktive among the children in this naberhood we have
it nough but it seams to be some milder not much feavor
        the crop of corn is vary good the best i have had sense i
have bin on the plase the coten crop is good oup to this
date and if we have a good fall and it matures well if we
all have good helth it will put us oup to save it it bids far
for a large crop we have made some clothing and have
cleared some land we are nough preparing for gethging

coten the stock all loucks as well as could be exspected
Most obedient

A month later, September 20, 1852, he sent the following letter, not in his own handwriting though signed by himself, and evidently written by the doctor in attendance:

we have had for the past week or two a great deal of sickness. The children have whooping cough — all doing well except one Eva's child, which will probably die in consequence of deep seated disease of the lungs. Among the grown ones Giles Wm Nevils, Caroline Harris and old Cloe have been very sick, but are now improving. Henry was severely attacked with Pneumonia on last friday — his disease seemed to be giving away under treatment until yesterday evening, when he got suddnly worse and died today. They all have an affection of the throats which is unattended with pain, but is of a fiery redness which in some cases spreads suddenly and rapidly throughout the system extending to the stomach and through the bowels also into the lungs, &c, &c, with excessive perspiration, great prostration, collapse and a speedy death. This was the case with Henry. The others will have the sore throat, although they do not seem to be aware of it, but with them it does not get worse or spread. It is in the large number of cases relieved by swabbing the throat with Spts Turpentine or solution Lunar Caustic and external rubefacient [?] applications. The Doctor calls it Erysipilas, or Saint Anthony's fire of the internal origin. It has been prevalent in the country for the last year or two, and he thinks most of the deaths that have occurred from Pneumonia in this section within that time have been in consequence of this sudden extension of Erysipilas to all the organs [through them (?)] of the system. We are making a tolerably fine crop of cotton and have been gathering very well until the recent interruption from sickness. Have 70 Bales packed

During the remainder of the year the letters of the overseer contained little that was interesting. November 1 he wrote: "I think we will make a plenty of corn to surply the farm we have 85 hogs to slaughter the stock all lucks as well as could be exspected we want to finish gethering the crop this month if the wether is favorable won of youre servents by the name of eavy has increased hur family on 13th of Oct calds hir child by the name of An marigh." November 12 he wrote: "Jane increas hir family on 8th has a daughter calds it by the name of vilete."

December 21, 1852, he wrote the following letter giving an idea of the results of farm operations for the year:

Mairm

i nough write you a few lins ireceved youre Leter dated 7th of this month thare is won or two of the negros sick but on the mend Old woman Sarah dyed yestaday morning got oup well and was taken sick dyed in 2 ours

We have a good deal of coten in the feld Packed 125 bags have 25 in the gin house i have sen you the nos. and wats in a leter bifore this thare ware 50 bags of your coten shipped from troy the 9 of this month and 75 the 18 of this moh i think we will rase a plenty of corn and meet To surply the plantation we will be late in gethering the coten and it will make us late in the somer clothing I thort it would be beter to by the somer clothing and we would get a start agane

Maj John W. Childress has i think the nams and ages of your negros he can arrange the number of hats and blank-

ets as well or beter than i can I have not receved a leter
from youre brother in some time the stock all lucks as well
as cold be exspected

Vary respectfully

The progress of cotton picking was very slow this year.
February 1, 1853, it had not been finished, due to the sickness of the slaves. March 3, 1853, it was all over and Mairs
wrote Mrs. Polk the following letter summing up the results
of operations during the preceding year:

MAIRM

i nough write you concerning your plantation And
people wone of your negros by the name of Agy increas hir
family the child was born ded and she dyed 5 days Afterwards the 27 of Febuary the balans of your people are in
reasonable helth it has bin vary sickly in yellowbushia
county a great many deaths youre surplis has all come
safe to hand youre coten has all bin shipped to New orleons
the Las shipment was 19 bags ship 13th of febuary we made
169 bags 1 of the bags was mots And marked on the hed
Mots 2 of the bags was vary inferure coten and i marked
them on the hed [A] won hundred and sixty nine bags in
all

We have sown the oats and preparing to plant corn we
are doughing the best we can Please rite me whin you receve this Leter   Vary Respectfully

April 18, 1853, Mairs made the following report to his
employer:

MAIRM

I have Received your leter dayted 13th of March we
have had a great deal of sickness this winter but the helth

of your people are nough improving and i am in hops will continue to improve we made a fine crop of coten and corn if we could of saved the coten but the hands was takin sick about the 15th of October and we have had more or less ever sense thare moust of bin 30 or 40 bags of coten wasted in the patch we never finished untwel the 14 of Febery though i have don to the best of my noledge all we picked out before we got sick was good youre com mishent murchant Rought me word that he had sold the two first shipments 50 bags at 11 cents the 2 ship 75 bags for 12 cts with the exception of a few bags falling in quality his leter was dayted 2th of January laste if I understand you to say 40 bales brought 11 and 12 cents if that be the case iam not pleased so far as iam concerned i have settled all the clam aganst the plantation that I nough of I have collected a part of the blacksmith actcounts i have not anofe yet to pay the negrose but if you wish for them to have some mony i will let them have it i can wate untwell your brother come down for mine wages we have a fine stand of corn and will finish planting coten in a few days   Most obedient

June 10, 1853, Mairs wrote to John W. Childers the following particulars of the progress of business on the farm:

Sir

       a few days ago i receved youre leter dated May 24th 1853 with an order drawn on Picket Perkins and Co Neworleans for five hundred and fifty dollars by Mrs. Jans K. Polk in my favor for my wages Last year i ragreate to learn you cold not visit the plantation i have payed the negros two hundred and ten dollars which i think will dough untwel you come done I have made good collection withe the black smith actcounts when you come down we will then settle it all' oup we have had some 4 or 5 cases of disentary but nough on the mend we have a far stand of coten and corn and in good order the corn and coten is small for the season we want rain vary much at this time i will finish Laying by corn in a few days and soing Peas the stock all lucks as well as coud be exspected the Negro boy by the Name of Joe has left me and takin bily Nevels with him bily got sick Joe brought him home the ware out six days went of without enny cause i have layed the case over to you idoughnot think chastising him will dough him eny good iam told that a man came on the stages a few day ago and he had the small pox and so won or two in cofevill had cort it of him 2 of Bakers servents had it you will please write me when you Receve this leter

Yours most obedent

The flight of Joe gave Mairs much anxiety for he believed that Joe had a bad influence on the remainder of the slaves. In a letter to Mrs. Polk dated July 9, 1853, he came back to the subject. His letter runs:

MAIRM

 i would of writen you before this but I have bin vary sick with the fluxe i am just giting about several of the negros have had it the are all well some of the casis was light mearier davis wone of your servents increased hir family May 10th calds hir child by the name of fanny We have had some fin rans the first of this month and the crop has improved the crop is good at this time both coten and corn and in good order the hands all seam to behave vary well but joe he has run away once and took bily nevels with him brought him home sick I have not touched him about it. I will tell you what I think Joe will ruin your young

[204]

men and mariner will ruin your young women Mariner is nough in the family way

Yours respectfully

August 16, 1853, Mairs wrote Mrs. Polk the following letter referring to the general state of affairs on the plantation:

MAIRM

I have Received your leter of July 30 i am Just giting so i can ride out Elisabeth tuck a back set but nough about again the rest of your servents are all well at present the crop of corn is good the best i have made sense I have bin on the plase the coten is good Groing rather large if eny thing thoug it depends on the season from this time out we have a fine young stock of hogs the stocks all lucks as well as could be exspected Mariner has increased hir family on the 3 of August Calds him by the name of Edwin i am in hops we will make a good coten crop the prosspects bid far at this time

Yours most obedient

The reader will doubtless have noticed the frequency of the birth of slave children on Mrs. Polk's plantation. Four had made their appearances between September 20, 1852, and the end of July, 1853, not to mention the child of the unhappy Aggy, which was born dead, carrying the mother to the grave five days later. Late in August, 1853, came two more. Said Mairs, writing on August 22, 1853: "Daphny has increased hir family on the 8th August calds hir child by the name of Pol Evy has increas his family on the 18th of August Calds his name Annanias." Thus in a year a plantation on which there were about 36 adults, men and women, saw an increase of its slave population by births of

[205]

six persons, which was unusual for such a group. On the other hand it will be observed that the letters contain frequent mention of the deaths of the infants of slave mothers, which has a tendency to lessen the rate of increase of the slave population through births.

The prospects for a fine cotton crop in 1853 were suddenly cut off by excessive rains and the ravages of the boll worm, which was not the same as the boll weevil of recent decades. Mairs described this situation in a letter dated October 15, 1853, as follows:

MAIRM

i nough write a few lins concerning your people and farme youre people are all well at present and behaving well at present i got filllup and manuelin a short time after the left the corn crope is turning out finely we have a fine pea crop we gethered a part of the corn and have got the hogs in the peefield the coten crop is cut short by the rans and bold worm it will be short in this naborhood we have about 60 Bags out i am trying to handle it so it will [bring a good price we will] rase aplenty of meat to surply the plantation the stock all lucks as well as could be exspected

Respectfully

Subsequent letters showed that not half a crop was raised. The yield was only 70 bales, with two more from the tolls taken at the plantation gin from the cotton ginned for other persons than the owner. In the preceding year 169 bales were shipped and at least 30 went to waste in the fields because the hands were sick and it could not be picked before it was spoiled. When at last the crop of 1853 was at Troy, the shipping point, and rains had raised the Yalobusha so the steamboats could come up, the owners of the boats announced that freight would be $4 a bale, which was so much higher than in ordinary years that Mairs refused to put the cotton on board and wrote to Mrs. Polk for instructions in the matter. The boat-owners evidently felt that since the crop was short they should have higher rates to save themselves from losses in operation. But the planters felt that an additional hardship had been placed upon them, who had already lost heavily through the short crop.

About this time an agitation began in Yalobusha County for a railroad, the county subscribing a portion of the cost. Mairs's reflections on the subject were probably typical of the men of his class. They appear in the following letter to Mrs. Polk, dated January 10, 1854:

MAIRM

i nough write you a few lins concerning your plantation and people youre people are all well iwrote you a letter Just befor chrismas we are giting on vary well with our work we are clearing making cloth ceivering[1] over some of the Negro cabins iam in hops this will be a good crop yeare for coten i want to make a good crop of cotten this year the people are trying to bild a rale road though Yellowbushia county the vote was takin last year it went to tax the people iam told i was not at the elexion iam told it is more tax than som of the people exspected the have put on three times more than the usual tax ihave mad collection and i am ready to Abide by your instrucktions Maj John W. Childress can in form you hough the rod will run Please an ser this Leter when you git it the yellowbusia River is lough nough Bots oup yet.

Vary Respectfully

---

[1] The uneducated people of the Old South in general said "kivver" for "cover."

Routine letters during the spring show that Mairs planted corn and cotton with the usual fear of cold weather and got a fair stand at last, which was the ordinary story. The health of the people also was good, as usual, and their behaviour was good. The first noteworthy letter in the correspondence for this year is dated July 6, 1854, and directed to Major Childress. It runs as follows:

DEAR SIR

inough write you a few lins concerning your sisters Plantation and people we hade some sickness among the children last weake and evey lost her youngist child by the name of anny niss it appears that she cant rase no children ihave them well nursed and medical ade the people are all well at present we hade a fine rane lost evening the corn began to neede it we have a fine crop of coten and corn ithink we will make a good crop if the seasons continues good the crop has bin well cultivated iam in hops we will make a good crope the negrose all behaving well working finely the stock all lucks as well as cold be exspected when youre sister gits returns for hir coten iwould like to nough hough it sold i think it rite as ihave the puting of it oup iwant to nough it will be but Litle truble to you we are nough making the winter clothing clearing some imentioned to you when you was down about clearing some land for myself i dyed not clear eny for myself igot Mr. Egleston overseer to clear me some this year iwould like nough to clear some with your sisters hands iwill give the same igive him or when you come down iwill dough what you think is Rite about it. Yours Respectfully

A letter from Mairs to Mrs. Polk dated September 3, 1854, gives us an idea of the quantity of cotton a good hand picked out in a day when working conditions were favorable. It runs as follows:

MAIRM.

I nough write you a few lins about youre Plantation and people youre people are all well and be having themselves well we have bin picking coten some 10 or 12 days the best pickers 200 lbs and 230 lbs though iam not Huring the wether is vary warme ithink we will make as much coten as we can gether in good time the bold worm has don some damage but i sey nough sin of them nough the corn crop is good ithink we will make aplenty to surply the farm and rase aplenty of bacon to surply the plantation the stock all lucks as well as could be exspected I shel not start the gin as urly as I have don hear to fore I had rather be later agining than picking out   Vary Respectfully

The winter and spring of 1854-1855 proved very unfavorable for shipping cotton. At no time was there enough rain to produce the usual rise in the Yalobusha. April 5 no cotton had been shipped from Troy. April 10, however, Mairs wrote: "Your coten is on acele [keel boat] the first bote that has loded at troy the people are giting oneasy some think the will not git ther coten of this season some has commens halling it iam in hops yours will git out safe and we may have a rise." The further fate of this cotton is related in the following letter from the overseer to Mrs. Polk dated May 12, 1855:

MAIRM

I have Received your leter dated April 20th youre servants are all well We have A good stand of corn the coten is not all oup we have had no rain sense we planted it it is comnig oup sloly if we could git a rain we would sound have a good stand of coten   Your surplys has all got oup safe

I surpose by this time you have hurd the balans of your coten 55 bg was burned on the steamer Texanner   I saugh Mr boswill he tuck it from troy   Says he put it on the Texaner put it in the hol that part of the Lode was all burnt he was on the bote at the time   I surpose your murchants had it inshorred at a good price   I wrote to Mr. Pickett that it was a nice artickle   sense the the other was burnt it was shiped to purkins Cambbell and Co pleas rite me when you git this leter   i want to no what it was in shed at

Vary Respectfuly

The operations of the year 1855 began with the usual routine. We have no information about the planting and growing of cotton until we come to a letter to Mrs. Polk dated June 17, 1855, in which the overseer writes in a less buoyant tone than usual. He says:

MAIRM

ihave Just Receved your leters 1 of 4th and 1 of 7th Your woman Jane had a child and at 2 weaks old overlyed it the rest of your servants are all well at present we have had some fivores for the last 3 weeks the wether is fine at present warm with some rane the crop lucks well thoug i had to plant over 40 acres but it groing finely if the seasons is good and a good fall ithink we will make a good crop I receved a draft drone on Messrs Purkins Campbell and Co for five hundred and fifty dollars in my favor you wanted to know hough much you had to pay your negros you in ginerly pay them About 200 hundred dollars at a time ihave not collected much of the black smith act counts the most of them got thir coten burnt Harry dous not git much

work to dough the most of the planters has a back smith
and makes out with them if you wish I will pay them some
of my oune mony stock sees a hard time corn is worth
$1.50 pur bushel I will try not to buy enny

Respectfully

August 29, 1855, Mairs wrote to Mrs. Polk as follows:

MAIRM

inough write you a few lins about your plantation
and sirvants your sirvants are all well at present your
woman evy increased hir family on 16th   calds hir child
Henry Polk We have had some dry wether sens irote you
the coten opeen vary fast the hands has picked finely the
crop of coten has bin cut short by the bold worm ihear goo-
deal of complaint in this naberhood idough not think we
will make a large crop nough but istill hope we will make
a far crop the corn is made it is good we had a fine rane
last evenig which will help the coten and pee crop and po-
taters the stock all lucks as well as cold be exspected iwill
dough my best   Respectfully

Mairs had good weather for picking cotton and the progress was satisfactory. Writing to Mrs. Polk on November
7, 1855, he said:

MAIRM

inough write you a few lins your servants are all
well at present we hald Ten Bags of your coten to troy to
day and will hall about 80 Bags before we stop we will stop
then untwel we ship some we have had a good deal of raine
and the Rivir is in good order for Boting the steamer unicorn has bin up all the summer will go out this rise is asking $4 four dollars pur Bag. ithink that is rather high cot-

ton is low perhaps we will dough beter yet on this rise your coten is in the care of Powell and Trummell troy Miss we have a good deal of Coten to pick out yet the negros behave themselve vary well we are doing the best we can write me when you git this leter   Vary Respectfully

The crop of 1855 proved fair, yielding a total of 148 bales. Mairs was able to ship it in three instalments; for the river was high enough to permit the passage of boats. November 29 he reported the shipment of 55 bales on a "ceal Bote," that is, a keel boat, named *Wave*,[1] known in the river as "Bryant's Boat." The load was apparently transferred to a steamboat on the Yazoo, to which the Yalobusha is a tributary. What happened to it there is described by Mairs in a letter to Mrs. Polk dated December 15, 1855, in these quaint words: "ilurn to day that the steam bote unicorne Burnt las weak on the asue [Yazoo] river She had 55 fifty Bags of your coten on bode it Burnt oup iam in hops you had good inshurrans on it." What happened with respect of the recovery of damages for this loss will be seen by perusing the chapter in this volume dealing with the cotton factor.[2]

Returning to plantation routine Mairs summed up the situation in a letter to Mrs. Polk dated January 7, 1856. It ran as follows:

John A. Mairs to Mrs. Sarah C. Polk

MAIRM   Okacheckina, Miss., January 7, 1856.

Inough writ you a few lins about your plantation and servants ireceved your leter of 15th and 18th of las

[1] So it seems in Mairs's letter, but the factors in reporting arrival at New Orleans call the keel boat the *Ware*.

[2] See below, pp. 239-243.

month 1855 ihave sent to Memphis after Harbard and
got him home Harbard is a bad boy idyed not rite you
word that he had left the plas he has left wons or twis before but dyed not stay out long come in himself iwill try
to ceap him at home and make him attend to his bisniss
the rest of your servants is at home and all well except
colds we are don picking out coten but not quite don gining ihave not shiped enny of your coten sens igot your leter
last iwill ship the balans to W. S. Pickett and Co. I have
made 3 ship ments the 1 = 52 bags 2 the 55 bags 3th 20
bags i lurn 55 bags was burnt on the unicorn i have 10
bags packed isurpose 8 bags more i will send you a list
of wats and number of bags when ifinish gining I am in
hops we will have good helth and a good season and iwill
try to make a good crope

Vary Respectfully

January 23, 1856, he wrote to his employer as follows:

Mairm

inough write you a few lins about your plantation
and people your servants are all well at present we ar don
the crop of coten made 148 bags isend you the nombers
and wats of the bags it is a lite crop of coten but idon my
best we made a good crop of corn and aplenty of Bacon
to surply the plantation

ihave got Harbard home and will try to keep him At
home all of your coten has bin shipped but the 21 Bals
iwill ship it on the first ris if enny chanc to do so and will
ship it to W. S. Pickett and Co New orleons at this time
the stock is doing tolerable well we have had vary cold
wether heare ever sence the sunday before chrismas and
vary cold at present iam in hop this year will be a good

year for crop and we may have good helth and iwill try to make you a good crop ihave collected some of the blacksmith act counts and settling oup the plantation act counts Please write me when you receve this leter so that imay nough you have receved it   Respectfully

Mairm

Pleas be so good As to ask your brother before he coms to your plantation to examin the papers of mine and Mr. J. T. Leigh setlement the 14 of January 1848 and the first of January 1849   Yours most obedent

Mrs Polk the reason imake this request I think thare has bin a miss stake in the setlement if so iam willing to curect it and ihave nough doubt your brother will dough the same the papers and Recets of Mr Leigh to the President will shoe
                              Respectfully

The recovery of Harbard did not stop his running away as is seen in the following letter to Mrs. Polk, February 23, 1856:

Mairm

          inough write you a few lins your servants are all well Wilson is not at home he left about 2 weeks ago and i have not heerd of him sense i surpose he has taken the same Rout that harbard tuck iexspect harbard got him of ihave this day got Mr. James Leigh to write to Mr. Harris of Memphis to nough whether he is thar I lurn that some negro give Harbard a pass and he went a part of the way on the ral cars and exspected to git on a bote at Memphis your coten has all bin shipped and if norting has hapen to it By this time is in neworleons we are nough preparing for another crop and if ilive iwill dough my best to your intrust and to make you a crop   Vary Respectfuly

The Overseership of John A. Mairs

Harbard, who was a "bad boy," was brought back to the plantation before January 7, 1856, and placed in irons. How long it was likely that a "bad boy" would stay in irons under such circumstances may be seen from the allusion to the subject in the following letter from Mairs to Mrs. Polk dated April 23, 1856:

MAIRM

I receved your leter of the 5 April   I was in troy today Mr Powell sayed your surplys was on akeel bote about 10 mils be Lough troy waiting for a ris in the river I have concluded to starte Munday Next after them with the wagons your servants are all well and all athome I have released Harbard of the irons I dough hope he will dough beter we have a fine stand of corn nough working of it on about 250 acres we have a good stand of coten we need a little rane and ithink we would sone have a full stand I have in a far crop and I hope we will have helth and a good season and may make you a good crope I will dough my best   Vary respectfully.

What was Harbard's record during the next four months does not appear for no letter from the overseer survives for that period, but he was not cured of running away. September 9 he was off again as may be seen in the following letter from Mairs to Mrs. Polk dated September 13, 1856:

MAIRM

inough write you a few lins about your plantation and servants Mariner and Caroline Johnson has ben havin chils and feavor but are nough redy for work. Jane has increas hir family has a son and calds his name Manuel bourn 25th of August last the servants has behaved well

all but Harbard, Manuel, and fonser, and Wilson Harbard
left on 9th and has taken thes boys along with him   And
some of the negros say he tryed to get 2 others along with
him   told them he cold of got away before but he thort he
wold stay with Mr. Sam Walker   ithink his am is to git to
Memphis thinking you may sel him thar   he liks to be in
a sity   ithink if you sel him thar when won gits displesed he
will put out for Memphis   I have sent to Hally springs
I will nough by to Night if I dount git them   ihave got a
man to way coten   iwill if nothing hapens be in Mem Phis
Tusday next   iwant to get him   if you wish to sel him let
me nough your prise

ithink we have a far coten crop   As good as ihave made
on the plase   the corn crop   ithink iwill make aplenty to
surply the plase   iwill try to ras aplenty of meet to surply
the plas   we have picked about sixty thousand pounds out
of the patch   have about 15 bags gined   will pack out today
Respectfully

This absence, however, was brief. Writing to his employer in a letter dated September 14,[1] 1856, the overseer said:

MAIRM

     inough write you a few lins about your plantation
and servants   your people are all well   But Wilson is not
got home   Harbard and Manuel and fonser is got home
iam in hops wilson will come home or imay here frome him
manuel and fonser sa Harbard was agoing to take them to
Memphis to sey there oncle   But the got afird and come
home   ihave not whipped nary wone of them   iwill try them
sey if the will dough without it   the wether is warm and

---

[1] The date may be wrong. It seems hardly likely that the fugitives would have
come in within twenty-four hours after the preceding letter was dated or that Mairs
would have written about it so promptly.

iwant to git the coten out But Harbard is a bad boy we
have had a good deal of rane and the coten has taken the
rote [rust (?)] some but istill think we will make a far av-
rige crop   Yours Respectfully

The yield of the plantation in cotton in 1856 was placed
by Mairs at 139 bales of good cotton, 4 bales of "traching,"
and 2 bales of moats. By "traching" he probably meant
cotton so full of trash that he would not let it go into the
regular ginning, but placed it by itself and ginned it as a
lot. Writing to Mrs. Polk on February 12, 1857, Mairs
said:

MAIRM
        i nough write you a few lins About your plantation
and people your servants are all well at this time and at
home your servant sally increased hir family and hir child
dyed lived only 8 days shiped the last of your coten on
the 7 of this m = 25 Bags on the steam Bote Trader iam
in hops you will git A good price for your coten ireceved
a leter from your merchant dated the 3 of January stating
he had Receved 90 Bags of your coten and he could git 12½
cents all round for it iam in hops he will still git more
        we are nough preparing for another crope clering some
land making some clothe ihope we will have good helth
and it may bea good year for croping and we may make you
a good crop I have not hurd enny thing frome your Brother
in some time   Vary Respectfully

The surviving letters from Mairs are now at wide intervals. Mrs. Polk seems to have got the habit of leaving much
to him so that he did not feel as keen a duty to report constantly as Polk had required of his overseers. Besides she
owed him back wages and perhaps that made a difference.

His letter to her of April 15, 1857, one of the last we have from him, deals with general affairs on the place. It runs as follows:

MAIRM

i have Received your leter March 5th your servants are all well But Betsia has a pain in on of hereys not much the mater [*sic*] will be at bisness in a few days I have Receved the surplise for the plantation all come safe I was in hops your merchant would of don a litle beter in the prise of your coten I have settled the Taxes and all the plantation dets ihave Bin Lucking for your brother but have not hurd eny thing frome him in som time you wish to nough if you can send my wages you can send it if your brother coms down or if you can send it saf another ways idough not want to run enny Risk myself in my settlement with your brother last year thar was due me $339.06 three hundred and thirty nine dollars an 6 cents you may all so sent that if it suts your convinents.

we have finished planting corn and iam ferfull we will have some of it to plant over last sunday was a weake ago we had asleet and snowe and ise the ground was frosed and inch or two deep deap frost most evry nit sense we will finish planting coten this weak inever commensed intwil 13th and am afered iam two sone nough

Respectfuly

May 11, 1857, we have the following letter from Mairs to Mrs. Polk briefly indicating what was going on at the plantation:

MAIRM

inough write you a few lins about your plantation and people your people are all well al fon ser toke a notion

to ran away a few days ago we have had a vary cold spring
the wether has moderated and we have some fine wether at
this time and ihope it will continue We have had a fine
rane we nough have a fine stand of corn But we had to
plant some thirty acres over 30 = it is oup finely we have
a good stand of coten oup and iam in hopes we will have a
good season from this out and we may make you a good
crop Inclose you a rect for the draft of five hundred an
fifty dollars Drone on Wm. S. Picket & Co. Please set [?]
writ me when you Receve this that imay nough it

Vary Respectfully

After the above letter we have none at all until we come
to the last that has had the fortune to survive.   It closes
this series of letters from overseers on the Polk plantation.
It is dated January 15, 1858, and runs as follows:

MAIRM

I nough write you a few lins Mairm I have receved
your leter of January 2th 1858 Mairm your servants are
all well and behaving well I have receved the surplise for
the Plantation I have finished the coten crop made 129
Bags and have shipped 115 of them to your merchant in
Neworleans and ithink will ship the balans in a few days I
am nough Preparing the land and fixing for a crop I am in
hops we will be more fortunate this year I will rite you
agane shortly and give you a list of the plantation expences

Vary Respectfully

In this letter is a tone of disappointment, as though the
writer of it was too much discouraged to write more. There
was much to warrant the feeling. Year after year he had set
out to make a good crop, that is, a crop in which no accident
should intervene to reduce the yield. Time and again he

[219]

had failed. The crop of 1857, at 129 bales, was at least 20 bales below the average. Rain or drought seemed to beset him at every effort, but he had been in the habit of rallying as each new year began. Probably he plucked up courage as the days passed and the intimations of a new season began to make themselves felt in his bones. Planting cotton was ever a thing of hope. One effort, with whatever it brought of failure or otherwise, was soon forgotten when it became time to prepare the land for a new planting. Then were formed the hopes for the new harvest. The stand, the fight against grass while the plants were small, the anxiety that the rain should be enough and not too much, the fortunate occurrence of a long sunny autumn for harvesting, and finally the possesion of good health by the slaves so that they could harvest the crop—all these were factors in a successful cotton crop. It was unusual for all to be present in one year. It was Mairs' misfortune that the one bumper crop he had during the thirteen years in which we have record of his stewardship was marred by the bad health of the slaves and the bad weather in the harvest time, with the result that in this year, 1852, he was not able to gather at least thirty bales which wasted in the fields. Such were the trials of a plantation overseer in the old South.

CHAPTER XII

The Planter and his Commission Merchant

OR the origin of the peculiar relation between the Southern planter and the commission merchants who sold his crops we must go back to the early years of Virginia history. The system grew up in a natural way in that colony and became so well established that it resisted the best efforts of the authorities to overthrow it.[1] It meant that the planter shipped the proceeds of his tobacco crop to England, entrusting it to a commission merchant, or factor, who sold it, bought with the proceeds the various articles of merchandise ordered by the planter and sent this merchandise back to Virginia when the ships were sent over for the next crop of tobacco.

One result of this method of trading was that the market for Virginia tobacco was more than 3000 miles from the place at which the crop was grown and that the shops in which the Virginians obtained clothing, implements, and the many articles they needed for personal use were an equal distance from their homes. In the Middle and Northern Colonies, as, for example, in Pennsylvania, the produce of the land was sold in colony seaports where large exporting and importing houses sprang up, thus establishing a trading class with all the financial and social activities that go with such a class. No such operations existed in

---

[1] The origin and operation of the factorage system in Virginia is treated in the author's paper "The Relation between the Virginia Planter and the London Merchant." *Report of the American Historical Association,* 1902, I, 551-575.

Virginia where the towns did not grow beyond villages and the life continued until after the revolution to be rural, isolated, and to a certain extent provincial.

The Virginia system as it developed contained many abuses. The planter was never at the market and had no way of telling that the price of tobacco returned to him was the best that could have been obtained. A small number of great Virginia merchants, as they were called, grew up in London, who seem to have acted more in agreement than otherwise. If the planter changed from one to another he was not sure of meeting better treatment. It was estimated that when expenses of freight, commissions, storage, and other charges were paid the planter received only 35.1% of the gross selling price of the tobacco. The freight was put at 17.9%. Tobacco growing in the colonial period was a profitable industry and the planter endured these abuses because he made large profits in spite of them. It was a careless kind of industry, with much of the flare of the speculator, playing for large stakes and not counting small losses.

The worst abuse arose from the tendency of the planter to become the debtor of the merchant. He sent over his crop in the confident hope that it would sell well, and with it frequently went orders for more merchandise than the proceeds of the sales would warrant. The merchant would allow him thus to overdraw, carrying the balance over to the next year. Too frequently these balances were continued from year to year, and as long as they ran the planter was morally bound to continue to send his tobacco to his creditor, who came to feel that he did not have to be careful in making sales. Over these luckless ones the merchant was likely to exercise a great deal of power, and his victims were wont to speak of their condition as industrial slavery.

From Virginia this system spread throughout all those parts of the South in which the large planter became the type. In the region of small farms, as in most of North Carolina, trade fell largely into the hands of marine hucksters who came down the coast from New England, their schooners filled with assorted stocks of goods which they traded for the tobacco, pork, and turpentine of the inhabitants living along the shallow sounds and rivers of the colony. The rice planters of South Carolina, however, depended more on towns than the tobacco planters of Virginia, and the trade centered in Charleston, as in Pennsylvania the wheat trade centered in Philadelphia. But the rice planters of South Carolina were a comparatively small part of the population. In the interior of the colony there was no staple crop, exports were very limited, and the planter class did not appear to an appreciable extent.

Shortly after the revolution cotton began to be raised in quantity in the uplands of the region south of Virginia and the result was the extension of the planter class to all parts of this vast area. Here was a great staple, comparable to, but far more important than tobacco in colonial times, and much the greater part of it was exported. The old habit of selling through commission merchants, followed by the Virginians with respect of their tobacco, was now adopted for cotton. But there was a difference. We were now an independent nation and had the markets of the world before us. The thing to do was to establish exporting ports whence the cotton was shipped to whatever buyers chose to have it. Here gathered the commission merchants as formerly they had gathered in London. Wilmington, Charleston, Savannah, Mobile, and New Orleans became the seats of operation of the factors who served the mass of cotton planters of the Southern interior. Of all these cities New Orleans was the greatest cotton export port, because the Mississippi River brought it the largest quantity of cotton.

The New Orleans commission merchant did not establish the same amount of authority over his clientele as the London merchant had exercised over the colonial Virginia planters, partly because the planter could keep informed steadily and quickly of market fluctuations, and partly because the customer could visit that city at selling time if he chose to go. Moreover, the New Orleans factor did not, like his London prototype, buy as well as sell for the planter. Orders might come to him for certain plantation supplies, as clothing, shoes, and blankets for the slaves, to be sent to the plantation, or for bagging and rope for packing the cotton, and these things might be sent in the spring and charged on account. But they were usually a small part of the value of the year's crop. The main part of the proceeds of the sale effected by the commission merchant went to the planters in drafts to be spent by them in the payment for articles bought in the towns that had sprung up in the cotton raising area in the wake of settlement. The result was that the factor did not establish a hold over the planter by becoming his creditor and gaining a claim to his patronage. In this respect the new type factorage was better than the old. Nevertheless, it was a most important part of the cotton business.

The largest factory demand for Southern cotton was in the region around Manchester, England, and it was here that the price in the ultimate market was fixed. For the Manchester area Liverpool was the importing city. Here were established the great cotton houses that bought and held stocks to be sold to the manufacturers as the raw cotton was needed. They sold to other countries than England and Scotland. The New England mills themselves looked to them to know the prices of the staple. The Liverpool houses had their buyers in the Southern towns and kept them advised of the quantities wanted and the prices to be paid. As cotton rose and fell in Liverpool it rose and fell in New Orleans, as quickly as the slow mails of the day could carry the information. The process through which the cotton went was, therefore, as follows: The overseer and the slaves made it for the planter, the planter passed it over to the commission merchant, the commission merchant sold it to the buyer, the buyer sent it to the great cotton dealer, and the dealer sold it to the manufacturer.

The planter could not escape the commission merchant. He might sell his cotton to some local purchaser, but such a purchaser would have to sell it to the commission merchant. The planter, therefore, had better go to the commission merchant himself and save the profit the local purchaser would take for his part in the process. Black man and white man had worked hard to make it for him. He put it on a boat and sent it off with fervent god-speeds. He committed it into the hands of the commission merchant and waited for returns with as much of the spirit of resignation as he could muster. He could do nothing else. Records exist of some planters who thought to escape the commission merchant by shipping a large combined lot to Liverpool itself. They did not repeat the experiment for Liverpool had more uncertainties than New Orleans, and the mystery of their diminutive returns was never penetrated.

In the letters received by James K. Polk and preserved

in his correspondence in the Library of Congress are occasional letters from his New Orleans factors; but they are not such as will afford consecutive information about his dealing with them. We learn from them that he sold his crop early in 1838 through the house of Caruthers, Harris and Co. in New Orleans. The members of the firm seem to have been Tennessee men and Harris seems to have been Polk's brother-in-law. A letter from this firm dated at New Orleans, June 8, 1838, shows the intimate personal relation between Polk and members of the firm. It runs as follows:

DEAR SIR:

We hand you herewith check on the Bank U. S. for $150 for acct. Dr. S. M. Caldwell who has doubtless instructed you on the subject. We did hope to have been able from our *own means* to have sent you the $500 you requested some time ago, inasmuch as the proceeds of your crop had been fully anticipated in Tennessee by your brother; but we are sorry to say that such is the state of things here, that it is with the utmost difficulty that we can realize from collections a sufficiency to meet our imperative and indispensable engagements; and now when the resources of the present season are nearly exhausted it is impossible to comply with your request without a misapplication of funds belonging to others. We have adjusted the loss of the 42 bales cotton with the underwriters on the best terms we could and will send all the accounts to Tennessee.

Very respectfully, etc.

The following extract shows what sudden changes could happen in the cotton market. It is from a letter written to Polk by W. S. Pickett and Company, then his New Orleans factors, December 31, 1844, and runs as follows:

The Planter and his Commission Merchant

We wrote you lately on the Subject of the Cotton market, and advising of the reception of 101 Bales of your Crop, which, believing there would occur no important improvement in prices during the season, we were in the act of preparing for sale this morning at the moment of the reception of the most disastrous news for the Cotton market we have yet received. The principal features of intelligence are, a heavy decline in Liverpool, holders pressing Sales, and manufacturers buying on their own terms. For further particulars we refer you to the Price Current which we shall send you tomorrow. What will be the effect upon our market after the excitement Subsides, we Cannot pretend to say. For the present we will offer none for sale.

February 3, 1845, the factors sold Polk's cotton to the amount of 101 bales and made to him the following returns:

DEAR SIR:

We hand you annexed acct sales of 101 Bales Cotton, nett proceeds to your credit $2,127.44. This cotton we placed upon the market some days ago under an active demand and improvement in prices, consequent upon the reception of favorable news from abroad, and having obtained an offer, full a ¼ ct. above the current rates (in honor of the mark) we did not think it proper to decline it.[1]

We did not intend for some time to have troubled you with the acct. sales of your cotton, as we presume you have your hands full, about this period, with more important

[1] The account sales attached to this letter shows that 50 bales sold at 6 cents, 15 bales at 5¼ and 36 bales at 4⅛ and the gross returns were $2,487.89. Of the expenses the freight was $1.75 a bale and with other shipping charges amounted to $197.45. Drayage, storage, weighing, etc., 50 cents a bale, amounted to $50.50; river insurance at 1½ per cent on $25 a bale was $37.87; and fire insurance at ½ per cent on the selling price was $12.44. Commissions were charged at 2½ per cent, $62.19. Total expenses, $360.45. Polk was then president-elect of the United States.

concerns, but our Mr. Walker (now in this city) prefers that you should be advised of the sale at once. We have on hand 28 Bales more which, with any further shipments for your acct, we will dispose of as may seem best for your interest. We are furnishing the necessary supplies for your plantation upon the orders of Col. Campbell and J. T. Leigh

Very respectfully, Your obt. servts.

During this period Polk was much in need of funds to prepare for the new station that awaited him. Between the beginning of November, 1844, and the end of the following March he drew four times on the factors, obtaining in all $4,100. His agent, R. Campbell, Jr., also received an advance of $150 through Samuel P. Walker the Memphis representative of the New Orleans firm. Supplies bought in New Orleans and paid for in cash by the firm had been sent to the plantation amounting to $243.45, and other cash items, as interest and postage, brought the advances, with the four drafts, up to $4,563.90. The credits from the sales of 129 bales of cotton came to $2,794.95, leaving a balance due to the factors of $1,868.95. One of the items excites special interest. It reads: "Commission on $1800.44 balance of acct to date   2 pct. $45.00."

This statement of acct. was sent to Polk March 7, 1845, and was filed as of that date. In a letter accompanying it the factors said they had sold the 28 bales for $567.51 net and that it was very inferior in quality.

No more reports of sales appear in the correspondence until after Polk's death in 1849 when the estate passed into the possession of Mrs. Sarah C. Polk, his widow. From that time they are fairly regular and give us a very good view of the relation between the factors and the owner of the Mississippi plantation. They begin with the sale of the crop of 1849. Writing on January 3, 1850, the factors, the firm is now Pickett, Perkins and Company, reported as follows:

DEAR MADAM:

We received some days ago the first shipment of your crop of cotton, 112 Bales, which we have today examined and classed particularly and find it a very good article, known in our classification as "middling fair" We could now get 11 cts for it, probably a fraction more if it suited in all respects; but as we are particularly anxious to get a *fancy price* for your Cotton, we shall not hasten the sale, but select a favorable time to sell, with reference to a demand for such Cotton. In the meantime we are asking 11½ cts for it and hope to get at least 11¼. You may rely upon our best exertions to promote your intersts[1]

Very respectfully etc.

Referring to the crop of 1850, which did not reach New Orleans until the following spring, owing to the low water in the streams in the winter, Pickett, Perkins and Company wrote Mrs. Polk on March 8, 1851, as follows:

DEAR MADAM:

A few days ago we received the first shipment of your crop of cotton pr steamer "Monroe," being 75 bales of which 56 bales are in quality a high order of "middling" to "good middling," and 19 bales "inferior" and stained badly. The 56 bales are worth at present 10½ and the 19 bales only 7 or 7½ cts. This is a wide difference in price, but such is the state of our market—and there is such a very large

---

[1] January 10, 1850, the firm reported that they had sold 100 bales at 11⅜ cents and 12 bales at 11 cents, total $6,407.57. Charges $509.13, a net sum of $5,898.44. May 9, 1850, they reported the sale of the last shipment of the crop 13 bales, with net proceeds of $662.46.

quantity of *stained* or *frost-bit* cotton here, that the sale and price of it is entirely arbitrary.

We very much regret that your plantation is so far off the great highway as to have prevented your Cotton getting to market some weeks sooner when prices were high. Our market has fallen about 4 cts pr lb from the highest point, and as your Cotton has just reached us, and prices are down so low that we think nothing could be made by letting it go in the present state of our market, we have not as yet offered it for sale.

We have today received a letter from M. Childress, of 25th Ulto. from Nashville in regard to your affairs, and are glad to perceive you coincide with us about selling your Cotton. We think it well to sell off the inferior Cotton, as that style will scarcely improve. And with the better quality we will exercise our judgment.

Very Respectfully yr. friends & servants

March 17, 1851, the senior member of the firm, who stood on terms of personal friendship with Mrs. Polk, wrote to her as follows:

Dear Madam:

I am rather inclined to sell your last shipment of Cotton (44 bales) to a customer who is anxious to get it and will give an outside or high price for it, probably 11¼ cts. If I sell, it will be because I can get a price above what the present market justifies and of course will be promoting your interest. Your Dft. to your overseer, Mr. Mairs, shall have due honor on presentation; and it will afford me pleasure to attend to any order of yours *outside of our regular business*. All well at home

Very Respfly. Yr. friend etc.

P. S.

I break the seal of my letter to say that I have just sold the 44 bales of your cotton at 11½ cts.

Mrs. Polk's entire crop of 1850, by the reports of the factors, was 137 bales, of which 32 bales were poor and 105 were very good. Of the poor cotton 21 bales were sold at 7 cents a pound and 11 at 7½. Of the good cotton 44 bales were sold at 11½ and 61 bales at 10¾ cents a pound. The entire net proceeds of the sales were $6,096.11. The 11 bales reported as poor and sold at 7½ cents a pound, said the factors, had the appearance of having been wet or sunk in the river and then dried and repacked. This was the cotton which was sunk at Troy, and we see that Mairs did not fool the New Orleans cotton men.[1]

The next year's crop sold at much smaller prices. The poorer grades were about two cents a pound lower than in the preceding season and the better grades were about three cents lower. Mrs. Polk's factors realized this state of affairs and desiring to prepare her for it they wrote her on January 5, 1852, as follows:

DEAR MADAM:

We write to hand you enclosed "the remarks on the market" for your information about cotton. You will observe, prices remain low, nor do we anticipate much if any improvement shortly, as the small rivers are now becoming navigable and heavy receipts are expected to follow.

We presume your Crop will shortly be on its way to us. We trust we shall find it as well handled as heretofore, and you may rely upon our best exertions to promote your in-

[1] See above, Mairs to Mrs. Polk, March 5, 1851.

terest in the sale of it. There is a good demand today at prices about the same as quoted in the enclosed.

Our city is full of company — the great Rail-Road Convention meets today; and we regret to find your state represented by only two delegates, Lucius J. and Geo. Polk

Very Respectfully
Yr. friends & C.

"Remarks on the Market" was a printed sheet of the prices of various commodities then ruling in New Orleans. It was issued at short intervals with blank pages on which the factor usually added such remarks as he thought advisable. It is interesting to note the following classification of the grades of cotton as they had become standardized in this market. It will be observed that they have little reference to the actual words used to designate them. The grades had become technically fixed and the cotton men in the city were expert in assigning a given lot to its proper rank. In the "Remarks" of January 3, 1852, appear the following grades and prices quoted for each:

Inferior 5 @ 5½
Ordinary 5¾
Good Ordinary 6½
Low Middling 6¾
Middling 7⅛
Good Middling 7¼ @ 7⅜
Middling Fair 7½ @ 7⅝
Fair 8¼ @ 8½
Good Fair   nominal
Good and Fine   nominal

January 30, 1852, the first shipment of Mrs. Polk's cotton had reached New Orleans. It was of such high grade that the factors, writing to her on that date, could not restrain their admiration. It is interesting to note that this cotton which they called at one time "very pretty" and "beautiful" was graded at "middling fair" to "fair." Their letter is as follows:

DEAR MADAM:

We wrote you on 21st Inst. informing you of a shipment of 85 bales of your Cotton on the way to us. We have since received it and find it opens remarkably well, classing fully "middling fair" to "fair." This is very pretty cotton, and we have succeeded today in getting a very pretty price for it — 9 cts pound being decidedly above the market quotations as you will observe by the enclosed review. It affords us great pleasure to report to you what we call a magnificent sale of your cotton, which may be partly attributed to the neat manner in which it has been handled and the present active demand for such cotton. The lower qualities are depressed and dull of sale[1]

Very Respectfully Yours

Mrs. Polk's second shipment reached New Orleans late in February. It contained 68 bales, 51 of which were graded at "Good Middling" and eventually sold at 8 cents a pound. Acknowledging its arrival the factors said, February 27, 1852, "Your overseer has handled your cotton remarkably well this season. The last shipment, which is good cotton, is much inferior to the first, which was *beautiful*." These words of praise for Mairs, the faithful overseer, recall to us his pathetic saying, so often encountered in

---

[1] The net proceeds of the sale were $3,210.50. Pickett, Perkins & Co. wrote February 4, 1852, that they could remit this sum in Tennessee credits at a profit to Mrs. Polk of 1 per cent; or they would hold it and allow her 6% interest, she drawing for it as she desired.

his letters to his employer, that he was doing the best he knew and that he was trying to make a good crop and put it up "nise." The net proceeds for the first shipment were $3,210.50 and for the second $2,198.46, a total of $5,408.96.

In the next season, 1852-1853, the same story was repeated. Writing on December 13, 1852, Pickett, Perkins and Company said:

DEAR MADAM

We write merely to hand you the enclosed remarks[1] on our market from which you will notice a decline in cotton. We regret that your crop, or a large portion of it, could not have reached us while prices were much better than at present, or are likely to be again shortly. However, we hope a reaction in our market will result to your advantage, but we fear we shall not see prices as high again this season as they have been. We shall in future endeavour to keep you informed of the state of our market, and shall take great pleasure in filling any order, or conforming to any instructions you may favor us with.

Very Respectfully
Your friends and ob. Servts.

A fortnight later, December 27, the factors, again rendering tribute to the faithful Mairs, ate some of their brave words in their preceding letter and reported sales of Mrs. Polk's shipment of "very pretty cotton" at a "very extraordinary price." The letter throws interesting light on the cotton trade in general. It runs as follows:

[1] In the "Remarks" prices of cotton are as follows: Inferior 6¾ @ 7, ordinary to good ordinary 7¼ @ 7⅝, low middling 8, middling 8¼ @ 8½, good middling 8¾ @ 9, middling fair 9½, fair 10¼ @ 10½, good fair — nominal, good and fine — nominal.

The Planter and his Commission Merchant

DEAR MADAM:

It gives us much pleasure to report the arrival of the first shipment of your cotton and its sale at a *very extraordinary price,* 50 bales at 11 cts less ¼ ct on *8 bales only* as pr. acct sales herein showing nett proceeds at your credit $2328.01. We were fortunate in selling this shipment *promptly,* and in meeting with a customer who wanted it badly. We know it will give you great satisfaction, the price being above the quotations for any cotton in the market. we will not however take all the credit to ourselves in this great sale. The large portion of the 50 bales was very pretty cotton, and your overseer deserves much praise for the beautiful manner he has prepared it for market. We hope the future shipments will turn out as well.

The enclosed price current will show you how our market stood up to Friday night last. Prices were *nominal,* as all parties were in suspense and waiting the arrival of the foreign accounts. Those accounts come yesterday — *very bad for cotton* and consequently our market today is down fully ½ ct below the quotations you will observe in the enclosed

Very Respectfuly Your ob. servt.

In the following statement the charges deducted by the factors from the gross proceeds from the sale of this cotton we may observe the rates of the several items of expense paid by the planter:

Freight 2.50 a bale —	$125.00
Shippers charges pr. B/L. $10.50 for the lot.	10.50
Dryage, storage, weighing & Labor @ 50 cts	25.00
River insurance — 2½% of $40. a bale	50.00
Fire ” on sale ½%	13.08
Comsns. on sale 2½%	65.43
	$289.01

During this season Mrs. Polk lost 33 bales of cotton and one bale of motes in a fire which destroyed the New Orleans warehouse in which they were stored. The loss was adjusted by her factors speedily by what regulations we do not know. The letter of the factors relating to the matter, March 5, 1853, is regrettably brief, and that part which deals with this subject is as follows:

DEAR MADAM:

The great fire which occurred in the Alabama Cotton Press on the 2d Inst., where we store, destroyed your two last shipments of Cotton, say 33 bales and 1 bale moats, for which we now enclose a statement adjusting the loss and showing nett proceeds of same at your credit $981.49. This adjustment is in accordance with the law and custom of the Insurance Companies here, and we hope will prove satisfactory to you. The Brokers declined to fix any value to the bale of moats as they were not aware that it was worth anything. We had been trying to sell it for some time, but without finding a purchaser at any price. We put it in your statement at $10 which we presume will be satisfactory under the circumstances. . . . . .

Putting together the facts on the subject in the reports of the factors it appears that the proceeds of the sale of the cotton crop in this season were as follows:

The first shipment, 50 bales,	$2,328.01
The second shipment, 75 bales,	3,185.07
The third shipment, 10 bales,	414.90
Paid by Insurance Company for cotton burned in warehouse,	981.49
Total proceeds,	$6,909.47

The Planter and his Commission Merchant

The year 1853 was an unlucky year for Mrs. Polk. The crop was cut off by boll worms and excessive rains until only 72 bales were shipped. Few as they were they arrived late in the market, just after prices had taken a decided drop. The financial return was meagre. W. S. Pickett,[1] writing on February 3, 1854, said:

DEAR MADAM

. . . . . . The cotton prospects have undergone a change for the worse since I had the pleasure of writing to you on the subject. The severe pressure in the money market, and the great difficulty in negotiating bills to pay for produce, are at present the most unfavorable points in the trade. For particulars we shall send you the usual review of the market tomorrow, hoping for a decided improvement by the time your crop reaches us. We shall of course exercise our best judgment as to the propriety of selling on arrival or holding for a better price

Very Resptfy Yours

March 1, 1854, Pickett's new firm, Pickett, Macmurdo and Company, wrote Mrs. Polk as follows:

DEAR MADAM:

. . . . . . The General Stokes brings us the first shipment of your cotton crop, 72 bales, in the quality of which, the writer is much disappointed, as it is greatly below your first shipment of the last season The 72 bales are

52 middling fair worth 10   to 10¼
20 good ordinary   ”   7¾ to   8   cts

As there is some prospect of cotton doing better, and as we are anxious to do better than the above figures, we shall

---

[1] Pickett was now in the firm of Pickett, Macmurdo & Co. which he had formed during the preceding year. The old firm was known as Perkins, Campbell & Co.

[237]

not be in a hurry to sell. Will keep you advised of what we may do. . . . . .

The days and weeks passed, prices still continued to fall and the factors held on to the cotton, waiting for the turn that usually comes in the spring. To keep up the spirits of their client they wrote her on May 22, 1854, as follows:

DEAR MADAM:

We fear you may become impatient in regard to the sale of your Cotton. When it arrived our market had declined considerably, and prices have since, we think, reached the lowest point of the season. We have therefore been inclined to hold on to your Cotton under the impression that prices would improve as the causes of depression disappeared. We are still of this opinion, and a more favorable feeling is now apparent, induced by rather lower freights, and a less stringent money market.

The enclosed review of our market for Saturday will show you its *lowest depression*.[1] Today there has been an active inquiry, resulting in the sale of about 10,000 bales at an improvement in prices. Your letter of 4th April was duly received submitting the sale entirely to our judgment. We trust it will not be long before we shall be able to report satisfactorily. In the mean time should you require to draw upon us, your Dft or Dfts at sight will be duly honored

It was not until spring had gone and summer had arrived that they were able to report a sale, at prices only a little below those that might have been obtained in Febru-

---

[1] Prices were: Inferior, 4 @ 5 cts.; ordinary, 5½ @ 6 cts.; good ordinary, 6¼ @ 6½ cts.; low middling, 6½ @ 7 cts.; middling, 7¼ @ 7½ cts.; good middling, 8¼ @ 8½ cts.; middling fair, 8½ @ 9 cts.; fair, nominal; good fair, nominal; good and fine, nominal.

ary when the cotton arrived. Their report of the sale, made
June 23, 1854, does not disguise the feeling of relief in
Pickett's mind that he had escaped as well as that. His let-
ter runs:

DEAR MADAM:

 We have to advise the sale of your crop of Cotton say
53 Bales middling fair at 10   cts
19   ”   very ordinary at 6½ cts
The late improvement in our market has enabled us to
realize a better price for your cotton than we could have
commanded at any time during several weeks past. It is
no more however than we could have obtained at the time
of its arrival, but hoping to do better, we were induced to
hold on; hence the loss of time is about all the damage we
have done you by the exercise of our judgment

The 19 Bales is of course very low Cotton, being stained
badly, and of inferior staple—the last pickings of your
Crop. In a day or two we will wait on you with act sale[1]

            Very Respfy Yr.
                Obt. Servts.

The year 1854 proved even more disastrous than 1853
for Mrs. Polk. So many things went wrong that it is difficult
to see what worse luck she could have had. In the first
place there was a short crop in the country at large and
knowing ones foretold good prices. Mrs. Polk made a fair
crop and it seemed that she stood to win. Then came the
Crimean War, which produced such anxiety by the autumn
of 1854 that the demand for cotton was lessened, with a
consequent loss in prices. The autumn was dry, as usual
the water was low in the Yalobusha River, and it was not

---

[1] The sale netted Mrs. Polk $2,755.14. Freight, $2.25 a bale; commission, 2½%.

possible to ship cotton until late. Mairs hauled it to Troy, as he was in the habit of doing, and stored it in one of the warehouses there against the arrival of the steamers with the rise of the river. When 100 bales were thus in storage fire broke out in the Troy warehouses and burned a large quantity of cotton. Thus was destroyed all of Mrs. Polk's 100 bales, and she had no insurance. But 55 bales remained to her. These were sent to market on what Mairs called the "ceal bote," *Wave,* but the factors call it the *Ware.* Whatever the name the keel boat sunk. Mrs. Polk's cotton was rescued, placed on another boat, the *Texana,* which started on its journey. But the *Texana* was burned in the Yazoo River. The result was that only one bale of the plantation's product reached the market that year. It was tantalizing to learn that this bale was of unusully good quality. For the 54 bales burned on the *Texana* insurance was collected at $50 a bale. March 7, 1855, W. S. Pickett wrote Mrs. Polk as follows:

Dear Madam:

In consequence of my absence of nearly three weeks on a trip to Memphis, your letter of 17th Ult, enclosing one from your overseer, Mr. Mairs, did not reach me until my return two days ago.

When I heard of the fire at Troy, I feared that some of your cotton might be there "in transitu", and I deeply regret now to learn that my fears have been realized, and to the extent reported by Mr. Mairs. I have no doubt it is a total loss to you, unless your *instructions* and *customs* heretofore has been to have your cotton insured against fire *at Troy previous to shipment.* This is so rarely done, indeed the chances of loss are considered so remote, that not one planter in a hundred thinks it necessary to adopt this precaution, and I presume you did not. I shall however write to Mr. Mairs for information on this point and do all that can be done to protect your interests

Your cotton is always covered by Fire Insurance *while in store here, as soon as it reaches our hands;* and this is the charge you observe in your acct. sales. I shall write you further when I hear from Mr. Mairs

The 55 bales of your crop have not yet reached Perkins, Campbell and Co.[1] Low water in the small rivers I suppose is the reason. I shall give the sale my attention. The market has improved a little as you will see by the enclosed slip.

Very Respfy   Your friend etc.

March 20, 1855, Pickett followed up this letter with another in which he said:

DEAR MADAM

I wrote you on 7th Inst. and have now to say, that I have heard from Mr. Mairs who informs me that no insurance was effected on your Cotton burnt at Troy. This is as I supposed. Shipping merchants in the interior never insure the Cotton of their customers while passing through their hands.

From my experience in a "big fire" that occurred here two years ago, I know well how to sympathize with you in the loss you have sustained, though it will not, I hope, subject you to serious inconvenience or force you to adopt the "credit system" which you seem so anxious to avoid. If it should, please bear in mind that I am always ready to supply your wants.

---

[1] Pickett seems to have gone out of regular business, but to have been looking after Mrs. Polk's affairs through the house of Perkins, Campbell & Co. One hundred bales of Mrs. Polk's cotton were burned. The 55 bales mentioned in this letter was the remainder of her crop.

The remainder of your crop has not yet reached this market. The low stage of the waters, is of course the cause of the delay. In the mean time, our market has improved considerably, prices having gone up ½ or ¾ cts within the past 10 days owing chiefly to advice from Europe of the death of the Czar and the increasing prospects for peace

Very Respfy and Truly Yours

Pickett's next addition to the bad news was embodied in a letter dated April 23, 1855, and runs as follows:

Dear Madam:

A fatality seems to attend your crop of cotton this year. The 55 bales *not burned* at Troy were shipped on a keelboat as soon as there was sufficient water in the river which keelboat was sunk in the Yallabusha before reaching a reshipping point. Your cotton was recovered in a damaged condition and again shipped on board the *Steamer Texana* and this boat took fire in the Yazoo river and was consumed with most of her cargo

I do not regard this loss as detrimental to your interest. On the contrary, I think it will result to your interest, as your cotton was insured at $50 p. bale, a high valuation and more than it would probably bring in the market, considering it was the last of your crop. I will attend to the adjustment of the loss and see that everything is properly done. In the mean time, you might as well instruct me what you will have done with the proceeds of the cotton — how you will have it remitted etc., etc.

Very Respfy Yr friend and ob. svt.

The end of this doleful matter is in the following statement rendered by Perkins, Campbell and Company, to whom the cotton was consigned:

MADAM:

We now wait On you with a statement of (1) your account current including sale and adjustment (2) of loss on 55 bales Cotton p Texana, all of which will, we trust be found correct and satisfactory. Leaving to your credit as requested to pay dft in favor of your Overseer, which has not yet been presented—$550.—we invest the balance due you in the enclosed (3) check of Joseph W. Allen Agt. on Bank of Tennessee for $1484.30 bought @ ½ % dis—$7.42 [making] $1476.88.

We supposed we had Our Insurance policy high enough to cover the value of your shipment but if the Cotton destroyed was as good as the bale received it would have brought *in a lot* even more than 12 cts, probably 13 @ lb and we presume its average weight was fully 470 lbs. The bale received brought as you will perceive $56.40

Very Respectfully

The crop of 1855 began to arrive in New Orleans in November, in time for the early prices. It was consigned to Perkins, Campbell and Company, although W. S. Pickett, still interested in the firm, kept a close oversight over it and wrote to Mrs. Polk about its disposal. His first letter of this season, written from New Orleans November 22, 1855, runs as follows:

DEAR MADAM:

On my return *home yesterday* I found your esteemed favor of 12th Oct. It is I hope, needless to say that my long absence from home (much longer than I anticipated) has caused the delay in replying to you.

I attended promptly to your request on my arrival at Memphis several weeks ago, about the Insurance of your cotton, by taking out a policy *against fire* while in the ware-house at Troy, and as I have policies to protect it against loss by navigation on the rivers and against fire while in store in this city, there is now, no interregnum of insecurity between its leaving your gin-house, and final disposition here. You need therefore give yourself no further uneasiness about it. All shall be right. The talk about "Condemned boats", "new regulations", etc is no new thing. The board of underwriters here, *condemn* and *reinstate* boats every season for some cause or other, but I have no idea that your agents at Troy will ship your cotton in such a manner as to vitiate the insurance upon it.

Our cotton market is doing well under all the influences bearing upon it. Such cotton as you have generally sent to this market, would now command about 11 cts

Very Respfy yr. ob. Svt

The first shipment of Mrs. Polk's cotton, 52 bales, arrived late in November and Perkins, Campbell and Company reported that it was of very good quality and that "nearly half of it is such as we expect to sell for a *fancy* price." A few days later, but in the month of December, W. S. Pickett wrote to her as follows:

Dear Madam:

Mr. Walker and Gov. Campbell left here on Sunday to return home. During their stay, we had a *general dissolution* and settlement of all our affairs in the house of Perkins Campbell and Co. Sam and Gov. Campbell retire altogether from the business, and I withdraw my means, receive a bonus for the last year's loss of time, and cancell my partnership agreement with Mr. Walker.

You will see from the above card, that I have branched

out on my own account, (free of all liabilities of the old house) and am now, I presume, a "commission merchant for life."

Your favor of 20th Ult came duly to hand. The shipment of 52 B/ Cotton in the hands of Mr. Perkins is not yet sold. The best offer had for it last week was 10 cts but I doubt if the offer will be repeated as our market has undergone a change for the worse. I see no reason however to hurry the sale, under the anticipation of much lower prices.

I shall esteem it a favor if you will order the remainder of your crop to be shipped to my new firm, and even to give me an order for the shipment now here. I am almost inclined to write to your overseer to ship to me believing it would meet your approbation[1]

Mary and the children came down with Sam about 2 weeks ago. She has been quite busy fixing up for the winter — desires to be affectionately remembered to yourself and Miss Childress.

Very Respfy your friend etc

The fire demon was still in pursuit of Mrs. Polk, but she now had no cause to fear him for her cotton was insured for more than it would bring in the market. This pleasing news came to her in a letter from W. S. Pickett dated January 3, 1856. It reads as follows:

Dear Madam:

Your esteemed favor of 18th Ulto came duly to hand and shall receive proper attention. The bill of sup-

---

[1] In an announcement printed at the head of the sheet on which this letter was written it was stated that W. S. Pickett had resumed the "Cotton factorage and General Commission Business" under the firm name of W. S. Pickett & Co. He spoke of his 12 years' experience in this kind of business.

plies as stated by Mr. Mairs for your plantation this year, shall be forwarded in due season, when navigation is most favorable. We have so informed Mr. Mairs.

We have today received from Perkins and Co $1969.41 at your credit with us being the proceeds of your first shipment 52 B/C as p. act. sales herein. Your next shipment of 55 bales, for which a bill of lading was received here, was burnt on the steamer "Unicorn" in Yazoo River, a total loss so far as has been ascertained. This is a "streak of *good luck*" as the Cotton was insured at $50 p. bale which, you will perceive, is more than the value of the first shipmt. The Insurance Office claims the usual 2 pct. discount for cash, or 60 days time after proof of loss. We shall allow *the time,* as you are not pressed for money, and 2 pct. is a heavy rate for 60 days. In the mean time, you may rely upon our attention to the adjustment of the loss. . . . .

Settlement was duly made with the insurance company and on as advantageous terms as Pickett anticipated. His letter to Mrs. Polk of January 12, 1856, gives an account of the completion of the settlement, as well as some other material information about the relation between factor and planter. It runs as follows:

Dear Madam:

Since our respects of 3d Inst we have received your favor of 3d. As your 55 Bales were consigned to Perkins & Co. and *insured under their policy,* we thought it best to use their name in the adjustment of the loss. The Insurance Company paid the money deducting only ½ pct, and we yesterday received the proceeds $2557.84 as p. statement

herein. We also enclose original of Jas. Robb and Co check
on New York endorsed by us for $4,561.45
Discount ¾ p. ct   34.20

                                    ——————— $4527.25

being a full payment as desired by you
for proceeds 52 B/C $1969.41
      "   55   "   2557.84

                                      ——————— $4527.25

This is the best remittance we can make you, and we
think it a very favorable one for your interest as the Bank
of Tennessee will no doubt allow you a small premium for
the check on New York, but if she allows no premium, the
¾ Discount is better than we can do for anything direct on
Nashville.

The Bill of Lading for 20 Bales is at hand transfered to
us. The cotton also came to hand yesterday; but as the
weather is awfully bad, and unfavorable for outdoor business, we may not be able to get it sampled and on the market for some days to come. The market is firm and there is
no danger, we think, of any immediate decline.

Your affairs in this quarter are all perfectly straight, and
your interest well looked after so you need give yourself, not
the slightest uneasiness in regard to them.[1] Hoping what
has been done so far will meet your approbation we are

                              Very Respfy Your friends etc.

Beside the 20 bales of cotton here mentioned other shipments of 21 bales in all arrived and were sold by the factors.
The net proceeds of the 41 bales came to $1,454.36, so that

[1] Perkins & Co. reported to Mrs. Polk, January 1, 1856, that they had closed up
he insurance matter of 55 bales and turned over the money to W. S. Pickett & Co.
is directed by Mrs. Polk. They said also that it was proper for her to transfer
her business to Pickett, adding "and in view of the relations existing between you and
Mr. Pickett's we could not ask or expect" to have her custom.

Mrs. Polk realized from her entire crop of 1855 the sum of $5,981.61.

The season of 1856 opened with the assurance that the crop was short and the stocks held in the great markets of the world smaller than usual. Mrs. Polk was lucky enough to have a fair crop, 143 bales. The letters of her factors give us quite a complete view of its sale, with some interesting glimpses of the relations that existed between the two sides of this kind of business. Writing on November 5, 1856, the factors, W. S. Pickett and Company, said:

DEAR MADAM:

Your favor of 9th Ulto came duly to to hand in which you request that the whole of your crop of Cotton may be received by us before we offer it for sale if not contrary to our judgment to withhold it from market.

Your suggestion on this point corresponds with our present opinions in regard to the future course of our market, and we feel no hesitation in conforming to your wishes. The principle cotton markets of the world are lightly stocked, and we think therefore that prices will advance, in the face of the present short crop, which appears to be considered as a fixed fact. The price current annexed will give particulars of our market, and we shall endeavour to keep you informed from time to time. We have effected insurance on your cotton while it remains in store at Troy, as last year

Very Respfy   Your friends etc.

December 24, 1856, W. S. Pickett and Company reported as follows:

DEAR MADAM:

The first shipment of your Cotton is now on hand — 90 bales — about one half is *low middling* and the other half *good middling* and worth at present 12⅛ @ 12¼ cts. We bear in mind your instruction to with hold your crop from market until it all arrives and you give orders for its sale. The market has been trending upwards, and the feeling in the cotton trade, is favorable for a further advance during the season. We shall advise you of the arrival of each shipment of your Cotton, and also the changes and prospects of the market   Very Respfly your friends etc

The next letter from the factors, dated January 21, 1857, runs as follows:

DEAR MADAM:

Your favor of 13 Inst. is received with the requisition of your overseer, Mr. Mairs, for the usual yearly supplies for your plantation. This shall have all proper attention. We presume it is your wish and expectation, as formerly, to have these supplies purchased and shipped at a time when the waters are up — navigation unobstructed — and freights low.

Since our last we have received a further shipment of your cotton — 30 bales, barely as good as the 90 bales first received. It is worth in our present market, 12 cts. The latest foreign advices are favorable for Cotton, but they were anticipated by us here, and have had no sensible effect upon our market. In fact, prices are not so firm or full as before, and we are beginning to entertain the idea of selling your crop under the discretion you give us, for fear of one of those "break downs" in the market that we have experienced before under similar circumstances.

Very truly yours.

The factors continued to watch the cotton market, which was lucky enough to escape one of the dreaded "break

downs." Early in February they began to feel that the time
to sell had arrived, and to prepare their client for such action they wrote her on the fifth of that month the following
letter:

DEAR MADAM:

We have shipped your plantation supplies in accord-
ance with the list made out by Mr. Mairs which you furnished us. Enclosed we hand you the invoice amounting to
$553.52 at your debit.[1] We hear of a considerable rise in
the Yallobusha river and trust your supplies will reach their
destination without unusual delay.

Our cotton market has advanced slightly—prices are
firm—and we are induced to place your crop on the market, under the impression that the present is about as
favorable a time to sell as we shall have. As we remarked
in a former letter, your crop does not come up in quality
and cleanliness to what it used to be; but we shall do the
best that can be done to obtain a high price. The average
value of it is 12¼ cts.   Very Respfy Yrs.

February 14, 1857, they wrote her as follows:

DEAR MADAM:

Your favor of 3d Inst. came duly to hand. We
thought it advisable last week to make sale of your crop of
cotton for which we hand you herein a/c sale 120 Bales
showing nett proceeds at your credit $6,227.93. You
will find this an average price of more than 12½ cts p. lb,
and we trust the sale will give satisfaction. The market re-

---

[1] The invoice shows that Mrs. Polk paid 18 cents a yard for bagging, 10½ cents
a yard for rope and 18 cents a lb. for twine. Shoes were $17.50 a dozen pairs and
4 dozen were ordered. Campeachy hats were $3.50 a dozen and 4 dozen were ordered.
766 lbs. "bacon sides" @ 11 cents. Slab iron was 6 cents a lb. and bar iron was 5
cents. Salt was 95 cents a sack.

mains about the same as when we sold. You direct us to remit in the "usual way", and presuming a sight check on New York will command a premium in Nashvle of about one pct. we hand you herein Jas. Robb and Co cks at sight on Robb, Hallett & Co. New York $5,714.24

Discount ⅞ pct.	50.00
	$5,664.24

This will balance your acct. at present. When we receive and dispose of the remainder of your crop we will send you statement in full of your a/c   Very Respfy

Twenty-three bales arrived a short time later, with two bales of motes, which both factor and overseer spelled "moats." Writing on March 9, 1857, W. S. Pickett and Company reported sale of the cotton as follows:

DEAR MADAM:

We have now to wait on you with the enclosed acct sales of your last shipment of Cotton, viz.

19 Bales "J. K. Polk"—	nett proceeds	$959.20
4 " |A|	do.	183.24

This cotton was quite low in quality. It has brought a high price not with standing, and we hope the sale will give you satisfaction. We have yet on hand of your crop 2 bales *of moats,* not sold. We shall probably get 8 @10$ p. bale for them.

We do not remit for this sale as in the first case, because exchange on N. York has got up to par and the inducements to remit in that way are not the same as before. Besides you have always heretofore reserved a certain amt. here for your overseer, Mr. Mairs. We shall therefore wait your instructions in regard to your funds now in our hands.

Very Respfy.

The allusion to the two bales of motes in the following letter written March 12, 1857, indicates with what contempt the dealer in cotton regarded them. In fact, they sold so low that it is a question if it would not have been better to have used them for bedding in the stables. Putting these returns with those made previously it is seen that the crop of 1856 sold for $6,818.14. The report of March 12 runs as follows:

DEAR MADAM:

Since we wrote you on 9th Inst. enclosing a/c sales of your last shipment of cotton, we have disposed of the 2 bales of *moats* as p. acct. sale herein, nett proceeds of same at your credit $11.46. we have also to acknowledge rect. of your favor of 5th Inst, and conforming to your wishes, we hand you herein A. Wheless ck. on Bank of Nashville $608.46; Discount ¾ pct. $4.56: at your debit $603.90. This you will perceive, closes your acct. to a point as P. statement herein, reserving $550 to meet your Dft. to Mr. Mairs as advised. Exchange on the North is *now at a premium* here, and it is rather to your advantage for us to remit in a check on Nashville.

Very Truly and Respfy Yrs

The insurance for *this year at Troy* I will charge when paid to your next year's a/c.

For some reason not revealed in the correspondence W. S. Pickett's firm did not outlast the season of 1856-1857. Retiring from business in New Orleans he joined an old and strong firm of cotton brokers in Memphis, Tennessee, operating under the name of Harris, Wormley and Company. This change was made in the summer, and July 7, 1857,

Mrs. Polk was advised of it. Pickett recommended her, if she wished to continue to sell in New Orleans, to deal with John Williams and Company. She did not, however, take his advice and returned to the firm of Perkins and Company with which she had done business while Pickett was a member. His letter of July 7, written from Memphis, contains the following interesting observations about the prospects of Memphis as a cotton market:

"I trust however this severance of our business connexion, will be of short duration. The cotton business of Yallobusha is fast concentrating at Memphis. Already there is a great deal of cotton from that county, hauled to within reach of the Mississippi and Tennessee Rail Road and thence to Memphis. In another year the Rail Road will perhaps penetrate as far as Grenada (its destined point) and it may be within a very short distance from your plantation. In that event, you will find it to your interest to send your cotton here, like everybody else, and order your supplies from this point. Memphis is the best market for cotton planters who are in reach of it by Rail Road Communication, as it is accessible at all times, and the charges are much less than in New Orleans."

Pickett continued to show an interest in Mrs. Polk's affairs. The last letter we have from him, written in Memphis, January 29, 1858, indicates that he was looking after the insurance of her cotton while it was stored at Troy, on the Yallobusha River. It runs as follows:

DEAR MADAM:

I ought to have advised you long since that I had renewed your Insurance on your Cotton Crop this season while it may remain in store at Troy as heretofore. Please excuse the omission. I am and have been very much pressed with labour which require attention nightly until 10 or 12 Ock. I find it much more labourious here than in N. Orls, because of the very many Cases of small planters and their orders — and the want of system and regularity of Conducting business.

I have paid the Insurance Agency here the premium for you on your last seasons crop as P statement herein of $23.34. This you can refund at your convenience. I only desired at present to let you know that I had not overlooked the more important matter of protecting your present crop while awaiting shipment at Troy. My family all well. Mrs. J. Knox W[alker] has been staying with us some days.

Very Respfy Yr. friend etc

Mrs. Polk's correspondence with Perkins and Company, of New Orleans, for the season of 1857-1858 begins with a letter from that firm dated October 13, 1857. It shows that the firm was having her gin-house, the cotton in it, and the cotton at Troy insured by underwriters in New Orleans. The letter runs as follows:

MADAM:

We have yours of 6th Inst and beg you to accept Our thanks for your patronage and confidence. We shall strive to prove Ourselves worthy.

We have effected insurance against fire on Cotton in your *Gin house* to amount of $2000 for 4 mos. from 1st Inst.[1] This will cover about 40 bales Cotton and will include the whole shipping season with you we presume. We write to your Overseer to know some particulars as to the

---

[1] February 10, 1858, Perkins & Co. rendered a bill showing that they paid $50 for insuring Mrs. Polk's gin-house for four months. The rate was 2½%. For insuring the cotton at Troy they paid at the rate of 1¾%.

ginhouse which have a bearing on the rate of insurance and have also requested him to give us notice in case he should find a stock exceeding $2000 in value accumulating in and around the gin

We have also taken insurance on Cotton to amount of $2000 on Cotton at your landing until the crop is shipped commencing with this date, estimating that you will not have more than 40 bales or 50 at the landing at One time. This last insurance has a condition that in case of loss you share one fourth. Our regular policies cover the Cotton from the time of shipment until sold and delivered. We have mentioned the *details* of these insurances for your reference (if necessary) hereafter, but in general terms we will say that we are endeavouring to protect you from loss by every possible means. We trust however that your full share of misfortune has already been realized.

Can you inform us whether your gin house is insured? And if not is it your wish that it should be done and for what amount? When we Once understand the position of these things we shall be able to give them due attention without troubling you   Very respectfully

December 4, 1857, the firm wrote, sending supplies ordered for her plantation, and referring to the state of the cotton market. The letter is as follows:

MADAM:

We received several days since yours of 23d Novem. with Order for plantation supplies, but until today we have had no Opportunity to ship them. The articles have now been shipped per steamer "Hope" as per enclosed invoice[1]

1 By this invoice the following prices were paid for the supplies: Bagging @ 12 cts. a yd., Rope 8½ cts. yd., Twine 17 cts., Salt 75 cts., Campeachy Hats $2.25 a doz., Clear sides, 14 cts. a lb., Russet brogans $18.00 a doz. pairs, Bar iron 5 cts., Slab iron 5 cts.

to your debit — $484.65. The Captain of the boat thinks he will be able to get to Troy but there is great uncertainty as to navigation to that point

We regret that a portion of your cotton at least had not come to hand to get the benefit of the good demand and very fair prices which have prevailed for the last two weeks. The market is now Completely unsettled by the Liverpool news received P. *America* and it is difficult to say what Cotton is worth, though we may say that the decline is not less than half a cent here. We sold a few days before receipt of this news all the Cotton we had on hand except about five hundred bales which we with held from the market by order of owners

Very respectfully

By New Years three shipments of Mrs. Polks cotton had arrived at New Orleans, in all 115 bales. As the market was not good the factors decided to hold it pending developments or instructions from the owner. This determination they reported to Mrs. Polk in the following letter dated January 2, 1858:

MADAM:

Within a few days we have received three shipments of Cotton from your plantation, say 65, 30, and 20 bales — together 115. The market is so very unsatisfactory we are not disposed to offer it for sale now. We may err in holding up but if so we shall err with good intentions. As yet we have samples of only the 65 bales in. This is beautiful Cotton and well ginned and handled. We do not know but think we could get a fraction over ten cents for it

Should you have any instructions or suggestions to give on the subject please communicate them freely. To undertake a prophecy as to the future course of the market would be folly in us as in times like these no reliable calculations can be made, but we incline to the Opinion that there is no danger in holding your Cotton. Since the publication of this morning's Price Current (annexed) we have news of a further decline of half penny at Liverpool equal to about one cent per pound here

Very Respectfully your servants

February 6, 1858, the factors reported that they had sold the first shipment, 65 bales. The report was made in the following words:

MADAM:

We sold a few days since your first shipment of Cotton 65 bales @ 12½ cts p lb. and shall deliver it either to-day or early next week. How shall we invest the proceeds? or shall we leave the amount subject to your draft? The later shipments fall short of this in quality, and at present we could not get over ten cents perhaps for it. We have Confidence in Cotton yet but did not feel justified in refusing 12½ as it is only now and then we have an opportunity of selling cotton at fancy prices. We sold to a buyer for France[1]   Very Respectfully

Mrs. Polk, like many other people, did not understand bank exchange, then sold at discount or premium, and she mistook the language used by her factors in settling for the first sale of the cotton. Her letter of protest, based on this misunderstanding, brought forth the following reply, dated at New Orleans March 13, 1858:

[1] February 11, 1858, Perkins & Co. reported that the net proceeds of the sale of the 65 bales were $3,415.53. They added: "The market has further improved, not for this grade, but for the medium and lower descriptions and we now hope to make the remainder of your crop pay a good price also."

The Plantation Overseer

Madam

We have just received yours of 6th Inst and regret to see that you are under a serious mistake as to the *exchange* in which we remitted your proceeds of cotton sold. Understanding that you relied on us to make the best exchanges we could we have felt more interest in the matter if possible than for our Customers generally. If you will take another look at the papers you will see that instead of *losing* you make $88.01 by the exchange, as you received a check at 3 per cent discount.[1] You may rest assured Madam that without special instructions we shall ever strive to promote your interests in all matters entrusted to us.

No other sale of your cotton has been made and we begin to fear that we have held a little too long, but with continued good news from Liverpool we had a right to expect an improvement instead of a decline here.

Very Respectfully

Exchange on Nashville now 1½% dis.

The remainder of Mrs. Polk's crop of 1857 was sold a short time afterwards. The two letters following summed up the transactions and transmitted funds in settlement of them. The first, dated March 27, 1858, runs as follows:

Madam:

We enclose account Sales of your last two shipments Cotton, 9+5 = 14 bales, netting $548.99 to cover which we enclose check on Bank Tennessee for $557.44 @ 1½% dis —$8.45—[costing you] $548.99. The best we can get Tennessee checks at is 1½% dis from Mr. Allen Agent of the Bank of Tennessee. We can buy checks on New York at

---

[1] That cheque was for $2,933.89 and it was charged in the statement for $2,845.88 which was at a discount of 3%.

about ¼ or ⅜% dis., but this must not be better for you nor as good as we understand the Nashville rates for checks on New York.

These 14 bales were the lowest of your crop and too full of dirt and dust to sell with the rest. We sold a few days ago the remainder 20 + 30 = 50 bales @ 11¾ around and after its weighing and delivery will wait on you with sales and remittances   Very truly

The second letter, dated March 31, 1858, is the last of the series before me. It closes this review of the dealings of the owner of the Polk plantation in the following words:

MADAM:

Confirming previous advices we now wait on you with account sales of the balance of your crop, say 20 + 30 = 50 bales[1] netting $2,324 79—from which we deduct for Mr. Mairs $850 and invest the balance say $1474.79 in the enclosed check on Bk. Tennessee for $1,497.25 @ 1½% dis —$22.46, [costing you] $1474.79.

What may be the future course of the market is uncertain. At present the tendency in Liverpool seems to be downward, the news by telegraph today being ½d decline there equal to a cent. We have thought it useless to wait for any further advances as we see nothing to justify the expectation of any *material* improvement. We trust that our course will meet your approbation.

Very Respectfully

---

1 It is interesting to note that on these shipments the freight is charged at $1.15 a bale, whereas in other years it had been more than twice as high.

CHAPTER XIII

The Lesson of the Letters

ROM 1833, when the first of these over-
seer letters was written, to 1858, when the
last was dated, was an even quarter of a
century. Through that period we have
constantly under observation an economic
unit of the Old South. There are a few
years in which the story breaks through failure of the letters, but there is no reason to believe that the omitted information was materially unlike what has been preserved.
It is safe to assume, therefore, that we have here a true and
fairly complete panorama of life on the plantation, so far as
it relates to the subjects dealt with in the letters. This
record is not to be disputed in the things which it reveals.

As for the things it does not take up, they are mostly the
ordinary matters of daily life. For example, there is not a
reference to the marriage of slaves in all the 275 letters that
have come into my hands.[1] Within this long period many
such unions must have occurred on the plantation, but no
overseer thought it worth his while to mention one. Also,
there may have been divorces or separations of husband
and wife. The letters contain no suggestion of such occurrences. The overseer wrote about the things that he
thought the owner ought to know. He doubtless assumed
that Polk had no concern with a negro marriage or a negro

[1] Of the letters copied from the Polk correspondence that might have been used in
this book, 84 were rejected because they were repetitions or unimportant. Of course
this aggregate includes many letters not written by overseers as these pages show.

divorce. Runaways were more to the purpose. His letters, therefore, said nothing about a large area of conduct that was intimately connected with the life of the slaves.

An expert in osteology will look at a fragment of a skeleton and reconstruct the whole of it. If a given part is thus and so the remainder is thus and so. It is like that with the evidence in these letters. They show us a fragment of plantation life. That fragment indicates the contour of the part that is omitted. It is of rugged shape and angular. It would not fit in with the very graceful contour that the romancers have given to the slave life of the past. I conclude, therefore, that the pictures drawn by the romancers are not true pictures of the life actually lived on the plantations.

What things are here indicated by the undeniable fragment of plantation life which we find in the letters? And that much ascertained what can be deduced from it about the general nature of such life? The question challenges the reader who will perhaps have his own peculiar reply. To me the following observations seem warranted:

In the first place we may consider the buildings in which the people lived. On this plantation on which the master did not live there was no "great house," or planter's residence. The buildings consisted of the overseer's house, a plain structure, no doubt, as overseers' houses were. It rarely had more than three rooms. Next were the slave cabins of one or two rooms. Besides these were the barns, the stables, the sheds for the carts and wagons, the shuck pens, which might or might not have roofs over them, and the gin-house with the tall armed cotton screw by its side.

Originally these buildings must have been built of logs taken from the place. The character of the buildings may be seen from the time it took to construct them. Writing to Polk January 10, 1835, Dr. Caldwell said that he remained on the place after taking the overseer and negroes to it for eighteen days and in that time he "put up a house for Beanland four Houses for the negroes a Smokehouse and a kitchen and made a lot for our stock." His statement of expenses is definite enough to show that he did not buy any sawn lumber, and he had with him no slaves who could be classed as carpenters. The work was doubtless done with the axes of the negroes directed by the doctor and Beanland. Boards may have been split for the roofs and floors and the chimneys were probably made of sticks daubed heavily with clay in the frontier fashion. The slave group consisted of eighteen men, ten women, seven children, and two boys who seem to have been about half grown, in all thirty-seven people crowded into four houses. Doubtless other houses were soon built for the slave residences, it being the practice on plantations to allow one cabin for each slave family. The trivial character of the buildings on the plantation is shown in the fact that a few years later, 1840, all these buildings were abandoned and others built in what was considered a more healthy situation. If one would try to imagine the life lived here he must place it in very simple homes.

Over this grouping of building and its inhabitants presided the overseer. The letters show us what kind of man he was. His education was very meagre. Of the facts one gets from reading books he had a scant supply. His stock of ideas was acquired in the experience of a workaday world, his own world of hard knocks. Negroes, cotton, the uncertainty of the seasons, and the routine of planting, cultivating, and harvesting made up his body of rules. He worked the slaves as regularly as he could, putting them at their tasks and keeping them there until the day was at an end. Of the humanizing side of labor he knew little. Slave labor could not be humanized from his point of view. To lift up the slave was to make him dissatisfied with slavery. To make him accept slavery and to work because he was told to work was the overseer's idea.

The *bête noire* of the overseer was the runaway slave. The letters show that there were always slaves who rebelled at the idea of bondage. Jack, Ben, Hardy, Gilbert, Harbart, Charles and Addison and those whom they influenced to follow their example represented this spirit of revolt. Caught and brought back to the plantation they took the whipping that was a matter of course and waited an opportunity for another flight. It always came, sooner or later. For them life was one attempt after another to escape, not to the land of freedom in the North, for they were too far away from the border line of slavery and freedom to think of that. They ran away merely to escape for the time from the hand of the overseer. A month in the woods, a brief sojourn in Tennessee, whence they came to Mississippi, was all they could expect. For this they underwent the arrest, the imprisonment in a jail, the journey in irons back to the plantation cabins and the punishment that awaited them. And for all their trouble they got only a brief respite from labor. None of the punishments seem to have broken their spirits or made them accept quietly the life of the slave.

The letters also show what were the problems of discipline. We cannot read them without seeing how necessary it was that the managers of the plantation should have the authority that every director of labor must have if he is to make a success of the business entrusted to him. Beanland and Dismukes alike have our assent when they say that the runaways must be sent back if discipline on the plantation is to be maintained. It was not so much that the overseer was hard but that the system he was set to administer was hard.

We must not forget, also, that an important part of the problem was the negro himself. A fundamental part of the slave problem was the negro problem. The African slaves were close to savagery. They were to learn much in the process of forced labor and they learned it very slowly. The finer feelings of advanced peoples were not for them. They had not developed such feelings in Africa — they could not be expected to acquire them in American slavery in one, two, or five generations. For them uplift was a thing that could only come gradually and painfully. The first generations died in order that those who came afterwards might make a slow and meagre advance in culture.

Of course there were exceptions among the slaves. In the letters here submitted to the reader we have a view of one only of this class, the blacksmith Harry. There may have been others, but we do not find trace of them. But Harry presents himself to our view as a man of great faithfulness. For thirty years and a half, he tells us, he had stood over the anvil. He had hammered out the tools with which his companions in slavery had dug riches out of the soil for the benefit of the master. Eleven children had he given to his owner, he and his wife, all representing wealth and the power to create more wealth. He did not rebel against his lot. To Polk he sent his loyal respect, to his old mistress he sent the cheering words, "Yours till death." Few men could offer a richer tribute. Slavery gave him the opportunity of manifesting an admirable spirit of faithfulness.

On the other hand is Eva, whom the overseers persistently called "Evy." We are not told in any letter who was her husband but it is well established that she was a fertile breeder. She was not able to raise her children. The overseer said that she did not have any luck in rearing or in keeping her offspring alive. What they died of we are not told. The statement is quite bare: Evy's child died last week or last night, that is all. But we may judge that a controlling cause was her inefficiency in taking care of them. Perhaps she did not feel much interest in their health. They were not hers, but her Master's. Why should she be interested in taking care of master's negroes? Here was mother love at a low ebb. Here was the inability to realize what was good for the child. Fortunately not all slave women were indifferent on this point.

Another thing about these letters that seems significant is the infrequent mention of deaths among the adult slaves. It has often been asserted that slaves were worked so hard in the Gulf State that they died rapidly, the master consoling himself that it was more profitable to work them hard and replace by purchase. It has also been said that this habit was especially pronounced on plantations under the sole control of overseers. If the assertion were well founded it ought to be supported by occurrences on Polk's Mississippi plantation. So far as the evidence in the letters here printed goes the assertion is erroneous. Deaths of infant slaves were common. In all the letters running from 1835 to 1858 there is mention of very few deaths of adult slaves. In fact, a larger proportion of the overseers died on the plantation than of the slaves.

Two facts should, however, be mentioned as serving to modify the weight of my statement. One is the incompleteness of the series of letters. It is possible that more adult slaves died and that the overseer reported the deaths to the employer in letters not now preserved. On the other hand, the gaps in the correspondence are long, the longest being for the four years of Polk's service as president of the United States. And by the same token there are long periods during which the letters preserved are fairly complete. By the law of probability we may expect that the condition affecting life and death would be the same for the first of these periods as for the second. On that basis it is safe to say that the death rate of adults on the plantation was low.

Another thing bearing on the argument is the fact that the group of men and women taken to the plantation in 1835 was composed of young and healthy slaves, selected for the purpose. Undoubtedly such persons could be expected to have a low death rate. That is what could have been expected and that is what resulted. But the argument against which I am protesting is that the slaves were worked so hard that they broke down and died, and if it were true we might expect that Polk's slaves would have broken down whether young people or not. The argument had it that the work was severe enough to break the strength of young and strong men. As to old or weak workingmen, a large per cent. of them continually break down in free labor.

To support the old assertion attention was called to the steady carrying of slaves into the gulf region from the older parts of the South. It was said that they went to replace those whom slavery had killed by hard labor. That there was a constant movement of slaves from the upper to the lower section of the South is undoubted; but it is sufficiently explained by the enlargement of the arable acreage in that region. Occurrences on Polk's plantation amply bear out this assertion. In 1839 the cleared land amounted to

271 acres, in 1842 it was 374 acres and in 1851 it was 566 acres. To cultivate this enlarged area required more slaves than could be supplied by the growing of young slaves into the age for working on the fields. What was happening on Polk's plantation was happening on a great many others.

Moreover, during the period covered by these letters there was in this part of the South a constant enlargement of the cultivated area through the taking up of land from the state. After the Choctaw, Chickasaw, and Creek Indians surrendered their ample lands in 1830, 1832, and 1833 respectively and moved to the region which became known as Indian Territory, the lands they had formerly occupied were put on the market. The best were seized on quickly. The patents for Polk's plantation, which he bought from the patentee, were dated October 31, 1833, and it was only a year and one month later that Polk paid ten dollars an acre for the land. After the first years of enthusiasm in which the best land was taken up there remained a large amount of less fertile ungranted land which came more slowly into private hands. As it was taken up gradually through the next twenty-five years there was an enlarging demand for slaves to work it. Probably it would not be as vigorous a demand as the size of the newly granted acreage would seem to imply; for the poorer land fell to the poorer men who did not use slaves to the same extent as the large planters. But they used a certain number and as they prospered they were sure to buy more slaves.

To recapitulate, these letters tend to show that slaves did not die in the far South through overwork, and they seem to indicate that there was enough progressive enlargement of the cleared areas on the first plantations to account for a large part of the migration of slaves to this

region. We may add that through a large part of our period
the entire arable region was being steadily enlarged through
the patenting of less fertile lands and enlarging the cleared
land on the farms already existing. It should not be forgotten that in 1860 a large portion of the gulf states were
as near the beginning of their frontier as Ohio in 1810.

The letters throw some light on the profitableness of the
operations on the plantation. They show what was the
ordinary return from a plantation that cost $8,800 in 1834,
with slaves then valued at about $16,000 — a total of say
$25,000. In good years and bad this place returned the
owners from $3,500 to $6,300 above cost of operations.
When it was sold in 1860 it brought, according to report,
$30,000 for the land and such slaves as were not otherwise
disposed of. Unfortunately we do not know how many
slaves Polk bought for the plantation, how many Dr. Caldwell withdrew of his original stock, and how many of those
who had been sent there and born there had been taken off
by 1860. On the face of things it seems that the place paid,
even as a non-resident plantation.

These letters tell something, not as much as we wish,
of the kind of clothing worn by the slaves. They do not
describe it with attention to detail, but they give us some
data from which to argue. They enable us to talk about the
subject in specific terms, which is much better than the old
habit of sweeping the subject aside and saying that the
clothing was issued regularly and was adequate.

When he owned the Fayette County, Tennessee, plantation Polk spoke of sending the "negro cloth" to that place
from Columbia. He did not say how much, nor what kind.
He said nothing about shoes and hats. But he had an account with one of the stores in Somerville and it is likely

that he bought at this store what he thought the slaves needed beyond the "negro cloth," which he sent from Columbia, because it was cheaper in that town.

As for the Mississippi plantation, there is nothing in the letters of the overseer or of the New Orleans factors to show that he had any considerable account at the local stores. The returns of the factors account for the disposition of the proceeds from the sale of the cotton. None of this sum went to Mississippi to pay any other account than the wages of the overseer. There was mention of a small account at the store in Coffeeville, but it was usually paid out of such sums as the overseer might have received from the sale of surplus corn, the money received from Harry's blacksmithing, or other small business. It does not seem possible that Polk bought in this way any considerable amount of clothing, for in the bill he made at the store must have been included such things as coffee, sugar, and flour for the sick slaves, occasional new harness, and other little things needed on a plantation. When we have glimpses of the bill it does not run beyond two hundred dollars a year.[1]

Every spring, however, the factor bought in New Orleans what came to be called "the supplies for the plantation" and sent them up the river while the water was high. We know that no other supplies were sent up but this spring shipment, for there is no mention of them in the letters and the accounts of the factors are silent about any shipment but the one made in the spring. By a process of elimination we have, therefore, made it seem likely that besides the clothing worn and made upon the place the main portions of the clothing furnished the slaves on Polk's plantation

[1] The year Polk broke up his place near Somerville to move to Mississippi, Dr. Caldwell paid his bill at a local store and it amounted to $170. (See above, Caldwell to Polk, February 10, 1835).

was those included in the spring shipment of "supplies for the plantation." Many of the invoices of these articles are preserved in the Polk correspondence and some are given in these letters. Here is one that is typical, reproduced in its entirety.[1] It is dated March 15, 1856, and is as follows:

1224 yds Ky. bagging @ 18	220.32
1438 " Rope @ 9½	136.61
15 lbs Twine @ 18	2.70
	359.63
drayage —	.75
	360.38
3 doz shoes — Russets — 7/10 8/2 9/2 10/10 11/3 12/3 13/6 @ 17.50	52.50
3 doz Compeachy hats @ $2.50	7.50
drayage	.25
	$60.25
25 prs. heavy grey Blankets @ 3.00	75.00
drayage & bale	.75
	$75.75
6 bars iron — 328 lbs. @ 5 cts	16.40
3 slabs " 348 " @ 6 "	20.88
1 Bundle Steel 50 " @ 11½ "	5.75
drayage	.25
	43.28
16 Sacks Co. salt @ 1.05	16.80

Out of this invoice the only articles that can be described as clothing are the shoes and "Campeachy hats." The hats cost twenty and five-sixths cents each. The shoes cost one dollar and forty-five and five-sixths cents a pair. For these articles of clothing, all that are in the invoice, Mrs. Polk

[1] See also Mairs to Mrs. Polk, February 10, 1851, above p. 189.

paid $60.25. The shoes were "Russets"—in some of the invoices they are called "Men's Russet Oak Tand. Brogans." The meaning was that they were made of leather that had not been blackened. The term "brogan," widely used in the Old South, indicated a heavy and stout work shoe cut low but slightly higher than the modern "Oxford," vary hard and clumsy. It is interesting to note the sizes. There were ten pairs of sevens, two pairs of eights, and two pairs of nines — these probably for the women — and there were ten pairs of tens, three pairs of elevens, three pairs of twelves, and six pairs of thirteens — for the men. They were probably ordered a little large, since it was not safe in ordering at such a distance to try for an exact fit. It was the general custom for men and women to go barefoot in warm weather. As nothing is said here about shoes for the children it may have been that they were expected to go barefoot all the year. It may have been, however, that the children were supplied from a local store where they could be fitted more successfully than in a distant market. In one of the letters the overseer speaks of getting shoes made by a local cobbler, but it is not clear whether the usual order went to New Orleans that year or not.

On the Mississippi plantation, after it became well established, Mariah was taught to weave and from that time on the cloth was made on the plantation that went into the negro clothing. As no sheep were mentioned as raised on the place I infer that the cloth was cotton, or mostly so. It was probably heavy for coats and trousers and lighter for shirts and the clothing of the women. The clothes were made up by the women on the place. There is nothing to show how many times a year the clothing was issued. The children, male and female, probably followed the custom

common everywhere to dress negro children in a single gar-
ment, a long shirt made of white cotton cloth.

In the invoice given above appears an item referring to
blankets. These articles were not distributed every year.
The price indicates that a good quality was ordered. How
long the slaves made them last we do not know. The invoices are not regular enough to make a deduction from the
frequency with which blankets appear in them. Of the arrival of these blankets at the plantation Mairs had the following to say in a letter to Major John W. Childress dated
May 6, 1856:

"Mrs. Polk surplys has got oup safe all to 6 blankets that
is 3 par we got 23 par that is 46 Blankets iunderstode
you to say you ordered 52 blankets iwent with the wagons
and come home with them the botehands mus have got
them iexamed the bal the ware in but dyed not discover it
had been opened think the beter way hear after is to put
them in a box we will be more apter to tell if it has bin
opeined."

In this connection I offer the following letter from Frank
L. Fowler to Mrs. Polk relating to the clothing of slaves
hired by the year. The writer seems to have been Mrs.
Polk's business adviser. The letter is without place or date,
but it was probably written in Nashville in the fifties. It
runs as follows:

"Mrs. Polk:
 The custom of hiring negroes by the year is that you
furnish them with such clothing as they may require. You
can be the better Judge of the number of prs. Shoes necessary. in regard to the Taxes and Medical Bills it is allways
the custom when you hire a servant to pay all expences that

may occur. I was engaged this morning and asked Mr.
Boyd to send you the notes. he misunderstood me and
sent you four notes to sign requiring a payment in advance
I hope the notes I have drawn will meet with your appro-
bation and this will be an apology sufficient for the mistake.
I am

Yours very Respectfully."

It is evident that neither of the overseers on the Polk
plantation thought it worth while to write about the religious
or moral instruction of the slaves; and it is noteworthy that
in all their letters no incident is mentioned that gives us
any evidence that such a thing as religious instruction existed on the plantation. It might have existed without direct reports on it. But it is not likely that it could have existed for twenty-five years without mention of some occurrence which had a connection with religion on the place.

No doubt the slaves fared better when the master was
himself resident on the plantation, or lived so close that he
visited it frequently. The reader should be warned that he
should not judge slavery as a whole by what he finds under
the régime of a non-resident master. And it is true that
non-residence was most found in the gulf region in the early
days of its settlement. As time passed it became more evident that it did not pay to conduct farming at such a distance from the owner of the land, and the non-resident type
of plantation receded as the owners sold one by one, as
Mrs. Polk finally sold, to men who lived nearer at hand.
The master-directed plantation was more typical, and in
making an estimate of slavery we should have this type in
mind. But the situation on a non-resident plantation was
not so far different from the situation on the other kind

that it can be ignored. The difference was largely in the moral oversight of the slaves and the exercise of a greater degree of humanity by the master, due to his superior interest in the higher forms of living.

Finally, we must not form the conclusion that the overseer was cruel or stupid because he was illiterate. Neither of the men whose thoughts are depicted here in their letters deserve to be called cruel or stupid. They were men of common sense and intelligence. So far as the letters show they were not pronounced cruel by the slaves in any other sense than that they punished severely, mostly for running away. One was accused of failing to encourage the slaves for good work, but it was evidently the idea of an aggrieved runaway who found it necessary to have an excuse. Another drank too much, and more than one had too much company. But by the men of the day these would have been considered minor faults in anyone other than an overseer.

The overseer's inherent fault was that he took a low idea of slavery. He did not see in the situation before him any suggestion that these stupid people under him could be improved. To him the thing to do was to have obedience, to get work done, and to keep the slaves in health and strength. These ends were to be accomplished by the exercise of will over the volition of the slaves. It was a thing natural to the times and the environment. The overseer was a development and a destiny. He and his place came out of the social necessities of a rural people who were trying to carry on the institution of slavery, making it work with the undeveloped African. As he had so large a part in directing the course of slave life he was in a position to determine to a large extent the destiny of its future. It was a vast power in the hands of a man who was not likely to use it with enlightenment. Slavery made him what he was and he used his best efforts to make slavery continue what it was.

Did slavery pay? This question has not been answered to the satisfaction of all. The experience of Mrs. Polk and her husband has some value as bearing on the matter. The records in the court house at Coffeeville contain this entry (filed February 18, 1860) :

"Mrs. Sarah Polk, Nashville, Tenn., to Jas. M. Avant, Rutherford County, Tenn., for $30,000, one-half of my estate in Yalobusha County, Miss. (Sec. 28 and N. ½ 33), consisting of 960 acres of land in one body and embracing a section and one-half section together with one other small tract of land containing 155 acres being near the above described tract of 960 acres, it being the tract conveyed to me by John A. Mairs on 20th of February, 1854, known as N. E. ¼ Sec. 20-24-5 E. Converting also the following slaves to wit: Pompey, Harry, Allen, Gilbert, Phillip, Addison, Garry, Giles, Perry, Manuel, Joe,* Alphonso, Billy, Wilson, Jason, Jim, Andy,* Jerry, Anderson, Turner, Lewis, Julius, Davy, Clay, Mariner, Evy, Betsy, Mary, Caroline, Daphny, Mariah, Rosetta, Caroline, Jane, Malinda, Sally, Angeline, John, George, Willis, Paul, Edward, Henry, Osbourn, Jack, Ted, Daniel, Little Manuel, Ananias, Ary, Carter, Lilly, Violet, Louisa, Susan, and Eliza, 56 in number."

For the original tract Polk and Caldwell paid $8,800, but it does not appear what was paid for the "small tract" of 155 acres bought from Mairs. On the original purchase the owners placed thirty-six slaves, valued at $16,050. Polk bought several others at later times, but it is not clear that he was not merely replacing slaves withdrawn by Caldwell when he sold his share, or by William H. Polk, when he sold out. At any rate, the plantation slaves increased in twenty-five years from 36 to 56, mostly through births. The price received for the half of the estate does not represent its value when sold under favorable circumstances. Mrs. Polk was in no position to get the best returns for the property, nor to sell it to an advantage, by virtue of her sex and her non-residence. Making reasonable allowances on these grounds, I am of opinion that the estate was a good investment.

INDEX

Index

Cooper, M. D. & Co., to Polk, Feb. 12, 1839, 118.

Cotton, selling, 224; expenses of selling, 227, n. 1, 235; prices and grades, 232, 234; excellent quality of Mrs. Polk's, 233, 234; Mrs. Polk's burned at Troy, 240; insurance of gin-house, 255.

Cowan, James, to Polk, July 2, 1839, 120.

Curry, James S., 34.

Dismukes, Isaac H., becomes overseer for Polk, 147; his discharge, 147; to Polk, Jan. 21, 1841, 148; to Polk, Feb. 1, 1841, 149; to Polk, March 9, 1841, 150; to Polk, April 1, 1841, 151; to Polk, April 5, 1841, 152; to Polk, Aug. 2, 1841, 154; to Polk, Sept. 1, 1841, 157; to Polk, Sept. 17, 1841, 159; to Polk, Feb. 1, 1842, 160; to Polk, May 17, 1842, 163; to Polk, June 1, 1842, 163; to Polk, June 26, 1842, 164; to Polk, Aug. 16, 1842, 164; to Polk, Sept. 13, 1842, 165; Leigh's testimony in regard to Dismukes' crop, 167; to Polk, Oct. 4, 1842, 168; to Polk, Oct. 12, 1842, 169; to Polk, Dec. 25, 1842, 170; to Polk, Jan. 14, 1843, 171; to Polk, Jan. 26, 1843, 172; end of his overseership, 172, 174; buys a slave, 173.

"Floats," 37, 46.

Gaines, Francis P., 10, n. 1.

Garner, John I., employed as overseer, 112; his overseership, 125-147; to Polk, Sept. 10, 1839, 125; to Polk, Nov. 3, 1839, 128; to Polk, Nov. 23, 1839, 129; to Polk, Dec. 11, 1839, 134; to Polk, Dec. 25, 1839, 130; to Polk, March 2, 1840, 138; to Polk, May 3, 1840, 138; to Polk, June 1, 1840, 139; to Polk, June 7, 1840, 140; to Polk, July 5, 1840, 142; to Polk, Oct. 4, 1840, 144; to Polk, Oct. 1, 1840, 145; end of his correspondence, 147.

Garrison, Wm. Lloyd, 14.

Graham, Major Daniel, agent for Mrs. Polk, 187, 188, 191.

Greenfield, G. T., buying slaves, 85.

Hammond, James H., 5.

Harris, A. O., 37, 52; to Polk, Dec. 30, 1833, 55; to Polk, Jan. 3, 1834, 56.

Harry, 137, 162, 210; to Polk, May 10, 1842, 161, 264.

Infant mortality, 265.

Jones, George, 33, 34.

Lane, Lunsford, 14.

Leigh, J. T., to Polk, Aug. 13, 1839, 122; to Polk, Sept. 28, 1842, 167.

McNeal, A. F., to Polk, June 15, 1838, 111; to Polk, Jan. 15, 1840, 135.

Mairs, John A., appointed overseer, 176; length of overseership, 176; his salary, 178; to Mrs. Polk, Aug. 19, 1849, 178; to Mrs. Polk, Sept. 20, 1849, 178; to Mrs. Polk, Oct. 29, 1849, 179; to Mrs. Polk, Jan. 12, 1850, 180; to Mrs. Polk, Feb. 1, 1850, 181; to Mrs. Polk, March 15, 1850, 181; to Mrs. Polk, April 12, 1850, 182; to Mrs. Polk, May 6, 1850, 183; to Mrs. Polk, June 7, 1850, 183; to Mrs. Polk, July 6, 1850, 184; to Mrs. Polk, Aug. 10, 1850, 185; to Mrs. Polk, Sept. 8, 1850, 186; to Mrs. Polk, Oct. 8, 1850, 186; to Mrs. Polk, Nov. 6, 1850, 187; to Mrs. Polk, Jan. 13, 1851, 188; to Mrs. Polk, Feb. 10, 1851, 189; to Mrs. Polk, March 5, 1851, 189; to Mrs. Polk, March 18, 1851, 191; to Mrs. Polk, April 16, 1851, 192; to Mrs. Polk, July 25, 1851, 194; to Mrs. Polk, Sept. 29, 1851, 195; to Mrs. Polk, Jan. 26, 1851, 195; to Mrs. Polk, April 3, 1852, 197; to Mrs. Polk, April 24, 1852, 198; to Mrs. Polk, Aug. 18, 1852, 199; to Mrs. Polk, Sept. 20, 1852, 200;

Index

Mrs. Polk, Nov. 5, 1856, 248; to Mrs. Polk, Dec. 24, 1856, 248; to Mrs. Polk, Jan. 21, 1857, 249; to Mrs. Polk, Feb. 5, 1857, 250; to Mrs. Polk, Feb. 14, 1857, 250; to Mrs. Polk, March 9, 1857, 251; to Mrs. Polk, March 12, 1857, 252.

Plantation, life on the, 9; see Overseers.

Planter, the, position, 1-3; on plantation management, 11; on plantation morals, 13.

Polk, Col. Thomas, 35.

Polk, Ezekiel, 35, 36.

Polk, James K., his plantation in Tennessee, 35-40; his ancestry, 35; purchase of Mississippi lands, 75; sells Tennessee plantation, 77; to his wife, Sept. 26, 1834, 77; removal to Mississippi, 81; partnership with Dr. Caldwell, 97; returns from his plantation, 133; wishes to sell the Mississippi plantation, 1843, 174; to Mrs. Polk, Oct. 26, 1843, 175; paying off debts, 176; buying slaves, 177; drafts on his factors, 228; finances in 1844, 228.

Polk, Marshall T., on transfer of slaves to avoid dividing the family, 197.

Polk, Mrs. Sarah C., sells her Mississippi plantation, 46, 268, 275; owner of the Mississippi plantation, 176; visit to the plantation, 181; succeeds Polk, 228; ill luck with her cotton, 237, 239; supplies for her plantation, 250, n. 1.

Polk, Samuel, 36.

Polk, Wm. H., 58, 61; buys half of Caldwell's share of the plantation, 100; his capacity, 101; to Polk, Dec. 17, 1836, 102; George Moore's opinion of, 103; as supervisor of the Mississippi plantation, 105, 110; to Polk, May 13, 1837, 106; to Polk, Dec. 2, 1837, 106; sells his share, 114; to J. K. Polk, Oct. 28, 1839, 127; inquires for runaway, 131; to J. K. Polk, Dec. 30, 1839, 131; to J. K. Polk, Dec. 4, 1840, 132.

Poor whites, social relations with the planters, 169.

Preaching to the slaves, 13-15.

"Remarks on the Market," 232.

Reserves, 46.

Runaway slaves, 263.

Shawnee Town, 78, 80.

Slavery, 86; and the negro problem, 264.

Slaves, their attitude towards overseers, 3, 8; routine life of, 12; religious instruction, 13-15; punishment of, 15-17; marriage of, 17; divorce of, 17; runaways, 18; influence of slave women, 20; taught by slavery, 21; rules on Weston's plantation, 23-32; "Lists," 25; tickets of leave, 25; allowances to, 25-27; tasks and labor of, 27; holidays, 27; sickness of, 28; division of families of, 197; dwellings of, 261; not diminished by overwork, 265; clothing of, 268; no deaths from overwork, 265; supplies for, 269; weaving by, 271; custom of hiring, 272; on non-resident plantations, 273.

Supplies for Mrs. Polk's plantation, 250, 255, n. 1.

Trade in the South, 223.

Virginia planters and London merchants, 221-223.

Walker, James, 36, 50, 52, 61, 63, 65; to Polk, March 18, 1836, 96; to Polk, Dec. 30, 1839, 133.

Washington, George, 7, 19.

Weston, Plowden C. J., 23-24.

Whatley, Jesse, 33, 34.

Yell, Archibald, 103, 134, and 134, n. 1.